New Models for
Population Protocols

New Models for
Population Protocols

Synthesis Lectures on Distributed Computing Theory

Editor
Nancy Lynch, *Massachusetts Institute of Technology*

Synthesis Lectures on Distributed Computing Theory is edited by Nancy Lynch of the Massachusetts Institute of Technology. The series will publish 50- to 150 page publications on topics pertaining to distributed computing theory. The scope will largely follow the purview of premier information and computer science conferences, such as ACM PODC, DISC, SPAA, OPODIS, CONCUR, DialM-POMC, ICDCS, SODA, Sirocco, SSS, and related conferences. Potential topics include, but are not limited to: distributed algorithms and lower bounds, algorithm design methods, formal modeling and verification of algorithms, and concurrent data structures.

New Models for Population Protocols
Othon Michail, Ioannis Chatzigiannakis, and Paul G. Spirakis
2011

The Theory of Timed I/O Automata, Second Edition
Dilsun K. Kaynar, Nancy Lynch, Roberto Segala, Frits Vaandrager
2010

Principles of Transactional Memory
Rachid Guerraoui, Michal Kapalka
2010

Fault-tolerant Agreement in Synchronous Message-passing Systems
Michel Raynal
2010

Communication and Agreement Abstractions for Fault-Tolerant Asynchronous Distributed Systems
Michel Raynal
2010

The Mobile Agent Rendezvous Problem in the Ring
Evangelos Kranakis, Danny Krizanc, Euripides Markou
2010

New Models for Population Protocols

Othon Michail, Ioannis Chatzigiannakis, and Paul G. Spirakis

ISBN: 978-3-031-00876-4 paperback
ISBN: 978-3-031-02004-9 ebook

DOI 10.1007/978-3-031-02004-9

A Publication in the Springer series
SYNTHESIS LECTURES ON DISTRIBUTED COMPUTING THEORY

Lecture #6
Series Editor: Nancy Lynch, *Massachusetts Institute of Technology*
Series ISSN
Synthesis Lectures on Distributed Computing Theory
Print 2155-1626   Electronic 2155-1634

New Models for Population Protocols

Research Academic Computer Technology Institute (CTI)
University of Patras
Patras, Greece

Research Academic Computer Technology Institute (CTI)
University of Patras
Patras, Greece

Research Academic Computer Technology Institute (CTI)
University of Patras
Patras, Greece

SYNTHESIS LECTURES ON DISTRIBUTED COMPUTING THEORY #6

ABSTRACT

Wireless sensor networks are about to be part of everyday life. Homes and workplaces capable of self-controlling and adapting air-conditioning for different temperature and humidity levels, sleepless forests ready to detect and react in case of a fire, vehicles able to avoid sudden obstacles or possibly able to self-organize routes to avoid congestion, and so on, will probably be commonplace in the very near future. Mobility plays a central role in such systems and so does *passive mobility*, that is, mobility of the network stemming from the environment itself. The population protocol model was an intellectual invention aiming to describe such systems in a minimalistic and analysis-friendly way. Having as a starting-point the inherent limitations but also the fundamental establishments of the population protocol model, we try in this monograph to present some realistic and practical enhancements that give birth to some new and surprisingly powerful (for these kind of systems) computational models.

KEYWORDS

computational complexity, distributed computing, wireless sensor network, passive mobility, population protocol, computational model, diffuse computation, mobile agent, space hierarchy, computational threshold

I once was deep in pain it seemed I couldn't find
The perfect interaction that would do
No agent was in state that would let him bind
My injured heart that was torn in two.

The scheduler at first was adversarial
Though Angluin et al. said that he had to be fair
So while my state was marked as "being in despair"
You show up as my interacting pair.

My plan was all too good but just in theory
You see our space was limited in range
But if we had some logarithmic memory
I couldn't wait for our first tape exchange.

Thank god I was to meet you one more time again
Compute with you the predicate of love
This time in a new model named PM
Let's stabilize our outputs to one.

Andreas Pavlogiannis, 2010

Never has so much money been transferred from so many to so few.

Joseph E. Stiglitz, China Daily, 2009

Now, it is probably the right time to study what fairness is all about...

Contents

Preface

Imagine a population of tiny (and possibly heterogeneous) artifacts that can interact only in pairs (e.g., when any two of them meet). Such a population (system) could be assumed to consist only of *mobile* artifacts, and then pairwise interactions happen when two artifacts meet in a *rendezvous* notion. Such meetings are usually being scheduled in an adversarial way (passive mobility). However, in order for the population to globally compute something useful, a notion of fairness should be imposed on the adversary that schedules such pairwise meetings.

It is also logical and desirable to assume that the code of each tiny artifact is of small size and independent of the population size (which may not be known in advance and even vary with time). In other words, *scalability* and *uniformity* are two desirable features for the programs of the elements of such populations.

An elegant abstraction capturing the above was first proposed by Angluin, Aspnes, Diamadi, Fischer, and Peralta in their 2004 seminal paper "Computation in networks of passively mobile finite-state sensors" [AAD+04]. This abstraction is known as "the Population Protocol model". In this abstraction, the protocol (for each tiny artifact and for all the population) is just a set of rules (grammar) mapping pairs of artifact states (q, q') to new pairs of states. Such rules indicate what happens in a pairwise interaction.

The work of [AAD+04] motivated several researchers (and the authors of this text) to think about extensions of the basic model that could enhance its practicality, while preserving the basic features of uniformity, scalability, and adversarial but fair interactions. Our monograph describes such extensions of the basic model.

The intellectual (but also practical) challenges of *how to compose protocols* and of *extending the computational power* of populations, lead us (and others) to propose adding some *memory* into the system. Such an enhancement of memory can be implemented in various ways (local identifiers, some non-constant memory per artifact, some passive global storage in the system). For example, a single bit of memory per interaction pair does not upset the constant size of the interaction grammar (the population protocol) since the grammar now maps triples (q, q', s) to triples (where q, q' are the states of the meeting artifacts and s is the single bit of the memory of the "link") instead of pairs (q, q') to pairs.

On the other hand, local memories of some size allow for local computations and, if size permits, for construction of identities. Non-constant local memory does not, necessarily, need to assume knowledge of the population size and in practice, all small devices have a lot of memory nowadays.

Such considerations, in fact, created a whole *theory* of *space-bounded distributed computations*, and lead to a hierarchy of classes of predicates that can be computed by populations. It is important to note here that the input (initial states) to a population "system" needs to be "symmetric" in the sense that it is of no matter which element of a population holds which part of the input. So, in fact, our monograph describes the start of a *theory of distributed computation of Symmetric predicates under the assumption of some available space*. This theory allows for comparisons with the classical theory of space-bounded computation by e.g. Turing Machines.

The monograph follows the basic idea of [AAD$^+$04] for *stable* computations (i.e., *converging* population states). Thus, we do not study here computation "time". In fact, the physical/logical notion of "time" in a distributed system is quite a deep issue and may even allow for Relativistic considerations (see [Lam78]). Adding time (and clocks) to population systems is currently being considered by many groups, and it is beyond the scope of this monograph. However, we devote a section within Chapter 3 to a particular version of fairness (probabilistic schedulers) which allows for measuring time efficiency in Population Protocols.

Most of the material described here is due to joint research of the authors and to the PhD Thesis [Mic10] of the youngest of us (O. Michail) and his advisor (P. Spirakis). However, the monograph also reviews the basic Population Protocol model, the Community Protocol model, and provides clear proofs (we hope!) and also exercises for students. Some of the exercises are open research and may motivate new and younger people to further contribute. We are deeply indebted to Jim Aspnes (and his team) for many inspirations, critique, and advices. We also wish to thank Nancy Lynch for giving us the opportunity to publish this monograph and for her encouragement for us to work on the protocol composition issue. We thank Diane Cerra for her support and encouragement as well as the support staff at Morgan and Claypool for their help in putting all the material together. We thank also Jim Aspnes, Shlomi Dolev and Alberto Marchetti-Spaccamela for reviewing the monograph and providing valuable feedback on improving its quality. We are greatly indebted to our students (now graduated!) Stavros Nikolaou and Andreas Pavlogiannis, whose undergraduate Diploma Theses contributed a lot in our joint research. We also thank Stavros for his valuable help in completing this monograph. We also wish to thank the ICT Project FRONTS of the European Union, under contract number ICT-2008-215270, and all of our Project Partners for providing the intellectual and material environment necessary for this research.

October 2010,
Paul G. Spirakis
on behalf of the authors

CHAPTER 1

Population Protocols

1.1 INTRODUCTION

A Wireless Sensor Network (WSN) consists of computational devices with sensing capabilities that are distributed in an environment in order to cooperatively monitor some metrics of interest. For example, such a network can be deployed by a Forest Service for fire detection. Nodes are equipped here with temperature sensors, and in case of fire, they wirelessly propagate an alarm message to some base station. WSNs are typically used in industrial and civilian application areas, including industrial process monitoring and control, machine health monitoring, environment and habitat monitoring, healthcare applications, home automation, and traffic control. So, the near computational future will possibly be full of tiny *computational agents* equipped with external sensors and limited memory and computational power, able to communicate with nearby agents and receive broadcasts from base stations, and which will be probably mobile.

Since WSNs consist of massive amounts of bulk-produced and usually tiny agents, the resources available to each agent are severely limited most of the time. Such limitations are not crippling if the system designer has fine control over the pattern, according to which agents interact. In this case, even finite-state agents can be regimented into von Neumann's cellular automata with computational power equivalent to linear space Turing machines (we usually abbreviate a Turing machine as TM[1]). On the other hand, if the system designer cannot control these interactions, then it is not clear what the computational limits are. The *Population Protocol* (PP) model aims to formally study these limits.

Consider a wireless sensor network in which the agents are moving according to some *mobility pattern* over which they have totally no control. This kind of mobility is known as *passive mobility*. Imagine, for example, that millions of such nodes are thrown into a hurricane in order to cooperatively study its various characteristics. Some metrics of interest could be the average or maximum barometric pressure, the highest temperature, or some collective data concerning the wind speed near the eye of the hurricane. In this scenario, the movement of the sensor nodes follows some collection of interchanging probability distributions which, as a result of some natural phenomenon, are in general totally unpredictable (any other phenomenon offering an abundance of kinetic energy could be representative). The nodes have to sense their environment according to the underlying query and then interact with the remaining population in order to make some cooperative decision or cooperatively compute a required function on the sensed inputs.

---

[1]The reader is encouraged to consult the complete list of acronyms included at the end of the monograph.

An interaction is established when two nodes come sufficiently close to each other so that communication becomes feasible (one within the range of the other). Communication is usually assumed to be *two-way*, though various modes of communication have been studied in the relevant literature. Additionally, the nodes are assumed to communicate in ordered pairs (u, v), where u plays the role of the *initiator* and v that of the *responder*. The distinct roles of the two participants constitute a fundamental symmetry breaking assumption.

1.2   A FORMAL MODEL

Definition 1.1   [AAD$^+$04, AAD$^+$06]   A *population protocol* (PP) is a 6-tuple (X, Y, Q, I, O, δ), where X, Y, and Q are all finite sets and

1. X is the *input alphabet*,

2. Y is the *output alphabet*,

3. Q is the set of *states*,

4. $I : X \rightarrow Q$ is the *input function*,

5. $O : Q \rightarrow Y$ is the *output function*, and

6. $\delta : Q \times Q \rightarrow Q \times Q$ is the *transition function*.

If $\delta(a, b) = (a', b')$ then $(a, b) \rightarrow (a', b')$ is called a *transition* and $\delta_1(a, b) = a'$ and $\delta_2(a, b) = b'$ are defined.

A simplification is that all agents concurrently sense their environment, as a response to a global start signal, and each one of them receives some input symbol from X. For example, X could contain all possible barometric pressures that the agent's sensors can detect. Then all agents concurrently apply the input function I to their input symbols to obtain their initial state. In this manner, the *initial configuration* of the system is formed. A (*population*) *configuration* in general, given a *population* of n agents, is a mapping $C : V \rightarrow Q$, describing the state of each agent in the population.

Formally, the agents are organized into an interaction graph $G = (V, E)$, which is a directed graph without self-loops and multiple edges, and where V is a population of $|V| = n$ agents and E describes the permissible interactions.

The crucial part is that the next interaction can be any interaction from E without the agents being capable of knowing which one will actually take place. This is interpreted as some inherent nondeterminism of the system. Not all interaction graphs are allowed in most practical scenarios. For example, if no obstacles are present, then we can assume that the interaction graph is always complete, which is the most commonly studied case. To the other extreme, we could have also considered only line graphs or even more complex collections of restricted graphs. Precisely, this *a priori* selection of all possible interaction graphs is captured by the notion of graph universes. A *graph universe*, also known as (a.k.a.) *graph family*, $\mathcal{U}$ is any set of graphs. Unless otherwise stated, it is assumed that the universes under consideration contain only *directed* interaction graphs without self-loops and multiple edges. We denote by $\mathcal{G}_{all}$ the graph universe consisting of all possible interaction graphs of any finite order that is at least 2 and by $\mathcal{G}_{con}$, the weakly-connected subset of $\mathcal{G}_{all}$. Given a graph universe $\mathcal{U}$, a PP runs on the nodes of some $G \in \mathcal{U}$.

Let C and C' be population configurations and let u and v be distinct agents. We say that C *goes to C' via encounter* $e = (u, v)$ and write $C \xrightarrow{e} C'$, if

$$C'(u) = \delta_1(C(u), C(v)),$$
$$C'(v) = \delta_2(C(u), C(v)), \text{ and}$$
$$C'(w) = C(w), \text{ for all } w \in V - \{u, v\}.$$

We say that C *can go in one step to C'* (or *yields C'*) and denote by $C \rightarrow C'$, if $C \xrightarrow{e} C'$ for some encounter $e \in E$. That is, C can go in one step to C' if there is some encounter via which C goes to C'. Having defined the binary relation "can go in one step to" on the set of population configurations, we can now easily define the relation "can go to" (in one or more steps) as its transitive closure. Formally, we write $C \xrightarrow{*} C'$, if there exists a sequence of configurations $C = C_0, C_1, \ldots, C_t = C'$, such that (s.t.) $C_i \rightarrow C_{i+1}$ for all i, where $0 \leq i < t$; in this case, we say that C' is *reachable from C*.

Mobility is modeled via an *adversary scheduler* that is a black-box to the protocol and simply selects members of E to interact according to δ (note that all agents apply the same global transition function). The only, but necessary, restriction imposed on the scheduler is that it has to be *fair* so that it does not forever partition the network into non-communicating clusters and to prevent the possibility of having agents interacting only at "inconvenient" times.

An *execution* is a finite or infinite sequence of configurations $C_0, C_1, C_2, \ldots$ such that $C_i \rightarrow C_{i+1}$ for all $i \geq 0$. An infinite execution is said to be *fair* if for all configurations C, C' such that $C \rightarrow C'$, if C appears infinitely often in the execution then so does C'. A *computation* is defined as an infinite fair execution.

The *transition graph* $T(\mathcal{A}, G)$ of a protocol $\mathcal{A}$ that is executed on an interaction graph G (or simply T when $\mathcal{A}$ and G are clear from the context) is a directed graph whose nodes are all possible configurations and whose edges are all possible transitions between those configurations. A strongly connected component of a directed graph is called *final* if and only if (iff) no edge beginning from some node of the component leads to a node of another component. One can prove the following (the proof is left as Exercise 1.1):

Theorem 1.2   [AAD+06, CDF+09]   *Let $\Xi = C_0, C_1, \ldots$ be an infinite execution of a population protocol $\mathcal{A}$ on an interaction graph G, $\mathcal{F}_\Xi$ the set of configurations that appear infinitely often in Ξ and $T_{\mathcal{F}_\Xi}$ the subgraph of $T(\mathcal{A}, G)$ induced by $\mathcal{F}_\Xi$. Ξ is a computation iff $T_{\mathcal{F}_\Xi}$ is a final strongly connected component of $T(\mathcal{A}, G)$.*

1.2.1 STABLE COMPUTATION

Computations of population protocols, by definition, do not halt. In fact, the definition itself captures the inherent inability of such systems to detect termination, which is mainly due to the *uniformity* and *anonymity* properties of population protocols. Uniformity requires protocol descriptions to be independent of n and anonymity that the set of agent states is enough small so that there is no room in it for unique identifiers. Instead, computations are required to stabilize to a correct common or distributed value. *Functions on input assignments* are used in order to formalize the *specifications* of protocols. For example, a natural question in our example could be whether at least 5% of the agents detect barometric pressure over some constant pressure c (which possibly partitions the pressures into low and increased). What we do expect from a protocol that solves this problem is to always *stabilize* (*converge*) in a finite number of steps to the correct answer. Since such a query has a binary range, making it a *predicate*, we want all agents to output 1 when the predicate is made true and 0, otherwise, which is a convention that we make for gathering the protocol' s output. Since our main aim here is to study the computational power of the models under consideration, we can without loss of generality (w.l.o.g.) focus on predicates (that no generality is lost is proved in Theorem 1.3 after some necessary definitions are presented), although there exist more general definitions for functions and also many other natural *output conventions*.

Formally, the *input* (a.k.a. *input assignment*) to a population protocol $\mathcal{A}$ may be any $x \in \mathcal{X}$, where $\mathcal{X} := X^* = \{\sigma_1\sigma_2 \ldots \sigma_k \mid k \geq 0 \text{ and } \sigma_i \in X\}$. In fact, any such $x = \sigma_1\sigma_2 \ldots \sigma_n$ may be the input to $\mathcal{A}$ when the latter runs on a population of size n. To make this possible, we assume an arbitrary ordering on the set of agents which is hidden from the agents themselves. For example, we could make the convention that $V = \{1, 2, \ldots, n\}$ and that agent i, $1 \leq i \leq n$, senses the symbol σ_i of x. We denote by $I(x)$ the initial configuration corresponding to input assignment $x = \sigma_1\sigma_2 \ldots \sigma_n$, that is $I(x)(i) := I(\sigma_i)$ for all $1 \leq i \leq n$. The specifications of protocol $\mathcal{A}$ are represented by a predicate $p : \mathcal{X} \to \{0, 1\}$ or by its corresponding language $L_p = p^{-1}(1) := \{x \in \mathcal{X} \mid p(x) = 1\}$; $p^{-1}(1)$ is the *support* of predicate p and denotes the set of all inputs that make the predicate true. Equivalently, any language corresponds to a predicate p_L over $\mathcal{X}$ defined as $p_L(x) = 1$ iff $x \in L$.

The *output* (a.k.a. *output assignment*) of a population protocol is a mapping $y : V \to Y$ describing the output of each agent. Let $\mathcal{Y} := Y^V$ be the set of all output assignments and similarly $\mathcal{C} := Q^V$ the set of all configurations. [2] Any configuration C corresponds to an output assignment y_C, resulting by the application of the output function O to the state of each agent under configuration C. To make this precise, y_C is the composite function $O \circ C$, that is, $y_C(u) = O(C(u))$, for all $u \in V$. We extend now O to a mapping from configurations to output assignments, $O : \mathcal{C} \to \mathcal{Y}$, by writing $O(C) = y_C$. $O(C)$ is called the output of configuration C. So, if q denotes the state of some agent u under configuration C (that is, $C(u) = q$), then the output symbol of u in the output assignment $O(C)$ is $O(q)$.

---

[2]Note that by assuming an ordering on V, we can define configurations as strings from Q^*, as we have already done for input assignments. In any case, the two definitions are equivalent for our purposes.

A configuration C will be called *output stable*, if $O(C') = O(C)$, for all C' that are reachable from C. Intuitively, from the computation viewpoint, reaching an output stable configuration C means that, no matter how the computation proceeds thereafter, the output of the forthcoming configurations will always be $O(C)$, so that the output of all agents remains unaffected.

A predicate p over $\mathcal{X}$ is said to be *stably computable* by the population protocol model in a graph universe $\mathcal{U}$, if there exists a population protocol $\mathcal{A}$ such that for any input assignment $x \in \mathcal{X}$, any computation of $\mathcal{A}$, on any interaction graph from $\{G \in \mathcal{U} \mid |V(G)| = |x|\}$, beginning from $I(x)$ eventually reaches an output stable configuration in which all agents give the output $p(x)$. By *eventually*, we always mean in a finite number of steps.

Note that, in general, any function $f : \mathcal{X} \to Y$, where Y is not necessarily binary, could be a possible candidate for stable computation. For such a function, given input assignment x, we want all agents to eventually output $f(x)$. We prove now that no generality is lost by restricting attention to predicates. Consider any such function f with range Y. For each $\omega \in Y$ define a predicate p_ω as $p_\omega^{-1}(1) = \{x \in \mathcal{X} \mid f(x) = \omega\}$. That is, given f, we create for each output symbol a predicate which is true for all input assignments that are mapped to this output symbol by f and false for the rest of them.

Theorem 1.3   [AR07]   *f is stably computable iff all p_ωs are stably computable.*

Proof. For the one direction, let f be stably computable by a protocol $\mathcal{A}$ and take any p_ω. Now replace the output map O of $\mathcal{A}$ by a binary one defined as $O'(q) = 1$ iff $O(q) = \omega$ for all $q \in Q$. If $p_\omega(x) = 1$ then $f(x) = \omega$, thus all agents eventually remain to states q_i such that $O(q_i) = \omega$ and we have that $O'(q_i) = 1$. Similarly, if $p_\omega(x) = 0$ all agents eventually output 0.

For the other direction, given that all p_ωs are stably computable, each by a $\mathcal{A}_\omega$ protocol, we must show that so is f. The idea is to construct a protocol $\mathcal{A}$ for f that executes the $\mathcal{A}_\omega$s in parallel. This can be done easily by having each $\mathcal{A}_\omega$ executed in a separate component of $\mathcal{A}$'s state while ignoring the operation of the remaining protocols. Note that this is legal because there is a finite (fixed) number of ωs in Y so $\mathcal{A}$'s state will also be finite. So the states q of $\mathcal{A}$ are of the form $(q_\omega)_{\omega \in Y}$. Let now O_ω be the output function of $\mathcal{A}_\omega$, for all $\omega \in Y$ and define the output map $O_\mathcal{A}$ of $\mathcal{A}$ as

$$O_\mathcal{A}(q) = \begin{cases} \omega, & \text{if } O_\omega(q_\omega) = 1 \text{ and } O_{\omega'}(q'_\omega) = 0 \text{ for all } \omega' \in Y - \{\omega\} \\ \omega', & \text{otherwise (for some fixed } \omega' \in Y). \end{cases}$$

In words, $\mathcal{A}$ outputs ω only if $\mathcal{A}_\omega$ outputs 1 and all other components output 0 and outputs something predetermined (arbitrarily), otherwise. Clearly, for all $\omega \in Y$, if $f(x) = \omega$, then only $\mathcal{A}_\omega$ eventually outputs 1, and all other components eventually output 0, thus $\mathcal{A}$ outputs ω. $\square$

Research initially focused on complete interaction graphs. It is worth mentioning that the completeness of the interaction graph, together with the fact that the agents are identical and are not equipped with unique identifiers, implies that stably computable predicates have to be symmetric (this is proved for another model in Lemma 4.6 of Section 4.1.2). A predicate p is called *symmetric* if for every $x = \sigma_1\sigma_2\ldots\sigma_n \in \mathcal{X}$ and any permutation function $\pi : \{1, 2, \ldots, n\} \to \{1, 2, \ldots, n\}$, it holds that $p(x) = p(\sigma_{\pi(1)}\sigma_{\pi(2)}\ldots\sigma_{\pi(n)})$ (in words, permuting the input symbols does not affect the predicate's outcome). Similarly, a language $L \subseteq \mathcal{X}$ is called symmetric if $x = \sigma_1\sigma_2\ldots\sigma_n \in L$ implies $\sigma_{\pi(1)}\sigma_{\pi(2)}\ldots\sigma_{\pi(n)} \in L$ for all π. For example, any language over an unary alphabet is symmetric and so is any language defined solely via some property of the *Parikh map* Ψ that takes $x \in \mathcal{X}$ to the vector $(N_{\sigma_1}, \ldots, N_{\sigma_k})$, where N_{σ_i} is the number of times σ_i occurs in x. For example, the language $L = \{x \mid x \text{ contains at least 5 } as\}$ is symmetric. On the other hand, the language $L = \{x \mid x \text{ begins with an } a\}$ is not symmetric since moving the initial a to another position results in a permutation that does not belong to the language.

We prove now a lemma showing that the terms "predicate" and "language" are equivalent for our purposes.

Lemma 1.4   *A predicate p is symmetric iff its corresponding language L_p is symmetric.*

Proof. If p is symmetric, then no permutation is missing from the support $p^{-1}(1)$ of p. However, $L_p = p^{-1}(1)$ (precisely those strings that make the predicate true), thus, L_p is symmetric. If L_p is symmetric, then $p^{-1}(1)$ is also symmetric and the same must hold for $p^{-1}(0)$, otherwise $p^{-1}(1)$ wouldn't be either (a permutation missing from $p^{-1}(0)$ would belong to $p^{-1}(1)$). □

Symmetry is inherent in population-protocol-like systems. This allows us to work with multisets instead of mappings. For example, the configuration $C : \{u_1, \ldots, u_6\} \to \{q_0, q_1, q_2\}$, defined as $C(u_1) = q_1$, $C(u_2) = q_2$, $C(u_3) = q_0$, $C(u_4) = q_0$, $C(u_5) = q_1$, and $C(u_6) = q_0$, can, without loss of information, be described by the multiset $\{q_0, q_0, q_0, q_1, q_1, q_2\}$, or equivalently by the vector $(3, 2, 1)$ from $\mathcal{C} = \mathbb{N}^Q - \{0\}$ (a $|Q|$-vector of natural numbers indexed by Q, representing the number of agents in each one of the $|Q|$ states). The same representation can also be used for the input assignments; that is, they can as well be described as vectors from $\mathcal{X} = \mathbb{N}^X - \{0\}$. Given two configurations $c, c' \in \mathcal{C}$ (we use lowercase for the vector representation of configurations), we may write $c \le c'$ if $c[q] \le c'[q]$ for all $q \in Q$. We can even generalize the reachability relation $\stackrel{*}{\to}$ as an ordering on $\mathcal{C}$ (not only relating configurations of same cardinalities as before) and require it to be reflexive, transitive, and to respect addition in $\mathbb{N}^Q$; that is, $c \stackrel{*}{\to} c'$ implies $c + d \stackrel{*}{\to} c' + d$ for all $c, c' \in \mathcal{C}$ and $d \in \mathbb{N}^Q$. Intuitively, this means that a partitioned subpopulation can still run on its own: the scheduler may deny interaction to agents corresponding to d and only let the agents corresponding to c interact until c becomes c' (in fact, not all computations convert c to c', but for $\stackrel{*}{\to}$ the existence of at least one such computation suffices). Finally, we may also write $x \stackrel{*}{\to} c$ for $x \in \mathcal{X}$ and $c \in \mathcal{C}$ if $I(x) \stackrel{*}{\to} c$. These alternative definitions will prove particularly useful for the discussion in Section 2.3.

We now present two examples in order to make the definitions, presented so far, clear.

Example 1.5   Flock of Birds [AAD⁺04]   Consider that we want to determine whether at least 5 birds in a flock are sick. For example, it could be the case that we consider a bird sick if its body temperature exceeds a specific threshold. To do that, we equip each bird with an agent capable of detecting elevated temperature. We also make the assumption that all birds may come close to each other, that an interaction may be established in any possible direction, and that the birds move according to some fair pattern (e.g., the uniform distribution). Here, the input alphabet of the protocol is the binary $X = \{0, 1\}$, where the values 0 and 1 correspond to normal and increased body temperature, respectively. This means that the input to any agent in the population will be 0 or 1, depending on the actual temperature of its carrier. So, an input assignment x to our protocol may be any string from $\{0, 1\}^*$, since our protocol may be executed on any complete interaction graph. In particular, given that we have n birds, the input assignment will be some string from $\{0, 1\}^n$, where the ith symbol of the string corresponds to the assignment for bird i (by assuming an ordering on the birds). Remember that the description of our protocol must be independent of the population size n, so that it is feasible to store the protocol in any agent of the population. The idea is this: when two agents interact, one of them (w.l.o.g. the one that initiated the interaction) keeps the sum of the values and the other keeps nothing, that is, goes to 0. Now the only thing that remains for the protocol to check is whether, at some point, one agent obtains a sum that is at least 5. If this happens, then that agent goes to an alert state whose output value is 1 and which is a propagating state, in the sense that all agents will eventually adopt it. Otherwise, all agents will forever remain to states giving 0 as output. Clearly, the specifications of the protocol in this example are described by the language $L = \{x \in \mathcal{X} \mid x$ contains at least five 1s$\}$, or equivalently by the predicate $p(x) = 1$ iff $x \in L$, because any input assignment can either satisfy or not satisfy the specifications. That is why the output alphabet of the protocol was chosen to be the binary $Y = \{0, 1\}$, and in order to have a system that makes sense, we agree that we want all agents to eventually provide the correct (with respect, of course, to the specifications) output, which is simply a convention that we make for the output of the protocol, or, more succinctly, an output convention. Of course, p is a symmetric predicate (and the same holds for L that describes its support) because no matter how we make the assignment of the input to the agents, the truth of the predicate only depends on cardinalities of symbols. The protocol that we have just described is formally presented as Protocol 1.

Protocol 1 *Flock of Birds*

1: $X = \{0, 1\}$
2: $Y = \{0, 1\}$
3: $Q = \{q_0, q_1, \ldots, q_5\}$
4: $I(0) = q_0$ and $I(1) = q_1$
5: $O(q_i) = 0$, for $0 \leq i \leq 4$, and $O(q_5) = 1$
6: δ:

$$(q_i, q_j) \rightarrow (q_{i+j}, q_0), \text{ if } i + j < 5$$
$$\rightarrow (q_5, q_5), \text{ otherwise}$$

We are now ready to give a formal proof that Protocol 1 stably computes the predicate

$$p(x) = \begin{cases} 1, & \text{if } N_1 \geq 5 \\ 0, & \text{if } N_1 < 5, \end{cases}$$

where, in general, N_σ denotes the number of agents that get input symbol $\sigma \in X$. Another way to write the predicate is ($N_1 \geq 5$), which specifies that the value "true" is expected as output by all agents for every input assignment that provides at least 5 agents with the input symbol 1.

There is no transition in δ that decreases the sum of the indices. In particular, if $i + j < 5$, then transitions are of the form $(q_i, q_j) \to (q_{i+j}, q_0)$ and leave the sum unaffected, while if $i + j \geq 5$ then transitions are of the form $(q_i, q_j) \to (q_5, q_5)$ and all strictly increase it except for $(q_5, q_5) \to (q_5, q_5)$ that leaves it unaffected. So the initial sum is always preserved except for the case where state q_5 appears. If $N_1 < 5$, then it suffices to prove that state q_5 does not appear because then all agents will forever remain in states $\{q_0, \dots, q_4\}$ that give output 0. Assume that it appears. When this happened for the first time, it was because the sum of the states of two interacting agents was at least 5. But this is a contradiction because the initial sum should have been preserved until q_5 appeared. We now prove that if q_5 ever appears then all agents will eventually get it and remain to it forever. Obviously, if all get q_5, then they cannot escape from it because no transition does this; thus, they forever remain to it. Now assume that q_5 has appeared in agent u and that agent $v \neq u$ never gets it. From the time that u got q_5, it could not change its state; thus, any interaction of u and v would make v's state be q_5. This implies that u and v did not interact for infinitely many steps, but this clearly violates the fairness condition (a configuration in which v is in q_5 was always reachable in one step but was never reached). Now, if $N_1 \geq 5$, then it suffices to prove that q_5 appears. To see this, notice that all reachable configurations c for which $c_{q_5} = 0$ can reach in one step themselves and some configurations that preserve the sum but decrease the number of agents not in state q_0. Due to fairness, this will lead to a decrease by one in the number of non-q_0 agents in a finite number of steps, implying an increase in one agent's state index. This process ends either when all indices have been aggregated to one agent or when two agents, having a sum of indices at least 5, interact, and it must end; otherwise, the number of q_0 agents would increase an unbounded number of times, being impossible for a fixed n.

Note that such proofs are simplified a lot when we use arguments of the form "if q_5 appears, then due to fairness, all agents will eventually obtain it," and "due to fairness, the sum will eventually be aggregated to one agent unless q_5 appears first" without getting into the details of the fairness assumption. Of course, we have to be very careful when using abstractions of this kind.

Example 1.6   Majority Protocol [AAD$^+$04]   The majority predicate becomes 1 (true) if there are more 1s than 0s in the input assignment, otherwise, becomes 0. We describe a protocol that stably computes the majority predicate.

The protocol is based on the *live bit* idea. The states of the agents consist of two components, where the first one is the counter bit and the second one is the live bit. Initially, each agent that reads input 0 sets its counter to -1, and each agent that reads 1 sets its counter to 1, while the live bit is initially 1 in all agents. Call an agent *awake* if its live bit is 1, otherwise, call it *asleep*. Notice that if under the initial configuration the sum of the counters is positive, then there are more 1s than 0s in the input, otherwise, the number of 0s is at least the number of 1s. When two awake agents interact, if the sum of their counters is in $\{-1, 0, 1\}$, then both set their counters to the value of sum and one of them becomes asleep, w.l.o.g. let it be the responder; otherwise, they do nothing. Therefore, the ineffective interactions are those between awake agents that both have counter 1 or both -1. Whenever some agent becomes asleep, it forever copies the counter of any awake agent that it encounters. Notice that interactions between two agents with counters 1 and -1, respectively, eliminate these values since one of them remains awake and keeps the value 0, while the other becomes asleep. Moreover, when a 0 interacts with a 1 or a -1, the sum is 1 or -1, respectively; it is copied by both agents and one of them becomes asleep; thus, 0 is eliminated by the awake subset of the agents. Eventually, a final set of awake agents will remain, which will not be capable of modifying their counters, since any pairwise sum will always lie outside $\{-1, 0, 1\}$, and in this equilibrium state, it is obvious that either all agents will have counter equal to 1, or all equal to -1, or all equal to 0 (even those that are asleep, since they will have copied it from the awake agents). Thus, if the output function is defined as $O(1) = 1$ and $O(-1) = O(0) = 0$, then this protocol stably computes the majority predicate.

To prove this formally, one has to notice that, in each step, the sum of the counters of the awake agents is preserved and is equal to the number of 1s minus the number of 0s in the input. The protocol keeps eliminating counters whose sum is equal to zero, and either there will remain awake 1s that have nothing to be eliminated with (which means that there were more 1s in the input), or only awake -1 that have nothing to be eliminated with (which means that there were more 0s in the input), or only one awake 0 that has no other awake agent to interact with (there was an equal number of 0s and 1s in the input). In any case, all agents obtain the correct counter value and the output function provides the correct answer in all agents.

The above protocol incorporates a generic idea for computing predicates of the form $(k \cdot N_1 - l \cdot N_0 \geq 0)$, where, recall that N_1 denotes the number of 1s in the input, N_0 the number of 0s in the input (that is $N_0 + N_1 = n$ for $X = \{0, 1\}$), and k, l are positive integers (fixed and independent of n). Consider the predicate p that is defined as $(k \cdot N_1 - l \cdot N_0 \geq 0)$. We have that $p(x) = 1$ iff the input assignment x satisfies the inequality. The states of the agents consist again of a counter and a live bit. The counter can take all integer values from $-l$ to k inclusive. Initially, all agents are awake, and those agents that obtain input 1 set their counter to k, while those that obtain 0 set their counter to $-l$. Notice that the initial sum of all counters is equal to $k \cdot N_1 - l \cdot N_0$. When two awake agents interact, if the sum of their counters is in $\{-l, \ldots, 0, \ldots, k\}$, then both set their counters to the value of the sum and one of them becomes asleep; otherwise, they do nothing. Each asleep agent simply copies the counter of any awake agent that it encounters. In this manner, the sum of the counters is always preserved and equals $k \cdot N_1 - l \cdot N_0$. At some point, any interaction between asleep agents will have no effect. This will mean that either all agents have positive counters, or all have negative counters, or there has remained a single awake agent whose counter is 0. Due to the fact that all asleep agents copy the counters of the awake ones, in the first case, the population will have positive counter, while in the other two cases nonpositive counter. The output of an agent is 1 if its counter is nonnegative and 0, otherwise (if instead of $\geq$ we wished to compute $>$, then the output should be 1 only if the counter was strictly positive). After the above discussion, it should be clear that the protocol we have just described stably computes the predicate $(k \cdot N_1 - l \cdot N_0 \geq 0)$.

Notice now that:

$$k \cdot N_1 - l \cdot N_0 \geq 0 \Leftrightarrow$$
$$k \cdot N_1 \geq l \cdot N_0 \Leftrightarrow$$
$$k \cdot N_1 + l \cdot N_1 \geq l(N_0 + N_1) \Leftrightarrow$$
$$N_1 \geq \frac{l}{k+l}n$$

Thus, predicate p is equivalent to the predicate that is true if at least $l/(k+l)$ of the input symbols are 1 and false, otherwise. Thus, due to the protocol we have just described, for any fraction of the agents that can be written as $l/(k+l)$ for strictly positive integers k and l (fixed and independent of n), the corresponding predicate, which is true iff at least $100l/(k+l)\%$ of the input symbols are 1, is stably computable by the population protocol model.

So, for example, it is easy now to determine whether there exists a protocol that stably computes whether at least 5% of the agents have detected elevated barometric pressure, because $l/(k+l) = 5/100 = 1/20 = 1/(19+1)$ (we reduce $5/100$ to its lowest terms, by dividing both the nominator and the denominator by $\gcd(5, 100)$, thus becomes $1/20$, in order to use the smallest possible counters); that is, $k = 19$ and $l = 1$; thus, it is the protocol that stably computes the predicate $(19N_1 - N_0 \geq 0)$, which has been already shown to exist. This answers a question posed at the beginning of the current section.

1.3   COMPUTATIONAL COMPLEXITY

The monograph is full of complexity classes. The reason is that for each model that we define, we are mainly interested in studying its computational power. To do that, we define the corresponding complexity class of stably computable predicates and usually try to associate it with some existing standard space complexity classes. We review here a few definitions from Complexity Theory that are required throughout the text.

Let us begin with the well-known *Big-Oh notation*.

Definition 1.7   [Knu76]   If f, g are two functions from $\mathbb{N}$ to itself, then we write

1. $f = \mathcal{O}(g)$, and say that f is *asymptotically at most* g, if there exists constants c, n_0, such that $f(n) \leq cg(n)$ for every $n \geq n_0$ (that is, for every sufficiently large n),

2. $f = \Omega(g)$, and say that f is asymptotically *at least* g, if $g = \mathcal{O}(f)$,

3. $f = \Theta(g)$, and say that f is asymptotically *the same as* g, if $f = \mathcal{O}(g)$ and $g = \mathcal{O}(f)$, and

4. $f = o(g)$, and say that f is asymptotically *strictly smaller than* g, if $\lim_{n \to \infty} \frac{f(n)}{g(n)} = 0$ or, equivalently, if for any $c > 0$, a n_0 exists, where $f(n) < cg(n)$ for all $n \geq n_0$.

To emphasize the input parameter, we often write $f(n) = \mathcal{O}(g(n))$ instead of $f = \mathcal{O}(g)$, and use similar notation for Ω, Θ, and o. [3]

In general, a *complexity class* is a set of functions that can be computed within given resource bounds, such as time and space. In the special case of Boolean functions (that is, predicates), we can think of a complexity class as containing *decision problems* or *languages*. When the resource under consideration is time, **P** is the class of all languages decidable by some deterministic TM in polynomial time (always as a function of the length of the input) and **NP** the class of all languages verifiable in polynomial time (or, equivalently, decidable by some polynomial time nondeterministic TM). A language is **NP**-hard if all languages in **NP** reduce to it in polynomial time and **NP**-complete if additionally belongs itself to **NP**. Now we turn our attention to the resource of space. Let $f : \mathbb{N} \to \mathbb{N}$ and $L \subseteq \Sigma^*$ for some finite alphabet Σ. We say that $L \in \textbf{SPACE}(f(n))$ if there is a (deterministic) TM deciding L in $\mathcal{O}(f(n))$ space. In general, a TM $\mathcal{M}$ decides a language L in $g(n)$ space, if $g(n)$ is the maximum number of tape cells that $\mathcal{M}$ scans on any input of length n. Similarly, for a nondeterministic TM $\mathcal{N}$, we require that, on any input of length n, $\mathcal{N}$ scans, at most, $g(n)$ cells on any branch of its computation. We say that $L \in \textbf{NSPACE}(f(n))$ if there is a nondeterministic TM deciding L in $\mathcal{O}(f(n))$ space. We also define the classes $\textbf{L} := \textbf{SPACE}(\log n)$ and $\textbf{NL} := \textbf{NSPACE}(\log n)$. When we place an 'S' in front of a complexity class **A**, (that is, write **SA**) we refer to the subclass of **A** consisting of all *Symmetric* languages in **A**. In particular, we define **SSPACE, SNSPACE, SL,** and **SNL** to be the symmetric subclasses of **SPACE, NSPACE, L,** and **NL**, respectively. Given a complexity class **A**, we define $\textbf{coA} := \{L \in \Sigma^* \mid \overline{L} \in \textbf{A}\}$, where $\overline{L} := \Sigma^* - L$ denotes the complement of L. A language L is **coNP**-hard if all problems in **coNP** reduce to it or, equivalently, iff its complement $\overline{L}$ is **NP**-hard.

Savitch's theorem is one of the earliest results concerning space complexity. It shows that deterministic TMs can simulate nondeterministic TMs by using a surprisingly small amount of additional space. Informally, this theorem establishes that any nondeterministic TM that uses $f(n)$ space can be converted to a deterministic TM that uses only $f^2(n)$ space.

Theorem 1.8   Savitch's Theorem [Sav70]   *For any function* $f : \mathbb{N} \to \mathbb{N}$, *where* $f(n) \geq \log n$, $\textbf{NSPACE}(f(n)) \subseteq \textbf{SPACE}(f^2(n))$.

The Immerman-Szelepcsényi theorem states that if a nondeterministic TM decides a language L, then $\overline{L}$ is also decidable by a nondeterministic TM in the same asymptotic amount of space. No

---

[3]Although the letter 'O' is usually used in the Complexity Theory literature for the Big-Oh notation, we have chosen here to use its calligraphic version '$\mathcal{O}$' in order to avoid confusion with the output function of protocols.

similar result is known for the time complexity classes, and, indeed, it is conjectured that **NP** is not equal to **coNP**.

Theorem 1.9   Immerman-Szelepcsényi Theorem [Imm88, Sze87]   *For any function $f : \mathbb{N} \to \mathbb{N}$, where $f(n) \geq \log n$,* **NSPACE**$(f(n)) = $ **coNSPACE**$(f(n))$.

Finally, the Space hierarchy theorem states that, given more space, TMs can compute strictly more languages. Call first a function f from $\mathbb{N}$ to itself, where $f(n) = \mathcal{O}(\log n)$, *space constructible* if the function that maps 1^n (a string of n 1s) to the binary representation of $f(n)$ is computable in $\mathcal{O}(f(n))$ space.

Theorem 1.10   Space Hierarchy Theorem [SHL65]   *For any space constructible function $f : \mathbb{N} \to \mathbb{N}$, a language L exists that is decidable in $\mathcal{O}(f(n))$ (non)deterministic space but not in $o(f(n))$ (non)deterministic space.*

Recently, it has been proven that in fact f need not be space constructible if we consider the unary alphabet $\Sigma = \{1\}$. This is captured by the following theorem.

Theorem 1.11   Symmetric Space Hierarchy Theorem [Gef03]   *For any function $f : \mathbb{N} \to \mathbb{N}$, a symmetric language L exists that is decidable in $\mathcal{O}(f(n))$ (non)deterministic space but not in $o(f(n))$ (non)deterministic space.*

1.4   OVERVIEW OF THE CONTENT

We begin the monograph with an extended introduction to the Population Protocol model. The next two chapters deal with the computational power of the population protocol model and discuss some first variants. One of them aims in solving the problem of protocol composition, the other makes a random scheduling assumption and studies efficiency in computation, and the last one is an enhancement that allows the agents to have unique identifiers (we usually abbreviate identifiers as *identifiers (ids)* and as *unique identifiers (uids)* when we want to emphasize that they are unique). However, the core of the monograph consists of two recently proposed new models for this kind of systems. The first is called the *Mediated Population Protocol* (MPP) model and the second the *Passively mobile Machines* (PM) model. Both constitute generalizations of the population protocol model. Our primary focus is on revealing the computational power of these models.

Each one of these models has its own special value. The MPP model, although less realistic, greatly reveals the cooperative power of these systems. Focusing on complete interaction graphs, we first show that the MPP model is computationally stronger than the PP model. To do this, we show that the former can compute a predicate that incorporates multiplication of variables. This is a first indication that the additional memory that we have allowed between each pair of agents can be used in a systematic fashion in order to allow wider computation. In the sequel, we show that the agents can get organized into a spanning line graph and operate as a distributed nondeterministic Turing machine that asymptotically uses the whole available space. This is a clearly unexpected result. Initially anonymous agents, beginning from a totally symmetric initial state of the system (due to the completeness of the interaction graph) manage to order themselves and exploit this ordering in order to visit their outgoing edges in a systematic fashion, precisely as a TM would visit its $\mathcal{O}(n^2)$ available cells.

The PM model has a value of a different flavor. According to our opinion, it constitutes the basic model of this research area. The reason is that population protocols have only covered the case in which the agent memories are of constant size, that is, independent of the population size. On the other hand, the PM model does not impose any restriction concerning the available memory and additionally assumes that each agent is a multitape TM equipped with communication capabilities. In this manner, the profit is twofold: the model better meets the need of contemporary technology, where each computational device is some sort of computer and additionally gives us the opportunity, possibly for the first time in sensor networks, to study the computational power as a function of the available memory. The latter, except for its theoretical interest, has also great practical importance. For each distributed system, we would like to know what can be actually computed as a function of the available memory. If given memory x in each agent, we can compute whatever belongs to a class $\mathbf{A}$, then it is always valuable to know what can be computed with memory $x \pm \varepsilon$. Does the corresponding class fluctuate? If yes, what is the relationship between the new class $\mathbf{B}$ and $\mathbf{A}$? If no, what is the minimum change in memory that would result in a new complexity class?

In this monograph, we present results that manage to provide satisfactory answers to most of these questions. In particular, we show that for memories strictly smaller than $\log \log n$ everything computable is semilinear (semilinearity is thoroughly discussed in Section 2.1), while for memories at least $\log \log n$ the computation of the first non-semilinear predicates begins. In other words, it turns out that population protocols not only model constant memories, but also memories that have some slight dependence on the population size. If memory exceeds $\log \log n$, then the class of computable predicates expands. Moreover, as we shall see, for memories $f(n)$, which is at least $\log n$, the class is in fact extremely wide: *it is the class of all symmetric languages in* $\mathbf{NSPACE}(nf(n))$. This provides a complete picture of what happens for these space bounds: *the more the available space grows the more we gain in computability*, a fact that answers in the affirmative the corresponding question of existence of some space hierarchy in the model and is of fundamental importance for any computational system. Moreover, we show that for $f(n)$ strictly smaller than $\log n$, the class becomes a proper subset of the class of symmetric languages in $\mathbf{NSPACE}(nf(n))$. This result makes the space bound $\log n$ outstanding: not only it constitutes a logical and realistic space requirement, but also it constitutes the first bound at which the computational behavior $\mathbf{NSPACE}(nf(n))$ begins, which happens to be the best behavior that we might had expected from this kind of systems (since the whole distributed memory is exploited in a nondeterministic TM simulation). In simple words, it turns out that $\log n$ is a golden section for the trade-off between memory and computational power.

At the end of this chapter, the reader can find tables summarizing all model abbreviations and all complexity classes that appear throughout the text.

1.5   ORGANIZATION OF THE TEXT

Chapter 2 studies the computational power of the Population Protocol model. In particular, the whole chapter is devoted to proving that the class of predicates computable by population protocols is precisely the class of semilinear predicates or equivalently the class of all predicates that can be defined in some first-order logical theory known as Presburger arithmetic.

Chapter 3 discusses some first variants of the Population Protocol model. In particular, the chapter briefly presents the variant with stabilizing inputs that mainly aims to formalize the composition concept of population protocols, the Probabilistic Population Protocol model that assumes a random uniform scheduler, and the Community Protocol model that allows the agents to have access to unique ids.

Chapter 4 defines the Mediated Population Protocol model and initially focuses on stable computation of predicates on complete interaction graphs. In particular, it is first proved that the class of computable predicates is wider than the class of semilinear predicates and in the sequel the main result is presented, establishing that the class is equal to the class of symmetric languages in $\mathbf{NSPACE}(n^2)$. In the sequel, the chapter deals with the MPP model from a completely different perspective. The goal is now the understanding of the ability of the model to stably compute graph properties. The focus is first on weakly connected graphs and the discussion provides closure results, shows the computability of several important graph properties and shows the inability of the model, when restricted to some class of state-stabilizing protocols, to compute a particular property. The rest of the chapter deals with the case in which the interaction graphs may well be disconnected. Here it is proved that no nontrivial graph property can be computed.

Chapter 5 defines the Passively mobile Machines model and focuses as well on the stable computation of predicates on complete interaction graphs. In the beginning, it focuses on agents whose memory does not exceed $\log n$. It turns out that the corresponding class is equal to the symmetric subclass of $\mathbf{NSPACE}(n \log n)$, a fact that makes this bound quite satisfactory. The proof shows that the agents, by exploiting the technique of reinitializing their computation, can assign unique consecutive ids to themselves and become organized into a distributed TM. Note that this space bound provides the required space for assigning unique ids. Then the chapter deals with the computational capabilities of the PM model for several different space bounds. In particular, it is proven that, for space bounds at least $\log n$, all resulting classes are similar in the sense that the agents can always obtain unique ids and as a result become organized into a TM that uses all the available space. For space bounds that are strictly smaller than $\log n$, it is shown that the above behavior ceases. For space bounds strictly smaller than $\log \log n$, it is proven that the class is precisely the class of semilinear predicates, while for bounds at least $\log \log n$ the computability of the first non-semilinear predicates begins.

Finally, Chapter 6 discusses some conclusions and many promising open research directions.

1.6   EXERCISES

1.1.   Prove Theorem 1.2.

1.2.   Show that the class of stably computable predicates is closed under complement, union, and intersection operations.

Hint: Fix an input alphabet and consider the operations over the supports of the predicates.

1.3.   This exercise asks you to prove a first upper bound on the class of computable predicates. Show that the class of computable predicates is in the complexity class **SNL**.

Hint: Show that a nondeterministic TM can determine the output of any population protocol on any input assignment to that protocol in $\mathcal{O}(\log n)$ space.

1.4.   Try to devise protocols for the predicates $(N_1 = 2^t)$, for some t, and $(N_c = N_a \cdot N_b)$ to get a feeling of what the model is not capable of doing.

1.5.   Show that if the interaction graph is always a directed (hamiltonian) line (that is, if $V = \{1, 2, \ldots n\}$, then E is of the form $\{(i, i + 1) \mid i = 1, 2, \ldots, n - 1\}$) then population protocols can simulate a linear-space Turing machine that decides some symmetric language; that is, **SSPACE**(n), is a subset of the class of predicates computable by population protocols on this kind of universe.

1.6.   Consider the following alternative definition of fairness: "all interactions occur infinitely often". Does this imply the definition of fairness that we have chosen to follow? Show also an execution that is fair (according to our notion), although some interaction never occurs.

1.7.   Consider that the interaction graph $G = (V, E)$ may be any weakly-connected digraph. It is possible to devise population protocols that stably decide whether the interaction graph on which they run has a specific property, for example, whether it is a directed cycle. By ignoring the inputs, define formally what does it mean for a protocol to stably decide a graph property. Then devise protocols to stably decide the following graph properties:

- G is a directed cycle.
- G has a node of in-degree greater than 1.
- G has a node of in-degree 0.
- G is an out-directed star (one node has in-degree 0 and all other nodes have in-degree 1 and out-degree 0).
- G is a directed line.

Add some more symmetry to the model by assuming that E is always symmetric, but keep the initiator-responder symmetry breaking assumption. Note that this is a way to define undirected graphs. Devise a protocol to stably decide whether G is an undirected star (one node has degree $n - 1$ and all other nodes have degree 1).

1.8. Given a population protocol $\mathcal{A}$, if Q is the set of $\mathcal{A}$'s states and if $\mathcal{A}$ runs on the complete interaction graph of n nodes, show that there are $(1 + \frac{n}{|Q|-1})^{|Q|-1}$ different configurations.

1.9. Devise a population protocol to stably compute whether there is an even number of 1s in the input.

Hint: Your parity protocol could incorporate the live bit idea of Example 1.6.

1.10. Consider the following *integer encoding convention*: Each $\sigma \in X$ corresponds to a k-vector of integers from $\mathbb{Z}^k$, denoted as $\rho(\sigma)$. Any input assignment $x = \sigma_1 \sigma_2 \ldots \sigma_n \in \mathcal{X}$ corresponds to the k-vector of integers $\rho(x) := \sum_{i=1}^{n} \rho(\sigma_i)$. We can similarly define the vectors *represented by* configurations and output assignments.

    (a) Do you see why by this encoding convention we can represent $\mathcal{O}(1)$ integers with absolute values bounded by $\mathcal{O}(n)$?

    (b) Define stable computation with respect to (w.r.t.) the integer encoding convention so that the population may now compute functions from $\mathbb{Z}^k$ to $\mathbb{Z}^l$.

    (c) Present a population protocol to stably compute the function $f(v) = \lfloor 2v/3 \rfloor$, that is, the integer quotient of $2v$ and 3 (for $v \in \mathbb{Z}^k$).

NOTES

The Population Protocol model was proposed by Angluin, Aspnes, Diamadi, Fischer, and Peralta in their 2004 seminal paper "Computation in networks of passively mobile finite-state sensors" [AAD+04]. The full paper appeared two years later [AAD+06] and also contained a proof of one direction of Theorem 1.2; the other direction appears in [CDF+09]. Examples 1.5 and 1.6 are based on stably computable predicates that appeared in these works. The name of the model was inspired by *population processes* in probability theory [Kur81]. It is worth mentioning that the population protocol model shares the fact that its reachability relation is *additive* (intuitively , as we shall in the subsequent chapter see, this means that subpopulations can run on their own) with many other models from divergent areas. These include vector addition systems [HP79, IDE04], some forms of Petri nets [EN94], and 1-cell catalytic P-systems [IDE04]. Theorem 1.3 appears in a survey of Aspnes and Ruppert [AR07]. The Parikh map was defined by Parikh in [Par66]. Savitch's theorem (Theorem 1.8) was, of course, proved by Savitch in 1970 [Sav70]. The Immerman-Szelepcsényi theorem (Theorem 1.9) was proven independently by Immerman and Szelepcsényi in 1987 [Imm88, Sze87]. For this result, Immerman and Szelepcsényi shared the 1995 Gödel Prize. For an elegant proof, the reader is referred to [Pap94] pages $151 - 153$. The space hierarchy theorem (Theorem 1.10) is due to Stearns, Hartmanis, and Lewis [SHL65]. Theorem 1.11 follows immediately from the unary (tally) separation language presented by Geffert in [Gef03] and the fact that any unary language is symmetric. An interesting future possibility is the construction of nano-scale agents. For an application example of outstanding importance, think of the possibility of deploying such agents in the human body (via, e.g., the blood vessels) for health monitoring and/or target treatment [SL05]. Exercises 1.2, 1.3, 1.4,

1.5, 1.9, and 1.10 are based on statements of [AAD⁺04], Exercise 1.6 on a statement of [AR07], Exercise 1.7 on statements of [AAC⁺05], and Exercise 1.8 is from [Spi10].

Any work like the present monograph is faced with the inconvenient situation to choose which of the many interesting results to leave outside. Here, for the sake of completeness and to minimally honor the corresponding researchers, we list some of the results that we have not been able to comprehensively present. However, some of these appear as exercises or as short statements in the text. Chatzigiannakis, Dolev, Fekete, Michail, and Spirakis proposed in [CDF⁺09] a generic definition of probabilistic schedulers and a collection of new fair schedulers, and they revealed the need for the protocols to adapt when natural modifications of the mobility pattern occur. Bournez, Chassaing, Cohen, Gerin, and Koegler [BCC⁺09] and Chatzigiannakis and Spirakis [CS08] independently considered a huge population hypothesis (population going to infinity), and studied the dynamics, stability and computational power of probabilistic population protocols by exploiting the tools of continuous nonlinear dynamics. Some other works incorporated agent failures. We know how to transform any protocol that computes a function in the failure-free model into a protocol that can tolerate $\mathcal{O}(1)$ crash failures. However, this requires some inevitable weakening of the problem specification. This result was proved in 2006 by Delporte-Gallet, Fauconnier, Guerraoui, and Ruppert [DGFGR06]. Additionally, Guerraoui and Ruppert [GR09] showed that any function computable by a population protocol tolerating one Byzantine agent is trivial. On the other hand, Angluin, Aspnes, and Eisenstat [AAE08b] described a population protocol that computes majority tolerating $\mathcal{O}(\sqrt{n})$ Byzantine failures. However, that protocol was designed for a much more restricted setting, where the scheduler chooses the next interaction randomly and uniformly (see the probabilistic population protocol model in Section 3.3). Moreover, in [GR09], Guerraoui, and Ruppert proved that their Community Protocol model, which, as we shall see in Section 3.4, extends the population protocol model with unique ids, can tolerate $\mathcal{O}(1)$ Byzantine agents [GR09]. Angluin, Aspnes, Fischer, and Jiang studied, in 2008, the *self-stabilizing* variant of population protocols [AAFJ08]. The reader is reffered to the book of Dolev [Dol00] for an introduction to the concept of self-stabilization. Recently, Bournez, Chalopin, Cohen, and Koegler [BCCK09a, BCCK09b] investigated the possibility of studying population protocols via game-theoretic approaches. For a brief but excellent introduction to the subject of population protocols see the 2007 survey of Aspnes and Ruppert [AR07] and for a survey on Mediated Population Protocols and their ability to decide graph languages see the 2009 survey of Chatzigiannakis, Michail, and Spirakis [CMS09d]. Very recently, Beauquier, Burman, Clement, and Kutten [BBCK10] gave a very interesting new insight by considering agents with heterogeneous speeds. They defined the speed of an agent as the number of interactions needed to interact with all other agents, called *cover time*. Then they proposed to study the worst-case complexity of protocols that have some limited access to the cover times (they do not know them but can tell if an agent is faster than some other) and applied their theory to a gathering problem. Finally, the *Static Synchronous Sensor Field* (SSSF) [ADGS09], of Àlvarez, Duch, Gabarro, and Serna, is a very promising recently proposed model that addresses networks of tiny heterogeneous computational devices and additionally allows processing over constant flows (*streams*) of data originating from the environment. The latter feature is totally absent from the models discussed in this monograph and is required by various sensing problems. Also, very recently, the relationship between the SSSF model and the MPP model has been studied via simulations by Àlvarez, Serna, and Spirakis [ASS10].

TABLES OF MODELS' ABBREVIATIONS AND COMPLEXITY CLASSES

MODELS' ABBREVIATIONS

PP	Population Protocol model
CP	Community Protocol model
MPP	Mediated Population Protocol model
SMPP	Symmetric Mediated Population Protocol model
GDMPP	Graph Decision Mediated Population Protocol model
PALOMA	Passively mobile LOgarithmic space Machines model
PM	Passively mobile Machines model
IPM	Passively mobile Machines with unique Identifiers model

COMPLEXITY CLASSES

General Classes	
P	All languages decidable by some deterministic TM in polynomial time
NP	All languages verifiable in polynomial time
NP-hard	Contains any language s.t. all languages in **NP** reduce to it in polynomial time
NP-complete	:= **NP**-hard $\cap$ **NP**
SPACE($f(n)$)	All languages decidable by some deterministic TM in $\mathcal{O}(f(n))$ space
NSPACE($f(n)$)	All languages decidable by some nondeterministic TM in $\mathcal{O}(f(n))$ space
L	:= **SPACE**($\log n$)
NL	:= **NSPACE**($\log n$)
SA	The symmetric subclass of any class **A**
coNP-hard	All languages whose complements are **NP**-hard
SEM	semilinear predicates

Community Protocol model	
CP (is proved equal to **NSPACE**($n \log n$))	Stably computable predicates by the Community Protocol model in complete interaction graphs
RCP (is proved equal to **CP**)	**CP** restricted to the case where agents can only have the uids $\{0, 1, \ldots, n-1\}$

Mediated Population Protocol model	
MPS (is proved equal to **NSPACE**(n^2))	Stably computable predicates by the Mediated Population Protocol model in complete interaction graphs and initially identical edges

Passively mobile Machines model	
PMSPACE$(f(n))$ $(=$ **NSPACE**$(n$ $f(n))$ for $f(n) = \Omega(\log n)$, $=$ **SEM** for $f(n) = o(\log \log n)$, $\supsetneq$ **SEM** and $\subsetneq$ **NSPACE**$(nf(n))$ for $f(n) = \Omega(\log \log n)$ and $f(n) = o(\log n))$	Stably computable predicates by some PM protocol that uses $\mathcal{O}(f(n))$ space in every agent
IPMSPACE$(f(n))$	Stably computable predicates by some IPM protocol that uses $\mathcal{O}(f(n))$ space in every agent
SIPMSPACE$(f(n))$	The symmetric subclass of **IPMSPACE**$(f(n))$

CHAPTER 2

The Computational Power of Population Protocols

This chapter is devoted to proving the following exact characterization of the computational power of population protocols on complete interaction graphs.

Theorem 2.1 [AAD$^+$06, AAE06] *A predicate is stably computable by the population protocol model iff it is semilinear.*

We begin by reviewing, in Section 2.1, the properties of Presburger arithmetic and the closely related semilinear sets. We will then show in Section 2.2 that any predicate that can be defined in Presburger arithmetic is stably computable by the population protocol model in complete interaction graphs and, finally, in Section 2.3 that this inclusion holds with equality, thus, arriving at the exact characterization of the computational power of population protocols of Theorem 2.1.

2.1 SEMILINEAR SETS AND PRESBURGER ARITHMETIC

Presburger arithmetic is a first-order logical theory that, in two words, contains addition and $<$. It is a decidable theory that allows the definition of predicates like those presented in the examples of the previous section. The common definition of Presburger arithmetic assumes a first-order logical language that contains a single functional symbol, "+", the constants "0" and "1", the predicates "=" and "$<$", the usual logical connectives "∧", "∨" and "¬", variables $x_1, x_2, \ldots$ and the quantifiers "∀" (universal) and "∃" (existential). The underlying set on which the quantifiers apply is the set of all integers $\mathbb{Z}$ (for example, formula $\exists x(x = 5)$, where 5 denotes $1 + 1 + 1 + 1 + 1$, is true since there exists an integer equal to 5, while on the other hand $\forall x(x = 5)$ is false since not all integers are equal to 5). The operation "+" is the usual integer addition. Constants "0" and "1" have their usual interpretation as integers. "=" and "$<$" are interpreted as the usual binary relations of equality and less than, respectively, on the set of integers.

A formula in Presburger arithmetic $\phi(x_1, \ldots, x_k)$ with free variables (not depending on any quantifier) $x_1, \ldots, x_k$ *defines* a predicate $p_\phi : \mathbb{Z}^k \to \{0, 1\}$ as follows: For any k-vector of integers $(u_1, \ldots, u_k) \in \mathbb{Z}^k$, it holds that $p_\phi(u_1, \ldots, u_k) = 1$ if formula $\phi(x_1, \ldots, x_k)$ becomes true whenever the variables $x_1, \ldots, x_k$ take the values $u_1, \ldots, u_k$, respectively, and $p_\phi(u_1, \ldots, u_k) = 0$, otherwise. A subset S of $\mathbb{Z}^k$ is called *Presburger-definable*, or simply *definable*, if there exists a logical formula $\phi(x_1, \ldots, x_k)$ with free variables $x_1, \ldots, x_k$ such that

$$S = \{(u_1, u_2, \ldots, u_k) \mid (u_1, u_2, \ldots, u_k) \in \mathbb{Z}^k \text{ and } \phi(u_1, u_2, \ldots, u_k)$$
$$\text{is true}\}.$$

We have shown that any Presburger formula ϕ defines a predicate F_ϕ. It is worth noting that the subset of $\mathbb{Z}^k$, consisting of all $(u_1, u_2, \ldots, u_k)$ for which $F_\phi(u_1, u_2, \ldots, u_k) = 1$ is definable. The same holds also for the definable subsets of $\mathbb{N}^k$, which are simply those definable subsets of $\mathbb{Z}^k$ that are in $\mathbb{N}^k$.

The predicates that can be defined in the above manner in Presburger arithmetic are closely related to the semilinear sets. A set $L \subseteq \mathbb{N}^k$ (similarly for $\mathbb{Z}^k$) is *linear* if there are vectors $v_0, v_1, \ldots, v_m \in \mathbb{N}^k$ (k-vectors of natural numbers) such that

$$L = \{v_0 + \alpha_1 v_1 + \ldots + \alpha_m v_m \mid \alpha_1, \ldots, \alpha_m \in \mathbb{N}\}$$
$$= v_0 + \{v_1, \ldots, v_m\}^*.$$

In simple words, a linear subset of $\mathbb{N}^k$ can be constructed by beginning from any k-vector $v_0 \in \mathbb{N}^k$, known as a *base point*, and adding to it an arbitrary number of times k-vectors from a finite set, e.g., 1 time v_1 and 0 times the rest, 2 times v_1 and 0 times the rest,..., 1 time v_1, 1 time v_2 and 0 times the rest, and so on.

A set is a *semilinear subset* of $\mathbb{N}^k$ if it is the union of a finite number of linear subsets of $\mathbb{N}^k$. Consider, for example, the sets

$$L_1 = (1, 2) + \{(3, 5), (7, 11)\}^*$$
$$L_2 = (1, 1) + \{(2, 3), (5, 7), (4, 0)\}^*$$
$$L = L_1 \cup L_2.$$

L_1 and L_2 are linear subsets of $\mathbb{N}^2$, and so L is by definition a semilinear subset of $\mathbb{N}^2$.

Let's see another example to make the above definitions clear.

Example 2.2   Consider the linear subset of $\mathbb{N}^2$, defined as $L_3 = \{(1, 0) + \alpha_1(0, 1) + \alpha_2(2, 1)\}$. This set consists of the base point $(1, 0)$, the point $(1, 1)$, resulting by $\alpha_1 = 1$ and $\alpha_2 = 0$, generally all points $(1, d)$, resulting by $\alpha_1 = d$ and $\alpha_2 = 0$ for any natural number $d \geq 0$, and more generally all points $(2l + 1, d + l)$, resulting by $\alpha_1 = d$ and $\alpha_2 = l$ for all natural numbers $d \geq 0$ and $l \geq 0$. Consider also the linear subset of $\mathbb{N}^2$, defined as $L_4 = \{(0, 2) + \alpha_3(2, 0)\}$. Here it is easy to see that L_4 consists of the points $(0, 2), (2, 2),\ldots,(2t, 2)$ for any natural number $t \geq 0$. In Figure 2.1, the black circles represent part of the points of the linear set L_3, while the gray circles represent part of L_4's points. The set $S = L_3 \cup L_4$ is a semilinear set consisting of all points of L_3 and L_4 (black and gray in Figure 2.1), and it equivalently consists of all satisfying assignments (x, y) of the formula

$$(\exists z : (x = z + z + 1) \wedge (y \geq z)) \tag{2.1}$$
$$\vee (\exists z : (x = z + z) \wedge (y = 1 + 1)), \tag{2.2}$$

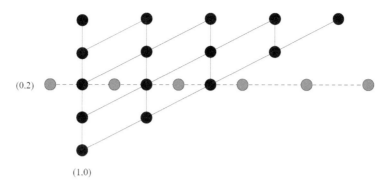

Figure 2.1: A semilinear set S (all circles), which is equal to the union of the linear set $L_3 = \{(1, 0) + \alpha_1(0, 1) + \alpha_2(2, 1)\}$ (black circles) and the linear set $L_4 = \{(0, 2) + \alpha_3(2, 0)\}$ (gray circles). This figure is from [AAE06] and is reproduced with permission of the authors.

where $a = b$ abbreviates $\neg(a < b \vee b < a)$ and $a \geq b$ abbreviates $\neg(b < a)$.

The following theorem, due to Ginsburg and Spanier, which we state without proof, establishes the equivalence between semilinear predicates and Presburger arithmetic.

Theorem 2.3 [GS66]   *A subset of $\mathbb{N}^k$ is semilinear iff it is definable in Presburger arithmetic.*

It is now immediate that:

Corollary 2.4   *Semilinear sets are closed under complement, finite intersection, and finite union.*

We saw what it means for a set to be semilinear. But when do we call a predicate semilinear? We say that *a predicate $p : \mathbb{N}^k \to \{0, 1\}$ is semilinear* if $p^{-1}(1)$ is a semilinear set. It is worth noting that due to closure of semilinear sets under complement it is equivalent to ask for $p^{-1}(0)$ to be semilinear. The class of semilinear predicates is often in this monograph denoted as **SEM**.

The following theorem, which we state without proof, is crucial since it allows us to restrict our attention only to formulas with no quantifiers (invoked by Theorem 2.12).

Theorem 2.5 [Pre29]   *Every predicate definable in Presburger arithmetic has an equivalent quantifier-free formula.*

2.2   SEMILINEAR PREDICATES ARE STABLY COMPUTABLE

We are now going to establish the first direction of Theorem 2.1. In particular, we will show that every predicate definable in Presburger arithmetic is stably computable, which, by also taking into account Theorem 2.3, implies that semilinear predicates are stably computable. Let $X = \{\sigma_1, \ldots, \sigma_k\}$ be an arbitrary input alphabet. Let a_i, c, and m be integer constants with $m \geq 2$. We will first establish (this is captured by Lemma 2.11) that the following predicates on nonnegative integers $N_1, \ldots, N_k$ (where, as usual, N_i denotes the number of agents with input σ_i) are stably computable by the population protocol model on complete interaction graphs:

1. $\sum_{i=1}^{k} a_i N_i < c$

2. $\sum_{i=1}^{k} a_i N_i \equiv c \pmod{m}$.

Call these the *threshold* and the *remainder* predicates, respectively. Then, in Theorem 2.12, we show that all Presburger formulas on nonnegative integers can be rewritten by using elementary combinations of the threshold and the remainder predicates, thus arriving at the required result.

　　　We only prove the stable computation of the threshold predicate. The proof that we present is constructive; that is, a parameterized protocol is presented that stably computes the generic threshold predicate. Exercise 2.2 asks you to do the same for the remainder predicate. However, since the two protocols are similar in spirit, we only leave to you the definition of the remainder's protocol transition function (which, for a hint, follows by a slight modification of that of the threshold protocol) and its proof of correctness. Let $s = \max(|c| + 1, m, \max_i |a_i|)$, where m is not needed in the case of the threshold predicate, and we consider it as 0. The set of states of both protocols is $\{0, 1\} \times \{0, 1\} \times \{u \mid u \in \mathbb{Z}$ and $-s \leq u \leq s\}$. Therefore, each state consists of two components that take binary values and a component that takes integer values. The first component is again called the *live bit* (the reader is strongly encouraged to revise Example 1.6 since the main idea of the protocols to be devised here is a generalization of the techniques employed in the majority protocol). An agent with live bit 1 is again called awake, and an agent with live bit 0 is called asleep. The second component is the output component used by the agents to store their output (in fact, each asleep agent sets its output component to the output value of any awake agent it interacts with). Finally, the third component is an integer counter. Initially, all agents are awake, their output value is 0, and each one of them that gets input σ_i sets its counter to a_i, which is the coefficient of N_i in the linear combination. Thus, the input function is defined as $I(\sigma_i) = (1, 0, a_i)$. If we now denote by $u_j(C)$, the value of agent's j counter under configuration C and by C_0 the initial configuration, then we have that

$$\sum_{j \in V} u_j(C_0) = \sum_{i=1}^{k} a_i N_i,$$

since σ_i is assigned to N_i agents, consequently, N_i have initially their counters set to a_i, for all $i \in \{1, \ldots, k\}$. The output function O simply maps $(\cdot, b, \cdot)$ to the output symbol $b \in \{0, 1\}$, and, obviously, the output alphabet is $Y = \{0, 1\}$.

We will present the transition function of the threshold protocol shortly. But let us first define, for any integers u, u' with $-s \leq u, u' \leq s$,

$$q(u, u') := \max(-s, \min(s, u + u'))$$

and

$$r(u, u') := u + u' - q(u, u').$$

Note that if the sum $u + u'$ is $-s$, or s, or between $-s$ and s, then $q(u, u') = u + u'$, if $u + u' < -s$, then $q(u, u') = -s$, and if $u + u' > s$, then $q(u, u') = s$. Intuitively, $q(u, u')$ stores as much as it can from the sum of u and u' without overflowing, that is without exceeding the bounds $-s$ and s. Now in what concerns $r(u, u')$, since by the second equation $r(u, u') + q(u, u') = u + u'$, if $q(u, u')$ managed to store the whole sum, then $r(u, u')$ is 0, otherwise $r(u, u')$ stores the part of the sum of u and u' that $q(u, u')$ did not manage to store. It is worth mentioning that $r(u, u')$ is always between $-s$ and s inclusive since $|u + u'| \leq 2s$, thus in the worst case $q(u, u')$ will defer for storing in $r(u, u')$ at most $|s|$. Let finally,

$$b(u, u') = \begin{cases} 1, & \text{if } q(u, u') < c \\ 0, & \text{otherwise.} \end{cases}$$

We are now ready to present the transition function δ of the threshold protocol. It is described by the general rule

$$(l, \cdot, u), (l', \cdot, u') \to (1, b(u, u'), q(u, u')), (0, b(u, u'), r(u, u')),$$

which applies if at least one of l and l' is 1 (that is, there is at least one awake agent in the interaction). If both agents are asleep, that is $l = l' = 0$, then the interaction has no effect. This completes the description of the threshold protocol. We will also make extensive use of the following definitions. Define $A(C)$ to be the set of awake agents under configuration C. Also recall that, for each agent j, $u_j(C)$ denotes the value of agent's j counter under configuration C and define $p(C) := \sum_{j \notin A(C)} |u_j(C)|$, which represents the sum of the counters of all agents that are asleep under configuration C. When no confusion may arise, we will write p instead of $p(C)$ and u_j instead of $u_j(C)$. Finally, only for this protocol, call a configuration C *stable* if there is a unique awake agent l (we use the letter l because another way to think of awake and asleep agents is as leaders and non-leaders, respectively) and one of the following three conditions is satisfied:

1. $p = 0$.

2. $u_l = s$ and $u_j \geq 0$ for all $j \neq l$.

3. $u_l = -s$ and $u_j \leq 0$ for all $j \neq l$.

Lemma 2.6 [AAD$^+$06]   *The threshold protocol converges to a unique awake agent.*

Proof. Initially, there are n awake agents, thus $|A(C_0)| = n$. Throughout the computation any interaction between two awake agents makes one of them asleep, thus reduces $|A(C)|$ by one, and no asleep agent ever wakes up. So, as long as $|A(C)| > 1$, $|A(C)|$ cannot increase, and it is always possible that it may decrease. Fairness ensures that it will eventually (in a finite number of steps) decrease, by guaranteeing that two continuously coexisting awake agents will eventually interact. □

From now on, l will denote the unique awake agent that remains.

Lemma 2.7 [AAD$^+$06] $\sum_{j \in V} u_j(C) = \sum_{i=1}^k a_i N_i$, *for every configuration C.*

Proof. We saw that $\sum_j u_j(C_0) = \sum_i a_i N_i$. We also show that during any interaction, no part of the sum is lost since, always, the sum of the counters after the interaction is equal to the sum of the counters before. Thus, the initial linear combination is always preserved as the sum of the counters of all agents (this is the value that we want to compare to c). □

Lemma 2.8 [AAD$^+$06] *Under a stable configuration, it holds that $u_l = \max(-s, \min(s, \sum_{i=1}^k a_i N_i))$.*

Proof. We simply inspect the three possible conditions for a configuration to be stable. In the first one, by Lemma 2.7, l has the linear combination, and since it can store it, obviously, $-s \le \sum_{i=1}^k a_i N_i \le s$. In the second, it has s, and since all remaining agents have nonnegative counters, $\sum_{i=1}^k a_i N_i \ge s$. Finally, in the third one, it has $-s$, and since all remaining agents have nonpositive counters, $\sum_{i=1}^k a_i N_i \le -s$. □

In simple words, the above lemma states that if $\sum_{i=1}^k a_i N_i$ happens to be between $-s$ and s inclusive, then the unique awake agent will have its counter set to the linear combination, while if $\sum_{i=1}^k a_i x_i < -s$, its counter will be $-s$, and if $\sum_{i=1}^k a_i x_i > s$, it will be s.

It remains to show that the threshold protocol always converges to a stable configuration. If we show this, then the protocol will be correct as follows: In the case where the counter of l is the linear combination, then all other agents have zero counters, and during every interaction between an awake and an asleep agent, the unique remaining awake agent will have its counter again set to the linear combination and both will set their output to 1 if $\sum_{i=1}^k a_i N_i < c$ and to 0, otherwise. Moreover, due to fairness, all asleep agents will eventually interact with l and will copy the correct output value. Similarly, if the final value of l is s, then the linear combination is at least s and therefore at least c since $-s \le c \le s$. In this case, all agents correctly output 0, eventually, since $q(u, u') \ge s \ge c$ in the comparison that determines the outputs during an interaction of an asleep agent with l. The $-s$ case is similar to the s one.

We will establish that the protocol converges to a stable configuration by first proving the following lemma.

Lemma 2.9 **[AAD$^+$06]** *From any non-stable configuration with a unique leader, there is a transition that reduces p and no transition increases p.*

Proof. Under any non-stable configuration with a single awake agent

1. There is a transition that reduces p:

    (a) Let $u_l = s$, and there exists some $j \neq l$, for which $u_j < 0$ holds (if it were $u_j \geq 0$ for all $j \neq l$ then the configuration would have been stable). In this case, an interaction between l and j sets the counter of the agent that remains awake after the interaction (this is the initiator) to $s + u_j$ and the other agent's (this is the responder) counter to 0. Consequently, p is reduced by $|u_j| > 0$.

    (b) Let $u_l = -s$, and there exists some $j \neq l$ for which $u_j > 0$ holds. In this case, an interaction between l and j sets the counter of the responder to 0 (while it was positive for j). Consequently, p is again reduced by $|u_j| > 0$.

    (c) Let $-s < u_l < s$, and there exists some $j \neq l$ for which $u_j \neq 0$ (again, if for all $j \neq l, u_j$ were 0, then $p = 0$ and the configuration would have been stable). When l and j interact, if (i) $u_j > 0$, the counter of the initiator becomes $\min(u_l + u_j, s) = u_l + \min(u_j, s - u_l)$, thus p is reduced by $\min(u_j, s - u_l) > 0$, and if (ii) $u_j < 0$, this case is symmetric and p is reduced by $\min(-u_j, s + u_j) > 0$.

    Therefore, under any non-stable configuration with a single awake agent, there is a transition that reduces p. Fairness then guarantees that such a transition will occur in a finite number of steps.

2. No transition increases p. The remaining possible transitions are the following:

    (a) Those between asleep agents. These have no effect and p remains unchanged.

    (b) Those where $u_l = s$ and the asleep agent j has $u_j \geq 0$. Again p remains unchanged, since the initiator sets its counter to s and the responder to u_j.

    (c) Those where $u_l = -s$ and the asleep agent j has $u_j \leq 0$. Again p remains unchanged, since the initiator sets its counter to $-s$ and the responder to u_j.

    (d) Similarly fo rthose where $-s < u_l < -s$ and $u_j = 0$.

$\square$

Lemma 2.10 **[AAD$^+$06]** *The threshold protocol converges to a stable configuration.*

Proof. By Lemma 2.9, under any non-stable configuration with a unique awake agent, there exists a transition that reduces p, and no transition may increase it. Moreover, by Lemma 2.6, the computation converges to a single awake agent. When this happens, if the computation contained a subsequence of infinite configurations in which p remains unchanged, then since the number of different configurations is finite, at least one of them, let it be C, must appear infinitely often in the subsequence. But, there is a configuration C', resulting from C via some encounter that reduces p, that does not appear in the subsequence since p remains unchanged, which leads as to the contradictory fact that the computation is not fair. This implies that, from the moment that the population remains with a unique awake agent, p will be reduced infinitely often, and it will be reduced at most $\sum_{i=1}^{k} |a_i| N_i$ times until it becomes 0. Thus, in a finite number of steps, either p becomes 0 or at least one of the other two conditions, defining stable configurations, is satisfied. In all these cases, it arrives and forever remains at an infinite sequence of stable configurations. □

Lemma 2.11 [AAD$^+$06] *The predicates*

1. $\sum_{i=1}^{k} a_i N_i < c$

2. $\sum_{i=1}^{k} a_i N_i \equiv c \pmod{m}$

on nonnegative integers are stably computable by the population protocol model on complete interaction graphs.

Proof. The second one follows from Exercise 2.2. For the first one, according to Lemma 2.8 and the explanations following it, stable configurations provide correct outputs w.r.t. to the predicate $\sum_{i=1}^{k} a_i N_i < c$, and by Lemma 2.10, the threshold protocol converges to stable configurations. Thus we conclude that the threshold protocol stably computes the threshold predicate. □

We next generalize Lemma 2.11 to all Presburger-definable predicates. As alluded to at the beginning of the section, the idea is to show that the quantifier-free equivalent (see Theorem 2.5) of any Presburger formula can be rewritten as an easy combination of the threshold and the remainder predicate. Then we can exploit their stable computability to easily stably compute any formula. But before proceeding with that, let us resolve another issue. You may have wondered why does $x \equiv_m y$ define a Presburger formula (in Lemma 2.11, we have $x = \sum_{i=1}^{k} a_i N_i$ and $y = c$). If it is not clear to you, then simply rewrite $x \equiv_m y$ as $\exists z \exists w ((x + z = y) \wedge t = z)$, where t is a first-order expression that adds together m copies of q, i.e.,

$$t = \underbrace{q + q + q + \ldots + q}_{m \text{ times}}.$$

A little thought reveals that the two expressions are equivalent. Moreover, by Theorem 2.5, there is also a quantifier-free equivalent of the above formula.

Theorem 2.12 [AAD$^+$06] *Any Presburger-definable predicate on nonnegative integers is stably computable by the population protocol model on complete interaction graphs.*

Proof. Given a Presburger formula ϕ, apply Theorem 2.5 to convert it to a quantifier-free formula ϕ'. ϕ' can be written in one of the following three general forms:

$$\sum a_i N_i + c_1 < \sum b_i N_i + c_2 \tag{2.3}$$

$$\sum a_i N_i + c_1 = \sum b_i N_i + c_2 \tag{2.4}$$

$$\sum a_i N_i + c_1 \equiv_m \sum b_i N_i + c_2 \tag{2.5}$$

It remains to show that all the above predicates are stably computable.

By rearranging terms, predicates of the form (2.3) can be rewritten as

$$\sum d_i N_i < c$$

where $d_i = a_i - b_i$ for all i and $c = c_2 - c_1$. This is the general form of the threshold predicate and thus Lemma 2.11 applies.

Now, those of the form (2.4) can be written as:

$$\left(\sum a_i N_i + c_1 < \sum b_i N_i + c_2 + 1\right) \wedge \left(\sum a_i N_i + c_1 > \sum b_i N_i + c_2 - 1\right)$$

Both parts are stably computable by the threshold protocol and so is their conjunction (we execute the two threshold protocols in parallel and output 1 iff both output 1).

Finally, predicates of the form (2.5) can be, similarly to case (2.3), rewritten as

$$\sum d_i N_i \equiv_m c.$$

These are again stably computable by the remainder protocol of Lemma 2.11. □

We can now immediately conclude, by combining Theorem 2.3 and Theorem 2.12, that:

Theorem 2.13 [AAD$^+$06]   *If a predicate p is semilinear then it is stably computable.*

This proves the one direction of Theorem 2.1.

2.3   STABLY COMPUTABLE PREDICATES ARE SEMILINEAR

We will now establish an exact characterization of the class of stably computable predicates by population protocols on complete interaction graphs. In particular, we will prove the other direction of Theorem 2.1, which is that any stably computable predicate is semilinear. The proof is based on abstract algebra, so we should begin by some necessary algebraic definitions.

A subset M of $\mathbb{Z}^d$ is a *monoid* if it contains the zero vector 0 and is closed under addition. A monoid M is *finitely generated* if there exists a finite subset $A \subseteq M$ such that every element of

M is a sum of elements from A. Monoids are not always finitely generated. Such an example of a non-finitely generated monoid is $M_{\sqrt{2}} = \{(i, j) \in \mathbb{N}^2 \mid i \leq \sqrt{2}j\}$. For any monoid M and any $v \in \mathbb{Z}^d$, $H = v + M$ is a *monoid coset* (a coset of monoid M).

We may now redefine linear and semilinear sets. A subset L of $\mathbb{Z}^d$ is *linear* if it is a coset of a finitely generated monoid in $\mathbb{Z}^d$, and is *semilinear* if it is a finite union of linear sets, that is, a finite union of cosets of finitely generated monoids. Finally, recall that a predicate $p : \mathcal{X} \to \{0, 1\}$ is semilinear iff its support $p^{-1}(1)$ is semilinear.

So, in order to prove that any stably computable predicate is semilinear, one will have to show that the support of any such predicate is a semilinear set, or equivalently that the support can be decomposed into a finite collection of cosets of finitely generated monoids. The idea is to first prove that the support can be decomposed into a finite collection of cosets of monoids that are not necessarily finitely generated and then show that any such decomposition can be further decomposed into a collection of cosets of finitely generated monoids. The second part is quite involved, so we restrict our presentation to the first one, which incorporates the core idea.

Higman's lemma states that for any infinite sequence $c_1, c_2, c_3, \ldots$ of members of $\mathbb{N}^d$, there exist $i < j$ such that $c_i \leq c_j$. In other words, that $\mathbb{N}^d$ is a *well-quasi-order*. The following are two useful (for our purposes) corollaries to Higman's lemma:

Corollary 2.14 [Hig52] *Every subset of $\mathbb{N}^d$ has finitely many minimal elements under the inclusion ordering $\leq$.*

Corollary 2.15 [Hig52] *Every infinite subset of $\mathbb{N}^d$ contains an infinite chain (i.e., an infinite totally ordered sequence).*

Let us now define a *truncation map* τ_k from $\mathcal{C}$ to itself, for each $k \geq 1$ as:

$$\tau_k(c)[q] := \min(k, c[q]) \text{ for all } q \in Q.$$

Obviously, this map truncates each component of its input to be at most k, for example, $\tau_5(10, 2, 5, 6, 7, 4) = (5, 2, 5, 5, 5, 4)$. It is easy to prove that the above truncation map respects both inclusion and addition, and we do so immediately.

Lemma 2.16 [AAE06] *For all $c, c' \in \mathcal{C}$ and $k \geq 1$, $c \leq c'$ implies $\tau_k(c) \leq \tau_k(c')$.*

Proof. Assume $\tau_k(c)[q] > \tau_k(c')[q]$ for some $q \in Q$. Then $\min(k, c[q]) > \min(k, c'[q])$ which implies that $c[q] > c'[q] \Rightarrow \neg(c \leq c')$, and the latter is contradictory. □

Lemma 2.17 [AAE06] *For all $c, c', d \in \mathcal{C}$ and $k \geq 1$, $\tau_k(c) = \tau_k(c')$ implies $\tau_k(c + d) = \tau_k(c' + d)$.*

Proof. Since $\tau_k(c) = \tau_k(c')$, we have that $\min(k, c[q]) = \min(k, c'[q])$ for all $q \in Q$, thus, either the minimum is k or $c[q] = c'[q]$. In either case, $\min(k, c[q] + d[q]) = \min(k, c'[q] + d[q])$ because in the first case, the minimum remains k, and in the second case, either it becomes $c[q] + d[q] = c'[q] + d[q] < k$ or $c[q] + d[q] = c'[q] + d[q] \geq k$, and it becomes k for both.   □

We will show now a very important property of output stable configurations of population protocols. In particular, in Lemma 2.20, we show that there is a truncation τ_k of fixed size $k \geq 1$ that returns an output stable configuration iff its input was an output stable configuration while preserving the output values. In other words, there is a constant upper bound on the number of agents in each state, such that any increase of a cardinality will not alter the output-stability properties of the corresponding configuration. Denote by S, only for this section, the set of output stable configurations and by $U := C - S$ the set of *output unstable* ones. Moreover, denote by $S_j \subset S$ the set of those output stable configurations that stabilize to the output $j \in \{0, 1\}$. We begin by showing that U is closed upward under inclusion, which, in simple words, means that even if we increase a component of an output unstable configuration, the configuration remains output unstable. Observe that, inductively, this means that we can increase by an arbitrary amount any number of components without altering stability.

Lemma 2.18 [AAE06]   *For all $c \leq c'$, if $c \in U$ then $c' \in U$.*

Proof. Even in the presence of new agents, the scheduler may ignore them for a finite number of steps and choose those interactions concerning c that lead to some modification of the output. Such a modification is guaranteed to exists since c is unstable.   □

We now prove that there exists a truncation τ_k of fixed size $k \geq 1$ that maps unstable configurations to unstable configurations and stable configurations to stable configurations.

Lemma 2.19 [AAE06]   *There exists $k \geq 1$ such that for all $c \in C$, $c \in U$ iff $\tau_k(c) \in U$.*

Proof. By Higman's lemma (in particular, by Corollary 2.14), we have that only finitely many elements are minimal in U, and let them be $u_1, u_2, \ldots, u_t$. So if $c \in U$, we have also that $u_i \leq c$ for some i because either c is minimal (so it is $\leq$ than itself) or it is not in which case it cannot be less than all minimal elements, as this would result in another minimal element not in the list. Moreover, the inverse also holds, that is if $u_i \leq c$ for some i, then $c \in U$ since $u_i \in U$ and by the fact that U is upwards closed (Lemma 2.18).

We set k to be the maximum component $u_i[q]$ for all $1 \leq i \leq t$ and $q \in Q$. We are now ready to prove the statement. If $c \in U$, then $u_i \leq c$ for some i, so by closure of the truncation map under inclusion (Lemma 2.16), we have that $\tau_k(u_i) \leq \tau_k(c)$. But $u_i = \tau_k(u_i)$, thus $u_i \leq \tau_k(c)$, which implies that $\tau_k(c) \in U$. For the other direction, if $\tau_k(c) \in U$, then $u_i \leq \tau_k(c)$ for some i, but also obviously $\tau_k(c) \leq c$, thus $u_i \leq c$ and $c \in U$.   □

Lemma 2.20 **[AAE06]**   *There exists $k \geq 1$ such that for all $c \in C$ and $j \in \{0, 1\}$, $c \in S_j$ iff $\tau_k(c) \in S_j$.*

Proof. The contrapositive of Lemma 2.19 gives $c \in S$ iff $\tau_k(c) \in S$. Moreover, it is obvious that the truncation map does not alter the output of the truncated configuration (only the cardinalities of the agents providing that output). □

Let us now define a map E from the set of all configurations C, the subsets of $\mathcal{X} \cup \{0\}$ (which, in fact, is $\mathbb{N}^X$) as

$$E(c) := \{x \in \mathcal{X} \cup \{0\} \mid c + x \overset{*}{\to} d \text{ for some } d \text{ s.t. } d \geq c \text{ and } \tau_k(c) = \tau_k(d)\}, \qquad (2.6)$$

where k is the constant chosen in Lemmas 2.19 and 2.20. But what does this set represent? Consider an output stable configuration c. Then $E(c)$ contains all input assignments x that when added to c (by adding new agents with their inputs specified by x) the new configuration will again reach an output stable configuration, giving the same output as c, or in other words, all input assignments by which c *can be pumped.* In fact, this means that the inputs to a stably computable predicate can be pumped in this manner without affecting its output. These input assignments are called the *extensions* of c.

Lemma 2.21 **[AAE06]**   *For all $x \in \mathcal{X}$ and $c \in S_j$, $j \in \{0, 1\}$, s.t. $x \overset{*}{\to} c$, we have that $p(x) = p(x + x')$ for any stably computable predicate $p : \mathcal{X} \to \{0, 1\}$ and any $x' \in E(c)$.*

Proof. $x' \in E(c)$ by definition implies that $c + x' \overset{*}{\to} d$ for some d s.t. $d \geq c$ and $\tau_k(c) = \tau_k(d)$. Since $c \in S_j$, by Lemma 2.20, we have that $\tau_k(c) \in S_j$ (remember that $E(c)$ uses the k chosen by that lemma), and since $\tau_k(c) = \tau_k(d)$, we have that $\tau_k(d) \in S_j$, and again by Lemma 2.20, we get $d \in S_j$. But d is reachable from $c + x'$, and c is reachable from x, thus, d is reachable from $x + x'$, and for p to be stably computable, it must provide the same output j for two input assignments, namely, x and $x + x'$, that both may reach output stable configurations that provide the same output, namely, c and d, that both provide output j. □

We next prove that $E(c)$ is a monoid, which means that it contains the 0 and is closed under addition. This shows that pumping operations can be composed.

Lemma 2.22 **[AAE06]**   *$E(c)$ is a monoid for all $c \in C$*

Proof. That $0 \in E(c)$ is trivial: simply set $d = c$. It remains to prove that $x_1, x_2 \in E(c) \Rightarrow x_1 + x_2 \in E(c)$. If $x_1, x_2 \in E(c)$, then $c + x_1 \overset{*}{\to} d_1$, and $c + x_2 \overset{*}{\to} d_2$, for some d_1, d_2 s.t. $d_1, d_2 \geq c$, and $\tau_k(c) = \tau_k(d_1) = \tau_k(d_2)$. Thus, since $\overset{*}{\to}$ is additive, we can add x_2 in both parts of $c + x_1 \overset{*}{\to} d_1$ to take

$$c + x_1 + x_2 \overset{*}{\to} d_1 + x_2 = (d_1 - c) + c + x_2 \overset{*}{\to} (d_1 - c) + d_2 = d_1 + d_2 - c.$$

It remains to show that $d_1 + d_2 - c \geq c$ and that $\tau_k(c) = \tau_k(d_1 + d_2 - c)$. That $d_1 + d_2 - c \geq c$ holds trivially because $d_1, d_2 \geq c$. That $\tau_k(c) = \tau_k(d_1 + d_2 - c)$ holds because $\tau_k(c) = \tau_k(d_2) = \tau_k(c + d_2 - c)$ and since $\tau_k(c) = \tau_k(d_1)$, we have by the fact that τ_k respects addition (Lemma 2.17) that $\tau_k(c + d_2 - c) = \tau_k(d_1 + d_2 - c)$. $\qquad\square$

We are now going to show that any stably computable predicate $p : \mathcal{X} \to \{0, 1\}$ *admits finite coset coverings*, meaning that for all $\mathcal{X}' = \{x_1, x_2, \ldots\} \subseteq \mathcal{X}$, there exists a finite set $\{(x_i, M_i)\}_{i \in I}$ (for some finite index set I) of pairs of input assignments and submonoids of $\mathbb{N}^X$ such that

- $\mathcal{X}' = \bigcup_{i \in I}(x_i + M_i)$ and

- $p(x_i + m_{ij}) = p(x_i)$ for all $i \in I$ and $m_{ij} \in M_i$.

The set $\{(x_i, M_i)\}_{i \in I}$ is called a *monoid coset covering* of $\mathcal{X}'$ w.r.t. p. Let us first define a map from $\mathcal{X} \cup \mathcal{C}$ to 2^S as $S(c) = \{c' \in S \mid c \xrightarrow{*} c'\}$; that is, $S(c)$ contains all output stable configurations that are reachable from c.

Lemma 2.23 [AAE06]   *Any stably computable predicate p over $\mathcal{X}$ admits finite coset coverings.*

Proof. If $\mathcal{X}' \subseteq \mathcal{X}$ is finite, e.g., $\mathcal{X}' = \{x_1, x_2, \ldots, x_t\}$, then consider the set $\{(x_i, \{0\})\}_{i=1,\ldots,t}$. Obviously, $\{0\}$ is a finite submonoid of $\mathbb{N}^X$, $\mathcal{X}' \subseteq \bigcup_{i=1,\ldots,t}(x_i) + 0$, and $p(x_i + 0) = p(x_i)$ for all $i \in \{1, \ldots, t\}$. So, in this case, we trivially obtain a finite monoid coset covering of $\mathcal{X}'$ w.r.t. p. It remains to show that the same holds for all infinite $\mathcal{X}' = \{x_1, x_2, \ldots\} \subseteq \mathcal{X}$. Assume that $x_1, x_2, \ldots$ is an enumeration of $\mathcal{X}'$ such that $x_i \leq x_j$ for all $i \leq j$. Let us now define a family of sets $B_i \subseteq \mathcal{X} \times \mathcal{C}$ inductively as follows:

$B_0 := \emptyset.$

$B_i := \begin{cases} B_{i-1}, & \text{if there exists } (x, c) \in B_{i-1} \text{ such that } x_i \in x + E(c) \\ B_{i-1} \cup \{(x_i, S(x_i))\} \cup \{(x_i, S(c + x_i - x)) \mid (x, c) \in B_{i-1} \text{ and } x \leq x_i\}, & \text{otherwise.} \end{cases}$

Let's see the above definition step by step, in order to make it clear. First of all, notice that for each x_i, we create a set B_i. What do we create for x_1? Since B_0 is empty, $B_1 := \{(x_1, S(x_1))\}$; that is, B_1 associates x_1 with all output stable configurations reachable from it. Now for x_2, there are two possible cases: if there is a pair (x_1, c) in B_1 such that x_2 belongs to the monoid coset $x_1 + E(c)$, then no associations for x_2 are added; otherwise, x_2 is associated with all output stable configurations that are reachable from it and also with all output stable configurations that are reachable from $c + x_2 - x_1$ for all output stable configurations c that are reachable from x_1 and provided that $x_1 \leq x_2$. And so on.

Let $B := \bigcup_{i \geq 1} B_i$. We claim that $T = \{(x, E(c)) \mid (x, c) \in B\}$ is a finite monoid-covering of $\mathcal{X}$ w.r.t. p. That it is finite will be proved at the end. We first show that it is, in fact, a monoid-covering of $\mathcal{X}$ w.r.t. p. As we have already shown in Lemma 2.22, $E(c)$ is a monoid for all $c \in \mathcal{C}$. We must also prove that $\mathcal{X} \subseteq \bigcup_{(x,c) \in B}(x + E(c))$, and that for all $(x_i, m_{ij}) \in T$, it holds that $p(x_i) = p(x_i, m_{ij})$.

The latter follows immediately from Lemma 2.21: for all $(x_i, m_{ij}) \in T$, we have that m_{ij} is output stable because the B_is only associate x_is with output stable configurations, and that $x_i \xrightarrow{*} m_{ij}$ because each x_i is either immediately associated by B_i with configurations that are reachable from itself or with configurations that are reachable from $(c + x_i - x)$, which by induction on i gives again those configurations must be also reachable from x_i. Thus the requirements of Lemma 2.21 are satisfied, and $p(x_i) = p(x_i, m_{ij})$ for all $(x_i, m_{ij}) \in T$. Take now for the former any $x_i \in \mathcal{X}$. If $(x_i, c) \in B$, then $(x_i, E(c)) \in T$, thus also $x_i = x_i + 0 \in \bigcup_{(x,c) \in B}(x + E(c))$ because $E(c)$ is a monoid, thus contains the 0. If $(x_i, c) \notin B$ for all c, then by definition of B, there exists $(x, c') \in B$ such that $x_i \in x + E(c')$, thus again $x_i \in \bigcup_{(x,c) \in B}(x + E(c))$ for $c = c'$.

It only remains now to prove that T is finite. It suffices to prove that B is finite (we do not care whether the monoid $E(c)$ is finite or not). First, observe that each B_i is finite (for finite i). If B_i is finite, then B_{i+1} is also finite since x_{i+1} and $c + x_{i+1} - x$ may reach only a finite number of output stable configurations, and there is a finite number of (x, c)s in B_i. Now assume to the contrary that B is infinite. Since the B_is are finite, it follows that infinitely many different elements of $\mathcal{X} = \{x_1, x_2, \ldots\}$ appear as first components of elements of B (infinitely elements from $\mathcal{X}$ with repetitions would not suffice because the union by which B is formed eliminates repetitions). By Lemma 2.15, there exists an infinite chain $z_1 < z_2 < \ldots$ of such elements. But for each such z_i, there exists a configuration c_i such that $(z_i, c_i) \in B$ and $c_i + z_{i+1} - z_i \xrightarrow{*} c_{i+1}$.

By applying Higman's lemma again, there must exist an increasing function f on $\mathbb{N}^{\geq 1}$ such that the sequences $(z_{f(i)})_{i \geq 1}$ and $(c_{f(i)})_{i \geq 1}$ are nondecreasing, which means that the sequence $\tau_k(c_{f(i)})$ reaches a maximum and becomes constant at some index $i = j$. This implies that $z_{f(j+1)} - z_{f(j)} \in E(c_{f(j)})$, which in turn implies that $(z_{f(j+1)}, d_{f(j+1)})$ cannot belong to B, thus a contradiction. We conclude that T is finite, and thus any stably computable predicate p admits finite coset coverings. $\square$

Finally, by using substantially more machinery, one can prove that:

Lemma 2.24 [AAE06]   *If a stably computable predicate p admits finite coset coverings, then $p^{-1}(1)$ is a semilinear set.*

And then by combining Lemmas 2.23 and 2.24, we obtain the inverse direction of the exact characterization of population protocols (Theorem 2.1):

Theorem 2.25 [AAE06]   *If a predicate p is stably computable then it is semilinear.*

2.4   EXERCISES

2.1. Cosider the Presburger formula

$$\phi := (\exists w_1 : (x = w_1) \wedge (z = w_1 + w_1) \wedge (y = 0)) \vee \tag{2.7}$$
$$(\exists w_2 \exists w_3 : (x = w_2 + w_2 + 1) \wedge (z = w_3 + w_3 + w_3 + 1) \wedge (y = w_2 + w_3)). \tag{2.8}$$

Write this as a semilinear subset of $\mathbb{N}^3$ and draw it in three dimensions.

2.2. Prove that the remainder predicate $\sum_{i=1}^{k} a_i N_i \equiv c \pmod{m}$ on nonnegative integers $N_1, \ldots, N_k$, of Lemma 2.11, is stably computable by the population protocol model on complete interaction graphs.

NOTES

In [AAD$^+$06], among other things, Angluin *et al.*, established that any *semilinear* predicate, or, equivalently, any predicate definable by some first-order logical formula in *Presburger arithmetic* is stably computable by the population protocol model (Theorem 2.13). Then, Angluin, Aspnes, and Eisenstat [AAE06] proved that this inclusion holds with equality (Theorem 2.25), which leads us to an exact characterization of the class of stably computable predicates on complete interaction graphs (Theorem 2.1). Example 2.2 is also from [AAE06]. Theorem 2.3 is due to Ginsburg and Spanier [GS66]. Kracht has given a more simplified proof recently [Kra03]. Presburger arithmetic is due to Presburger [Pre29], who also proved that it is a consistent, complete, and decidable theory. One fact that makes Presburger arithmetic famous is that Fischer and Rabin, in their 1974 paper [FR74], proved that any decision algorithm for Presburger arithmetic has a worst-case runtime of at least $2^{2^{cn}}$, for some constant $c > 0$, where n denotes here the length of the binary encoding of the Presburger formula. This makes the decision problem of Presburger arithmetic one of the very few known problems that have been proved to require more than exponential computational effort. Higman's lemma is due to Higman [Hig52] and constitutes a fundamental tool in well-quasi-order theory.

CHAPTER 3

Enhancing the model

3.1   INTRODUCTION

The work of Angluin *et al.* on population protocols shed light and opened the way towards a brand new and very promising direction. The lack of control over the interaction pattern, as well as its inherent nondeterminism, gave rise to a variety of new theoretical models for WSNs. Those models draw most of their beauty precisely from their inability to organize interactions in a convenient and predetermined way. In fact, the population protocol model was the minimalistic starting-point of this area of research. However, due to the minimalistic nature of the population protocol model, the class of predicates computable by it is fairly small. In particular, the class **SEM** of semilinear predicates does not include multiplication of variables and exponentiations, which are some natural and common operations on input variables.

The next big step is naturally to strengthen the population protocol model with extra realistic and implementable assumptions, in order to gain more computational power and/or speed-up the time to convergence and/or improve fault-tolerance. Several promising attempts have appeared towards this direction, partly motivated by the need to more accurately reflect the requirements of practical systems. In each case, the model enhancement is accompanied by a logical question: *What is exactly the class of predicates computable by the new model?*

One idea is to allow some heterogeneity in the model, so that some agents have more computational power and/or more storage capacity than others. For example, a base station can be an additional part of the network with which the agents are allowed to communicate. Another interesting possibility is to study what is computable when the inputs are not fixed from the beginning, but it is guaranteed that they will eventually stabilize to a final assignment. One more is to allow the agents access to read-only unique ids, which they are only allowed to compare. Finally, we can even think of the agents as Turing machines with unlimited storage capacity and classify our protocols according to their memory consumption. In this chapter, we present the stabilizing inputs variant that, as we shall see, allows the composition of protocols, the Probabilistic Population Protocol model that makes a random scheduling assumption, and the extremely powerful Community Protocol model that allows access to ids. The rest of the monograph is devoted to the Mediated Population Protocol model that allows the existence of a base station with special storage capabilities and to the Passively mobile Machines model that considers the agents as multitape Turing machines with unbounded storage.

3.2   COMPOSITION OF PROTOCOLS: STABILIZING INPUTS

An interesting possibility is to allow the inputs to the population oscillate, and only require that this oscillation ceases after some finite time. This is the *stabilizing inputs* variant of population protocols. The transition function is now of the form $\delta : (Q \times X) \times (Q \times X) \to Q \times Q$. Each agent has two components in each state, where the first one is its actual state from Q, and the second one plays the role of an input port whose symbol may change arbitrarily between any two interactions, but it will eventually stabilize. Here all agents are assumed to be initially in some *initial state* q_0 and to have arbitrary inputs. The output function is applied to the state components of the agents.

The stabilizing inputs model does not only serve as another model of passively mobile computation where it is possible that the environment provides streams of data that eventually stabilize to their final value. It also has a more practical contribution. Think of the idea of composing (sequentially) two population protocols $\mathcal{A}$ and $\mathcal{B}$. To do that, of course, it must be the case that $Y_{\mathcal{A}} \subseteq X_{\mathcal{B}}$ (where by $Y_{\mathcal{A}}$ and $X_{\mathcal{B}}$, we denote the output alphabet of $\mathcal{A}$ and the input alphabet of $\mathcal{B}$, respectively), since $\mathcal{B}$ will obtain as input the output provided by $\mathcal{A}$. The first thing to solve is to have the output of $\mathcal{A}$ in some component so that $\mathcal{B}$ can read it. This can be done easily by extending $Q_{\mathcal{A}}$ to be $Q_{\mathcal{A}} = \{(q, y) \mid q \in Q \text{ and } O_{\mathcal{A}}(q) = y\}$ and $\delta_{\mathcal{A}}$ as $\delta((q_1, O_{\mathcal{A}}(q_1)), (q_2, O_{\mathcal{A}}(q_2))) = (q_1', O_{\mathcal{A}}(q_1')), (q_2', O_{\mathcal{A}}(q_2'))$ iff $\delta(q_1, q_2) = q_1', q_2'$. In a similar fashion, we could extend the state set of $\mathcal{B}$, $Q_{\mathcal{B}}$, to take into account the outputs of $\mathcal{A}$ as its own inputs. But there is a small problem in this construction: $\mathcal{B}$ does not know when the outputs of $\mathcal{A}$ will converge in order to apply its own input function to them once and for all. It has to always apply the input function whenever some output of $\mathcal{A}$ is modified, hoping that $\mathcal{A}$ will eventually stabilize. In some sense, any computation that $\mathcal{B}$ performs before it obtains its final fixed inputs is meaningless. So, it is important to know what can be actually computed by protocols with stabilizing inputs in order to know what can the second protocol in a composition of two protocols compute, where the stabilizing inputs to the second protocol are the stabilizing outputs of the first protocol.

It is known that all semilinear predicates can be computed with stabilizing inputs. Since population protocols can only compute semilinear predicates, this implies that *any population protocol for fixed inputs can be adapted to work with stabilizing inputs*. However, no general constructive proof of this fact has been proposed yet, and it seems tricky in practice to convert population protocols to their versions that work with stabilizing inputs. Moreover, by Lemmas 2.23 and 2.24, we obtain as a corollary that nothing more than semilinear predicates can be computed by the stabilizing inputs variant. This means that population protocols and population protocols with stabilizing inputs are totally equivalent in terms of computational power, and we can, in principle, compose population protocols by replacing the second stably computing protocol in the composition by its stabilizing inputs version.

Example 3.1   Majority with Stabilizing Inputs [AAC$^+$05]   Let us now show how the majority protocol of Example 1.6 can be modified to work with stabilizing inputs. Keep in mind that this construction is *by no means global*, in the sense that it cannot be used as a general procedure for creating stabilizing inputs variants of population protocols. However, it incorporates some techniques that may be useful in adapting other protocols to the stabilizing inputs setting. In fact, Exercise 3.10 asks you to generalize these ideas to arrive at a general constructive proof for adapting population protocols to work with stabilizing inputs.

An interesting way to start is to ask why the majority protocol for fixed inputs fails to work with stabilizing inputs? Clearly, it might be the case that two awake agents, both with counters 1, interact and that the input of one of them has changed from 0 to 1. In this case, the awake agents cannot preserve the input difference, which is equal to the number of 1s minus the number of 0s appearing in the input ports. The reason is that a 0 has changed to 1, thus the input difference must change by 2, and the counters of both interacting agents have already obtained their maximum value (both should become 2 or one of them 3, which would cause a counter to overflow). So clearly, some additional mechanism is needed.

We now present the protocol that works with stabilizing inputs. The counter is now extended to take integer values from -2 to 2. An *input component* stores the current input at the beginning of every interaction (of course, there is no real "beginning" since there is a single state update, but it is equivalent to think of single state updates as finite deterministic sequences of actions). Initially, all agents have input component 0, counter -1, and are all awake. The main idea is similar as before: we must ensure that the sum of the counters of the awake agents is always equal to the number of 1s minus the number of 0s of the input components and that there is never some awake agent with a negative counter and input component 1 or with positive counter and input component 0 (these are what are called *preserved invariants*). The latter eliminates the inconvenient situation outlined in the previous paragraph, where a modification of the current input could leave us with no space in the counters for storing it. Clearly, any protocol that always preserves these two invariants stably computes the majority predicate with stabilizing inputs.

During an interaction, the agents first perform some update of their components, and then they proceed with the actual interaction (w.l.o.g., sequencing of actions is done for the sake of clarity). If the current input of the agent has not changed, then the agent performs no updating; otherwise, it does the following:

1. It sets its input component to the current input.

2. If it is asleep:

    (a) Becomes awake.

    (b) If the input component is 1 it sets the counter to 2, otherwise to -2.

3. If it is awake:

    (a) If the input component is 1 it adds 2 to the counter, otherwise subtracts 2 from it.

Of course, a change in the input of an asleep agent must cause it to become awake in order for the set of awake agents to count for this change. If the input component is 1, the counter is set to 2 because a 0 has changed to 1, and the preserved input difference must increase by 2; otherwise, it must decrease by 2. On the other hand, if the agent is awake, then restoring its counter might cause loss of information; that is why in this case, 2 is added or subtracted from the current counter value. In either case, given that no overflow occurs when the agent is awake, the input difference is clearly preserved.

During the actual interaction, the following might happen:

1. If both agents are asleep, nothing happens.

2. If one is awake and the other asleep, the asleep copies the counter value of the awake.

3. If both are awake:

   (a) If both counters are positive or both negative nothing happens; otherwise, both set their counters to the sum of the counters.

   (b) One becomes asleep subject to the following conditions:

   - If the other has negative counter, then its input component must be 0.
   - If the other has positive counter, then its input component must be 1.

All operations are the same as in the majority protocol for fixed inputs. The only difference is that an agent becomes asleep subject to two conditions. These conditions ensure that no awake agent remains with a negative counter and input component 1 or with positive counter and input component 0, as needed, thus clearly no overflow might occur during any subsequent update step. It remains to prove that this is always feasible, which is left as Exercise 3.1.

Example 3.2   Let us now compose the protocol of Example 3.1 with another protocol in order to present composition in action. Consider, only for this example, that the interaction graph G is any weakly connected digraph; that is, not necessarily complete. Consider also Protocol 2 below. A little thought reveals that Protocol 2 always stabilizes to an output assignment in which the agents that output 1 form a vertex cover of G of cardinality at most 2 times the optimum vertex cover of G. In the Approximation Algorithms terminology, Protocol 2 is a *2-factor approximation protocol* for the cardinality vertex cover problem, which is formally defined as follows.

Problem 3.3   Cardinality Vertex Cover   Given a weakly connected interaction digraph $G = (V, E)$, find a minimum cardinality *vertex cover*, i.e., a set $V' \subseteq V$ such that every edge has at least one end point incident at V'.

Now, if we modify the stabilizing inputs majority protocol of Example 3.1 to work also for non-complete interaction graphs (you are asked to prove that this is possible in Exercise 3.2), then, by composing the two protocols, we may stably compute whether the constructed vertex cover uses more than half of the nodes of G.

Protocol 2 *Vertex Cover*

1: $X = \{0\}$
2: $Y = \{0, 1\}$
3: $Q = \{q_0, q_1\}$
4: $I(0) = q_0$
5: $O(q_i) = i, i \in \{0, 1\}$
6: $\delta\colon (q_0, q_0) \to (q_1, q_1)$ // Only effective interactions are presented (only one in this case)

3.3   PROBABILISTIC POPULATION PROTOCOLS

The *eventual* stabilization guarantee provided by the population protocol model is insufficient in most practical situations, e.g., when time for convergence is also an issue. Stronger guarantees require additional constraints and assumptions on the interaction pattern between members of the population. One such assumption is to consider that the adversary selects the next ordered pair of interacting agents randomly and uniformly. By additionally assuming that the interaction graph is complete, we obtain the *probabilistic population protocol* model. The above random pairing assumption is sufficient to guarantee fair executions with probability 1 so that any protocol that stably computes a predicate p in the basic fair model, also computes p with probability 1 on every input in the corresponding random-pairing model, assuming executions on the same population.

The probabilistic assumption allows us to consider computations that are correct with high probability and to describe the expected number of interactions for convergence that is the total number of pairwise interactions until all agents have the correct output value, considered as a function of n, the number of agents in the population. Given a function $f : \mathcal{X} \to \mathcal{Y}$, where $\mathcal{X}$ and $\mathcal{Y}$ are the sets of all input and output assignments, respectively, a population protocol $\mathcal{A}$, and an input x, the probability that $\mathcal{A}$ computes f on input x is defined as the probability of all computations beginning with $I(x)$ that stabilize with output $f(x)$. In addition, *parallel time* can be considered in the sense that interactions occur in parallel according to a Poisson process, but each agent participates in an expected $\Theta(1)$ interactions per time unit. It can be easily seen that this time measure is asymptotically equal to the number of interactions divided by n since each agent u in the population can interact with at most one other agent v independently to the interactions that take place between the other (than u, v) agents. Thus at most $\lfloor n/2 \rfloor$ interactions can happen independently.

Example 3.4 Leader Election   Let us now examine the classic leader election problem for the population protocol model where all agents of the population are initially leaders, and the requirement is that eventually only a unique leader remains, and the rest of the population consists of followers. The protocol's state set is $Q = \{L, F\}$ (Leader, Follower), and the only effective transition in its transition function is $(L, L) \to (L, F)$. The time (that is, the expected number of interactions) for a single leader to remain in the population is equal to the sum of the times until two leaders meet with $n, n - 1, \ldots$ leaders. This sum is:

$$\sum_{i=2}^{n} \frac{\binom{n}{2}}{\binom{i}{2}} = (n-1)^2.$$

Therefore, the protocol's time is $\Theta(n^2)$ and parallel time $\Theta(n^2)$. Note that this is the fastest known, w.r.t. the number of interactions, leader election protocol for the probabilistic population protocol model. Whether a leader can be elected significantly faster is still an open problem.

It can be proved [AAE08a] that given a leader in the form of some unique input agent, the population can be organized in an array of registers that can hold values linear in the size of the population. This simulation is achieved through controlled use of self-timed epidemics that disseminate control information rapidly through the population. The simulation, however, is quite involved, and thus we will only briefly present two basic tools which play a fundamental role on the construction and convergence speed. The first tool is the *one-way epidemics*, and the second is the *3-state one-way approximate majority protocol*.

Note that the protocols presented in this section are probabilistic, and they include tuning parameters that can be used to adjust the probability of success. A statement holds *with high probability* if for any constant c there is a setting of the tuning parameters that causes the statement to hold with probability at least $1 - n^{-c}$. The cost of achieving a larger value of c is a constant factor slowdown in the number of interactions (or time) used by the algorithms.

3.3.1   EPIDEMICS

We consider *one-way* (only the responder of an interaction may change its state) epidemics with state space $\{0, 1\}$ and transition rule $(x, y) \rightarrow (x, \max(x, y))$. Any agent that is in state 0 is considered as being *susceptible* and any agent that is in 1 is considered as being *infected*. The protocol corresponds to a simple epidemic in which the transmission of the infection occurs if and only if the initiator is infected and the responder is susceptible. It can be shown that the number of interactions for the epidemic to finish (that is, infect every agent) is $\Theta(n \log n)$ with high probability.

To achieve that bound, the number of interactions of the epidemic protocol is reduced to the number of operations in the well-known coupon collector problem, in which balls are thrown uniformly at random into bins until every bin contains at least one ball. Based on an occupancy bound of [KMSP95], the following bounds on the number of operations to fill the last k of n bins can be shown. Note that because of the high variance associated with filling the last few bins, only the case $k \geq n^\epsilon$ for $\epsilon > 0$ is considered.

Lemma 3.5   [AAE08a]   *Let $S(k, n)$ be the number of operations to fill the last k of n bins in the coupon collector problem. Then for any fixed $\epsilon > 0$ and $c > 0$, there exist positive constants c_1 and c_2 such that for all sufficiently large n and any $k > n^\epsilon$, $c_1 n \ln k \leq S(k, n) \leq c_2 n \ln k$ with probability at least $1 - n^{-c}$.*

Proof.   Observe that each step of collecting a specific k of n coupons can be split into (a) choosing to pick on of the k coupons with probability $\frac{k}{n}$ and (if (a) is successful) (b) choosing the specific coupon to pick. The number of steps of type (b) before all coupons are collected is exactly $S(k, k)$. It is easy to see that $E[S(k, n)] = \frac{n}{k}E[S(k, k)]$, and a simple application of Chernoff bounds shows that $S(k, n) = \Theta(\frac{n}{k}S(k, k))$ with high probability (assuming k is polynomial in n).

Now it will be shown that $S(k, k) = \Omega(k \log k)$ with high probability. Theorem 2 of [KMSP95] states that with m balls tossed uniformly into n bins,

$$Pr[|Z - \mu| \geq \rho\mu] \leq 2 \exp\left(-\frac{\rho^2\mu^2(n-\frac{1}{2})}{n^2-\mu^2}\right),$$

where Z is the number of empty bins and $\mu = E[Z] = n(1 - 1/n)^m = \Theta(ne^{-m/n})$.

The goal is to bound the probability $Z = 0$, i.e., that all coupons have been collected after m operations. By substituting $n = k$ and $m = (1/4)k \ln k$ in the μ equation, we have that $\mu = \Theta(k \cdot k^{-1/4}) = \Theta(k^{3/4})$. For Z to equal 0, we must have $|Z - \mu| \geq \mu$ or $\rho = 1$. So

$$Pr[Z = 0] \leq 2 \exp\left(-\frac{\mu^2(k-\frac{1}{2})}{k^2-\mu^2}\right)$$
$$= 2 \exp\left(-\Theta\left(\frac{k^{3/2}k}{k^2}\right)\right)$$
$$= 2 \exp\left(-\Theta(k^{1/2})\right).$$

For k polynomial in n the probability that $S(k, k) \leq \frac{1}{4}k \ln k$ is exponentially small, which means that $S(k, n - 1) = \Omega(\frac{n-1}{k} \cdot k \ln k) = \Omega(n \ln k)$ with high probability.

For the upper bound, if $m = ak \ln k$ and $n = k$ then $E[Z] = k(1 - 1/k)^{ak \ln k} \leq ke^{-a \ln k} = k^{1-a}$ can be made an arbitrarily small polynomial in n by choosing a sufficiently large, and by Markov's inequality this bounds $Pr[Z \geq 1]$. $\square$

Let $T(k)$ denote the number of interactions to infect the last k agents in a one-way epidemic. To get concentration bounds for $T(k)$, the number of interactions for an epidemic is reduced to the number of operations for coupon collector. The intuition is that once half the agents are infected, the problem becomes a coupon collector problem (collecting susceptible responders) that is delayed by, at most, a factor of two by occasionally choosing uninfected initiators. When fewer than half the agents are infected, the symmetry of the waiting times for each new infection is used to apply the same bounds.

Lemma 3.6 [AAE08a]   *Let $T(k)$ be the number of interactions before a one-way epidemic starting with a single infected agent infects k agents. For any fixed $\epsilon > 0$ and $c > 0$, there exist positive constants c_1 and c_2 such that for all sufficiently large n and any $k > n^\epsilon$, $c_1n \ln k \leq T(k) \leq c_2n \ln k$ with probability at least $1 - n^{-c}$.*

Proof. Observe that the probability that an interaction produces $i + 1$ infected nodes starting from i infected nodes, which is $\frac{i(n-i)}{n(n-1)}$, is also the probability that an interaction produces $n - i + 1$ infected nodes starting from $n - i$ infected nodes. It follows that the distribution of $T(i + 1) - T(i)$ is identical to the distribution of $T(n - i + 1) - T(n - i)$ and, in general, that the distribution of

$T(k) = T(k) - T(1)$—the number of interactions to infect the first $k - 1$ susceptible nodes—is identical to that of $T(n) - T(n - k + 1)$-the number of interactions to infect the last $k - 1$.

Next, Lemma 3.5 is used to bound the number of interactions to infect the last k susceptible nodes. Consider each step of the epidemic process as consisting of (a) a random choice of whether or not the initiator is infected and (b) a random choice of a responder. Then step (b) makes progress with probability $k/(n - 1)$, exactly the same probability as in the coupon collector problem with k remaining coupons out of $n - 1$. Step (a) corresponds to a random choice (with probability $(n - k)/n$ lying between $1/2$ and 1) of whether to draw a coupon or not. A straightforward Chernoff bound argument applied to (a) then shows that the number of interactions to infect the last k susceptible nodes lies with high probability between $S(k, n - 1)$ and $2S(k, n - 1)$ where $S(k, n - 1)$ is the time to collect the last k of $n - 1$ coupons. From Lemma 3.5, it holds that $S(k, n - 1)$ lies between $c_1(n - 1) \ln k$ and $c_2(n - 1) \ln k$ with high probability, which simplifies to $\Theta(n \ln k)$ as claimed. □

3.3.2 3-STATE APPROXIMATE MAJORITY PROTOCOL

The *one-way 3-state approximate majority protocol* is defined above (Protocol 3).

Protocol 3 *3-State Approximate Majority Protocol* [AAE08b]

1: $X = \{x, y, b\}$
2: $Y = \{0, 1\}$
3: $Q = \{x, y, b\}$
4: $I(b) = b, I(x) = x, I(y) = y$
5: $O(x) = O(y) = 1, O(b) = 0$
6: δ: // Only effective interactions are presented

$$(x, y) \rightarrow (x, b)$$
$$(x, b) \rightarrow (x, x)$$
$$(y, x) \rightarrow (y, b)$$
$$(y, b) \rightarrow (y, y)$$

Protocol 3 considers three inputs, x, y and b, where b is the blank state and decides which symbol (x or y) dominates the population. Note that if all agents are blank (*blank configuration*), no further interactions are effective, thus the configuration is stable. However, any non-blank configuration (at least, one agent is in x or y) cannot reach a blank one since no interaction can eliminate the last x or y. Moreover, the population, starting from any non-blank configuration, can only reach one of the all x's or all y's configurations, which are also stable.

Intuitively, the process can be viewed as two competing epidemics (x's and y's) trying to spread on each other's subpopulations. The "undecided" b-agents are immediately converted by the x, y-initiators to their respective states whereas the x, y-responders become undecided.

It can be shown that the above protocol converges from any non-blank configuration to a stable configuration (either all x's or all y's) in $\mathcal{O}(n \log n)$ interactions with high probability. The main idea is to divide the non-blank configurations' space in four areas: three for the configurations where the x, y or b agents dominate the population, and one where the three populations have close cardinalities. It can be shown that the number of interactions for convergence in each of the above areas is bounded by $\mathcal{O}(n \log n)$ with high probability. To achieve that a family of supermartingales (stochastic processes which are used to model fair games) is constructed which have the form $M = e^{aS/n} f(x, y)$ where $a > 0$ is a constant, S counts the number of a particular type of interactions, f is a appropriately selected potential function defined across the entire configuration space and x, y (and b) are extended to denote the corresponding number of agents in a configuration.

Let τ_* denote the time at which the protocol converges. Assuming that f does not vary too much over the configuration space, the supermartingale property $E[M_\tau] \le M_0$ can be used to show that $e^{aS_\tau/n}$ is small and through Markov's inequality to get the corresponding bounds on the number of interactions. The total number of interactions is given by summing the bounds of each region. Unfortunately, the detailed proof of the protocol's convergence is too much involved and thus we only present the convergence theorem:

Theorem 3.7   [AAE08b]   *Let τ_* be the time at which $x = n$ or $y = n$ first holds. Then for any fixed $c > 0$ and sufficiently large n,*

$$Pr[\tau_* \ge 6754n \log n + 6759cn \log n] \le 5n^{-c}.$$

In addition, Protocol 3 correctly computes the dominant non-blank value in its input provided that there is a large enough initial majority. The following theorem shows that it correctly computes the initial majority x or y value, provided that the agents that carry this value in the initial configuration are $\omega(\sqrt{n \log n})$ more than those that carry the opposing value.

Theorem 3.8   [AAE08b]   *With high probability, the 3-state approximate majority protocol converges to the initial majority value if the difference between the initial majority and initial minority populations is $\omega(\sqrt{n \log n})$.*

Proof. Without loss of generality, assume that the initial majority value is x. Consider a coupled process (u_t, u'_t) where $u_t = (x_t - y_t)$ and u'_t is the sum of a series of fair ± 1 coin flips. Initially, $u'_0 = u_0$. Later values of u'_t are specified by giving a joint distribution on (Δ_u, Δ'_u). Let p be the probability that $\Delta_u = 1$ and q the probability that $\Delta_u = -1$. Then let

$$(\Delta_u, \Delta'_u) = \begin{cases} (0,0), & \text{with probability } 1 - p - q, \\ (1,1), & \text{with probability } \frac{1}{2}(p+q), \\ (1,-1), & \text{with probability } p - \frac{1}{2}(p+q), \\ (-1,-1), & \text{with probability } q. \end{cases}$$

The probability in the third case is non-negative if $p/(p+q) = Pr[\Delta_u = 1|\Delta_u \neq 0] \geq \frac{1}{2}$. This holds as long as $u \geq 0$; should u ever drop to zero, the process is ended.

Observe that unless this event happens, it holds that $u_t \geq u'_t$. By summing the cases, it can be also verified that Δ_u rises with probability exactly p and drops with probability exactly q, and that Δ'_u rises or drops with equal probability $\frac{1}{2}(p+q)$. So we have $E[\Delta'_u] = 0$ and that $|\Delta'_u| \leq 1$, the preconditions for Azuma's inequality.

Theorem 3.7 states that the process converges before $\mathcal{O}(n \log n)$ interactions with high probability. Suppose the process converges at some time $\tau = \mathcal{O}(n \log n)$. Then by Azuma's inequality, we have that $|u'_\tau - u'_0| = \mathcal{O}(\sqrt{n \log n})$ throughout this interval with high probability. So if $u'_0 = u_0 = \omega(\sqrt{n \log n})$, it follows that $u_0 \leq u'_0 \leq 0$ throughout the execution, and, in particular, that the process does not require before convergence and that u is not-negative at convergence. But this excludes the $y = n$ case, so the process converges to the initial majority value.   □

3.3.3   VIRTUAL REGISTER MACHINE SIMULATION

The tools previously described, along with some other techniques and tools, can be used to simulate virtual register machine. The simulation is deeply involved and cannot be presented here, but we provide a major consequence for the probabilistic population protocol model. We refer the reader to [AAE08a] for details. A consequence of this simulation is that any semilinear predicate can be computed without error by a probabilistic population protocol that converges in $\mathcal{O}(n \log^4 n)$ interactions with high probability. The result is formally described by the next theorem.

Theorem 3.9 [AAE08a]   *For any semilinear predicate P, and for any c > 0, there is a probabilistic population protocol on a complete graph with a leader to compute P without error that converges in* $\mathcal{O}(n \log^4 n)$ *interactions with probability at least* $1 - n^{-c}$ *and in expectation.*

Note that in [AAE08a] the per-step parallel time (of the simulation) was $\mathcal{O}(n \log^4 n)$ and was improved later [AAE08b] by the approximate majority protocol to $\mathcal{O}(n \log^2 n)$.

3.4   COMMUNITY PROTOCOLS

In this section, we present another extension of the population protocol model, known as the *Community Protocol* model. In fact, this, recently proposed, model makes the assumption that the agents are equipped with unique ids and are also allowed to store a fixed number of other agents' ids. The term "community" in the model's name is used to emphasize the fact that the agents here form a collection of unique individuals similar to the notion of a human community, in contrast to a population which is merely an agglomeration of nameless multitude. We will show that the community protocol model is extremely strong: the corresponding class consists of *all symmetric predicates in* **NSPACE**$(n \log n)$, where n is the community size. The proof is based on a simulation of a modified version of *Nondeterministic Storage Modification Machine* (NSMM), as defined by Schönhage.

3.4.1 THE MODEL

We start again with a formal definition of the model, and then a somewhat informal description of its functionality follows.

Definition 3.10 [GR09] Let U be an infinite ordered set containing all possible ids. A *community protocol* is an 8-tuple $(X, Y, B, d, I, O, Q, \delta)$, where X, Y, and B are all finite sets and

1. X is the *input alphabet*,

2. Y is the *output alphabet*,

3. B is the set of *basic states*,

4. d is a nonnegative integer representing the number of ids that can be remembered by an agent,

5. $I : X \rightarrow B$ is the *input function* mapping input symbols to basic states,

6. $O : B \rightarrow Y$ is the *output function* mapping basic states to outputs,

7. $Q = B \times (U \cup \{\perp\})^d$ is the set of *agent states*, and

8. $\delta : Q \times Q \rightarrow Q \times Q$ is the *transition function*.

If $\delta(a, b) = (a', b')$, we call $(a, b) \rightarrow (a', b')$ a *transition*, and we define $\delta_1(a, b) = a'$ and $\delta_2(a, b) = b'$.

The first obvious difference between this and the population protocol model is that the agent states are allowed to contain up to d ids. Additionally, each agent is assumed to have its own unique id from the industry (which is an element of U). As in the population protocol model, initially, each agent $i \in \{1, \ldots, n\}$ receives an input symbol from X. Note that the ith agent is the agent whose id is in position i in the ascending ordering of agent ids. An input assignment is again any $x \in \mathcal{X}$. Moreover, let id_i denote the actual id of agent i and $b_i = I(x_i)$ (that is, the initial basic state of agent i). Then the *initial state* of each agent i is of the form $(b_i, id_i, \perp, \perp, \ldots, \perp)$. Thus initially, each agent i is in basic state b_i, contains its own unique id id_i in the first position of its list of ids, and the remaining list is filled with $d - 1$ repetitions of the symbol $\perp$.

A *configuration* C may be viewed now as a vector in Q^n of the form $C = (q_1, q_2, \ldots, q_n)$, where q_i is simply the state of agent i for all $i \in \{1, \ldots, n\}$ (this is equivalent to the function representation of Chapter 1). Thus, the *initial configuration* corresponding to input assignment x is

$((b_i, id_i, \bot, \bot, \ldots, \bot))_{i=1}^{|x|}$, where again $b_i = I(x_i)$ and id_i is the actual id of agent i. The notions of *execution*, *computation*, and *fairness* are defined in the same way as in the population protocol model, the interaction graph is again always complete, and the scheduler choosing the interactions is again assumed to be *fair*.

The output of an agent at any step of the computation is the output of its basic state. For example, the output of an agent in state $(b_i, id_i, 1, 5, \ldots, \bot)$ is $O(b_i) \in Y$. A community protocol is said to *stably compute* a function $f : \mathcal{X} \to Y$, if for any $x \in \mathcal{X}$ and any assignment of the symbols in x to the nodes of the complete interaction graph of $|x|$ nodes, all agents, independently of the fair computation followed, eventually stabilize to the output $f(x)$; that is, a configuration is reached under which all agents output $f(x)$ and continue doing so forever, no matter how the computation proceeds thereafter (such a configuration is, as usual, called an *output stable* configuration).

As population protocols, community protocols are *uniform* (but, clearly, not *anonymous*). The reason is that their description makes no assumption of the *community size n*, thus their functionality remains identical for all complete interaction graphs. That's why the set of ids U is infinite. The suspicious reader would notice that if we do not impose further restrictions on the model then the agents can use their d slots to store arbitrary amounts of information (by exploiting the fact that U is defined to be infinite), which is artificial. To avoid this, we impose a *local knowledge* constraint, according to which agents can only store ids that they have learned from other agents via interactions with them. To formalize this, let $l(q)$ denote the set of different ids appearing in the list of ids of state q. If $\delta(q_1, q_2) = (q_1', q_2')$ and $id \in l(q_1') \cup l(q_2')$ then $id \in l(q_1) \cup l(q_2)$ (in words, no new ids appear in the outcome of an interaction).

Additionally, an *operational* constraint is imposed that allows no other operations except for comparisons to be performed on ids by the agents. This constraint is only imposed to keep the model minimal because it turns out that, even in the presence of this constraint, the model is surprisingly strong (computationally). Intuitively, if $((b_1, \ldots), (b_2, \ldots)) \to ((b_1', \ldots), (b_2', \ldots))$ is a transition in δ, then any transition with precisely the same basic states in which the ids of the left-hand-side are replaced by ids that preserve the order (which, according to the local knowledge constraint, implies that also the ids in the right-hand-side will preserve the order) also belongs to δ. Since this may be a little subtle, another way to think of it is the following. All interactions that do not differ w.r.t. the basic states of the agents and whose lists of ids contain ids that preserve the order, provide the agents with the same new pair of basic states and with new lists of ids that do not differ w.r.t. the order of ids.

To make this precise, let $\delta(q_1, q_2) = (q_1', q_2')$. Moreover, let $id_1 < id_2 < \ldots < id_k$ be all ids in $l(q_1) \cup l(q_2) \cup l(q_1') \cup l(q_2')$ and let $id_1' < id_2' < \ldots < id_k'$ be ids. If $\rho(q)$ is the state obtained from q by replacing all occurrences of each id id_i by id_i', then we require that $\delta(\rho(q_1), \rho(q_2)) = (\rho(q_1'), \rho(q_2'))$ also holds.

Example 3.11   Assume that $\delta((b_1, 1, 2, \bot), (b_2, 7, \bot, \bot)) = ((b_1', 1, 7, \bot), (b_2', 2, 2, 1))$. Then it holds that $\delta((b_1, 2, 5, \bot), (b_2, 8, \bot, \bot)) = ((b_1', 2, 8, \bot), (b_2', 5, 5, 2))$. The reason is that $1 < 2 < 7$ and $2 < 5 < 8$, and we have replaced 1 by 2, 2 by 5, and 7 by 8, thus, preserving the order of ids.

Generally, $\delta((b_1, id_1, id_2, \bot), (b_2, id_3, \bot, \bot)) = ((b_1', id_1, id_3, \bot), (b_2', id_2, id_2, id_1))$ must hold for all $id_1, id_2, id_3 \in U$, where $id_1 < id_2 < id_3$, for the same reason.

3.4.2   COMPUTATIONAL POWER

The community protocol model turns out to be extremely strong in terms of its computational power. In fact, it turns out that any predicate is stably computable by the basic community protocol model if and only if it belongs to **SNSPACE**$(n \log n)$, where, as usual, n denotes the community size.

Definition 3.12   Let **CP** denote the class of all predicates that are stably computable by the community protocol model on complete graphs.

CP obviously contains only symmetric predicates because the identifiers of the model cannot be used to order the input symbols, thus a protocol's functionality on complete graphs has to be identical for any permutation of the inputs w.r.t. to the agents' ordering. First of all, we prove that any stably computable predicate p is in **NSPACE**$(n \log n)$.

Theorem 3.13   [GR09]   **CP** *is a subset of* **NSPACE**$(n \log n)$.

Proof. We will construct a nondeterministic TM $\mathcal{N}$ that decides the language $L_p = \{x \in \mathcal{X} \mid p(x) = 1\}$, using at most **NSPACE**$(n \log n) =$ **NSPACE**$(|\langle x \rangle| \log |\langle x \rangle|)$ cells on any branch of its computation. The reason that the latter equality holds is that the input of p consists of n input symbols, picked from the set X whose cardinality is independent of n. This means that for any input x to the machine $\mathcal{N}$ (any element of L_p) it holds that $|\langle x \rangle| = \mathcal{O}(n)$, where n is the community size.

First of all, we make the following natural assumption: n agents have w.l.o.g. the unique ids $1, 2, \ldots, n$. This implies that each id occupies $\mathcal{O}(\log n)$ cells in a TM. Moreover, there are d id slots in an agent's state, and since d is independent of n again, $\mathcal{O}(\log n)$ cells suffice to store the list of ids of any state. The cardinality of B is also independent of n, thus we conclude that $\mathcal{O}(\log n)$ cells suffice to store any state of Q. A configuration is simply a vector consisting of n states, thus a configuration will occupy $\mathcal{O}(n \log n)$ cells of memory storage.

To accept input x, $\mathcal{N}$ must verify two conditions: that there exists a configuration C reachable from $I(x)$, in which all basic states output $p(x)$, and that there is no configuration C' reachable from C, in which some basic state does not output $p(x)$.

The first condition is verified by guessing and checking a sequence of configurations, starting from $I(x)$ and reaching such a C. $\mathcal{N}$ guesses a C_{i+1} each time, verifies that $C_i \rightarrow C_{i+1}$ (begins from $C_0 = I(x)$, i.e. $i = 0$) and, if so, replaces C_i by C_{i+1}, otherwise, drops this C_{i+1}. The second condition is the complement of a similar reachability problem. But, according to the Immerman-Szelepcsényi theorem (Theorem 1.9), **NSPACE** is closed under complement for all space functions $\geq \log n$. Thus, by taking into account that only one configuration is kept at any step of any branch and that the size of any configuration is $\mathcal{O}(n \log n)$, we conclude that $\mathcal{N}$ decides L_p in $\mathcal{O}(n \log n)$ space. $\square$

A *Storage Modification Machine* (SMM), as defined by Schönhage, is a kind of pointer machine (not a distributed system). Its memory stores a finite directed graph of constant out-degree with a distinguished node called the *center*. The edges of the graph are called *pointers*. The edges out of each node are labeled by distinct *directions* drawn from a finite set Δ. For example, a reasonable implementation of Δ could use all nonnegative integers up to the maximum out-degree in the graph minus one. Any string $x \in \Delta^*$ can be used as a reference to the node that is reached if we begin from the center and follow the pointers whose labels are indicated by the sequence of symbols in x. We denote the node indicated by $x \in \Delta^*$ by $p^*(x)$. The basic operations of an SMM allow the machine to create nodes, modify pointers and follow paths of pointers. We now formalize the above description.

Definition 3.14 [Sch80]   A *Nondeterministic Storage Modification Machine* (NSMM) is a 3-tuple (Σ, Δ, P), where Σ, and Δ are both finite sets and

1. Σ is the *input alphabet*,

2. Δ is the set of *distinct directions*, and

3. P is the *program*, which is a finite list of instructions.

Inputs to the SMM are finite strings from Σ^*. Programs may use instructions of the following types:

- *new*: creates a node, makes it the center, and sets all its outgoing pointers to the old center.

- *recenter x*, where $x \in \Delta^+$: changes the center of the graph to $p^*(x)$.

- *set $x\delta$ to y*, where $x, y \in \Delta^*$ and $\delta \in \Delta$: changes the pointer of node $p^*(x)$ that is labeled by δ to point to node $p^*(y)$.

- *if $x = y$ then goto l*, where $x, y \in \Delta^*$: jumps to (program) line l if $p^*(x) = p^*(y)$.

- *input $l_1, \ldots, l_r$*, where $l_1, \ldots, l_r$ are (program) line numbers: consumes the next input symbol (if there is one) and jumps to line l_i if that symbol is σ_i.

- *output o*, where $o \in \{0, 1\}$: causes the machine to halt and output o.

- *choose l_0, l_1*, where l_0 and l_1 are line numbers: causes the machine to transfer control either to line l_0 or to line l_1 nondeterministically.

When a node becomes unreachable from the center, it can be dropped from the graph since it plays no further role in the computation. Space complexity is measured by the maximum number of (reachable) nodes present at any step of any branch of the machine's nondeterministic computation.

It can be proved that any language decided by a nondeterministic Turing Machine, using $\mathcal{O}(S \log S)$ space, can be decided by an NSMM using S nodes. Thus, to prove that all symmetric predicates in **NSPACE**($n \log n$) also belong to **CP**, it suffices to show that there exists a community protocol that simulates an NSMM that uses $\mathcal{O}(n)$ nodes. We show in an abstract level how to achieve this, just after presenting the statement of the theorem. Now by taking into account Theorem 3.13, we get the following exact characterization.

Theorem 3.15   [GR09]   CP *is equal to the class of all symmetric predicates in* **NSPACE**($n \log n$).

Since the construction is quite involved, we only present the main idea of the proof, and you are asked to try a formal complete version in Exercise 3.11. As already mentioned, one direction follows from Theorem 3.13. For the other, in order for the agents to simulate the NSMM, they first organize themselves into a virtual ring. To do this, each agent tries to locate the agent with the smallest id that is larger than its own. In this manner, they are eventually ordered (clockwise) by their ids. However, they cannot know when the ring structure has stabilized. To overcome this, the *reinitialization technique* is applied. [1]

The main idea of this technique is to execute the simulation from the beginning of some construction and reinitialize it whenever that construction changes, where here the construction is the ring. In this manner, we can guarantee that when the last modification of the construction occurs, a final reinitialization is executed, and then the simulation is executed for the last time from the baginning without being interrupted again. However, this entails reassuring that the simulation can be restarted correctly in all agents (after the last modfication of the construction). The same technique is also used for adding some nondeterminism to the simulation. The idea is that we allow the distributed computation to follow some path of the nondeterministic TM (similarly, NSMM) computation, and whenever the TM (NSMM) reaches a rejecting state, we reinitialize the simulation. Note that fairness guarantees that all possible paths will be eventually followed, unless some accepting state is reached, in which case the population (similarly, community) also accepts.

It is not hard to see that the eventual ring structure enables a correct reinitialization of the simulation without allowing interactions between reinitialized and nonreinitialized agents. Reinitializations can, e.g., propagate from the smallest id to the largest. It remains to ensure that a community protocol can indeed simulate a SMM (we can temporarily forget about the nondeterminism as this is handled by the reinitialization technique). The idea is to exploit the existence of a unique leader p, let it w.l.o.g. be the agent with the lowest id. The leader stores a program counter that describes the line of the SMM program it is simulating. Moreover, it keeps an id-index pair that locates the SMM graph center. The other agents store the remaining graph data structure. Recall that the out-degree of each node [2] is constant, thus a community of size n can store a SMM graph of n nodes (each agent stores a node and a constant number of pointers to other nodes). For a convincing example that the simulation is feasible, consider the *recenter* instruction (you will have to show how to simulate the remaining instructions in Exercise 3.11). To simulate *recenter* x, the leader follows one by one the

---

[1] This technique is used in most of the simulations presented in this monograph. The reader can, e.g., find a more in detail application of the reinitialization technique in Chapter 4.

[2] By "node", only for this discussion, we refer to a node of the graph data structure of an SMM.

pointers described by x (for each symbol of x, it traverses the ring waiting to encounter the pointed id, which it remembers). When x is exhausted, the leader updates its center field to point to the new center that is described by the id-index pair of the last visited node.

Finally, by assuming that faults cannot alter the unique ids and if some necessary preconditions are satisfied, then the above simulation (with substantial more machinery) can be adapted to tolerate $\mathcal{O}(1)$ Byzantine agents. However, faults are out of the scope of this monograph.

3.5   EXERCISES

3.1. This exercise concerns the majority protocol for stabilizing inputs of Example 3.1. Prove that any awake agent that appears throughout the computation satisfies one of the following conditions:

- It has a 0 counter.

- It has a negative counter and its input component is 0.

- It has a positive counter and its input component is 1.

3.2. Prove that any population protocol that stably computes some predicate p on complete interaction graphs, either with or without stabilizing inputs, can be adapted to also stably compute p in the family of all weakly connected interaction graphs.

3.3. Adapt the parity protocol that you devised in Exercise 1.9 to work with stabilizing inputs.

3.4. Consider the transition function δ of a community protocol and let $\delta(q_1, q_2) = (q_1', q_2')$ be any transition. Let b_q denote the basic state of state q, and $id_{q,j}$ the jth id in the id list of q. δ is defined as follows. If $b_{q_1} = b_{q_2}$, then nothing happens. If $b_{q_1} \neq b_{q_2}$ then

- If $id_{q_1,j} > id_{q_2,j}$ and $id_{q_1,j}, id_{q_2,j} \neq \bot$ for some $j \in \{2, \ldots, d\}$, then $id_{q_2',i} = \bot$ and $id_{q_1',i} = id_{q_2,i}$ for all $i \in \{2, \ldots, d\}$, and $b_{q_1'} = b_{q_2'} = b_{q_1}$.
- Else $id_{q_1',i} = \bot$ and $id_{q_2',i} = id_{q_1,i}$ for all $i \in \{2, \ldots, d\}$, and $b_{q_1'} = b_{q_2'} = b_{q_2}$.

Does δ satisfy the local knowledge and operational constraints? Support your answer with a formal proof.

3.5. Assume that the adversary scheduler selects each interaction independently and according to the random uniform distribution. Prove that this scheduler, called the *random uniform scheduler*, is fair with probability 1.

Consider now the following generic definition of probabilistic schedulers: "A *probabilistic scheduler*, w.r.t. a transition graph $T(\mathcal{A}, G)$, defines for each configuration $C \in V(T)$ an infinite sequence of probability distributions of the form $(d_1^C, d_2^C, \ldots)$, over the set $\Gamma^+(C) = \{C' \mid C \to C'\}$ (the possibly closed out-neighbourhood of C), where $d_t^C : \Gamma^+(C) \to [0, 1]$ and such that $\sum_{C' \in \Gamma^+(C)} d_t^C(C') = 1$ holds, for all t and C."

Now, a probabilistic scheduler is called *consistent* if for all configurations $C \in V(T)$, it holds that $d^C = d_1^C = d_2^C = \ldots$. Prove that any consistent probabilistic scheduler is fair with probability 1.

3.6. This exercise aims to familiarize the reader with the problem of algorithmically verifying population protocols. Generally speaking, computer-aided verification of distributed protocols is a crucial part of the design, specifically when the protocols are about to be applied in critical scenarios, like, for example, health, space, and fire detection applications. Consider the following problem:

Given a population protocol $\mathcal{A}$ whose output alphabet $Y_\mathcal{A}$ is binary, a first-order logical formula ϕ in Presburger arithmetic representing the specifications of $\mathcal{A}$, and an integer $k \geq 2$ (in binary), determine whether $\mathcal{A}$ stably computes ϕ on the complete interaction graph of order k.

(a) Prove that PPVER is **coNP**-hard.

(b) Generalize this for the case where k is not provided as part of the input and general verification (for all complete interaction graphs) is sought.

(c) Devise an exponential algorithm for PPVER based on searching of the transition graph of $\mathcal{A}$ for k agents.

3.7. Define nondeterministic population protocols by extending the transition function to return sets of candidate transitions. Then show that any nondeterministic protocol can be simulated by a deterministic one.

3.8. Suppose that the interaction graph may be any d-colorable digraph. Show that there is a simple nondeterministic protocol that always stabilizes on a d-coloring of the interaction graph.

3.9. (Research Question (RQ)) What is the computational power of the enhancement of the PP model in which each agent is *probabilistic* in the sense that it has access to some internal random process (e.g., it may flip a coin during every interaction, and the result of the flip will determine the transition to be followed)?

3.10. Generalize the ideas of the majority protocol of Example 3.1 to arrive at a general constructive process for adapting population protocols to work with stabilizing inputs.

3.11. Give a formal proof of Theorem 3.15 (by completing and formalizing the proof idea that was presented there), that is, show that there exists a community protocol that simulates an NSMM that uses $\mathcal{O}(n)$ nodes.

NOTES

The fault tolerance of population protocols was studied by Delporte-Gallet, Fauconnier, Guerraoui, and Ruppert in 2006 [DGFGR06]. The stabilizing inputs extension of the population protocol model is due to Angluin, Aspnes, Chan, Fischer, Jiang, and Peralta [AAC+05]. In that work, they stated that all semilinear predicates can be computed with stabilizing inputs (however, the general constructive proof was deferred to the full paper that, to the best of our knowledge, has not appeared yet) and also studied the computability of graph properties by the population protocol model. Example 3.1 is also from [AAC+05]. The *probabilistic population protocol* model was proposed in [AAD+04, AAD+06]. Some recent work has concentrated on performance, supported by this random scheduling assumption (see, e.g., [AAE08a]). The community protocol model was proposed in 2009 by Guerraoui and Ruppert [GR09]. The initial idea to allow some heterogeneity in the model, by assuming that some agents have more computational power than others is due to Beauquier, Clement, Messika, Rosaz, and Rozoy [BCM+07]. In particular, they assumed the existence of a base station that is capable of computing the population size n. The stabilizing inputs part of Exercise 3.2 appears as a statement in [AAC+05], and the fixed inputs part is proved in [AAD+04, AAD+06]. The generic definition of probabilistic schedulers of Exercise 3.5 is due to Chatzigiannakis, Dolev, Fekete, Michail, and Spirakis [CDF+09]. The problem PPVER of Exercise 3.6 was defined and studied by Chatzigiannakis, Michail, and Spirakis very recently [CMS10a]. Nondeterministic protocols (Exercises 3.7 and 3.8) were first discussed in [AAC+05]. In particular, the simulation of Exercise 3.7 and the protocol of Exercise 3.8 appear there.

CHAPTER 4

Mediated Population Protocols and Symmetry

We discuss in this chapter an extension of the population protocol model, which seems to be of its own theoretical interest. The main additional feature is that the agents are allowed to store pairwise information into some global storage, like, e.g., a base station, called the *mediator*, that provides a small fixed slot to each pair of agents. Before interacting, the agents communicate with the mediator to get informed of their collective information, and this information is updated according to the result of the interaction. Another simplified way to think of this system is that agents communicate through fixed links which are capable of storing limited information. We think of each link (u, v) joining two agents u and v as being itself an agent that only participates in the interaction (u, v). The agents u and v can exploit this joint memory to store pairwise information and to have it available during some future interaction (see Figure 4.1 for an example).

In the first part of this chapter, we present the the *Mediated Population Protocol* (MPP) model, the name being inspired by the idea of the mediator. Section 4.1 provides a formal definition of the MPP model. Section 4.1.2 focuses on the computational power of the model by studying what predicates on input assignments are stably computable in the *fully symmetric case*, in which the interaction graph is complete and all edges are initially in a common state. First, Section 4.1.2.1 proves that the MPP model is strictly stronger than the population protocol model by showing that the former can stably compute a non-semilinear predicate. Then in Section 4.1.2.2, it is shown that the MPP model can turn itself into a deterministic TM with linear space. Section 4.1.2.4 first extends the techniques developed in Section 4.1.2.1 to show that the MPP model can simulate a NTM of $\mathcal{O}(n^2)$ space and then, by showing that the inverse inclusion also holds, it establishes the following exact characterization for the class of computable predicates by the MPP model: *it is precisely the class of symmetric predicates in* **NSPACE**(n^2). Thus, unexpectedly, while preserving both *uniformity* and *anonymity*, the MPP model turns out to be an extremely powerful enhancement: it dramatically extends the class of computable predicates, from semilinear predicates to all symmetric predicates computable by a nondeterministic TM in $\mathcal{O}(n^2)$ space.

In the second part of the chapter, we go one step further and study what properties of inter-action graphs are computable by the MPP model. To understand properties of the interaction graph is an important step in almost any distributed system. In particular, we temporarily disregard the input notion and make the assumption that all agents simply start from a common *initial state* q_0. Also, as in the SMPP model, we make a similar assumption for the edges, that is, $\iota(e) = s_0$ for all

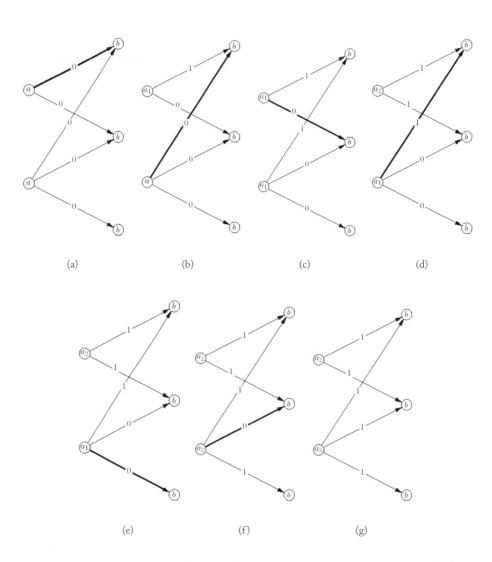

Figure 4.1: An example showing the Mediated Population Protocol model in action. Each agent is in one of the states $\{a, a_1, a_2, a_3, b\}$ and each edge in one of the states $\{0, 1\}$. Initially, we have some agents in state a and some other in b, while all edges are in state 0. The a agents exploit the new capability of storing on the edges in order to count the number of their b neighbors. Each time that an a encounters a b via a 0 edge, it counts it by incrementing an index (e.g., by becoming a_1) and makes the state of the edge 1 in order to remember not to count the same b again in the future. In the PP model, the agents would have to store something on a b agent, thus conflicting with the other a agents that share the same b as a neighbor. The bold edges indicate the next interacting pair.

$e \in E$ (recall that ι denotes the edge initialization function). Here the interest is in protocols that when executed on any interaction graph G of a given graph universe, after a finite number of steps stabilize to configurations where all agents give 1 as output if G belongs to a graph language L, and 0, otherwise. This is motivated by the idea of having protocols that eventually accept all interaction graphs (on which they run) that satisfy a specific property, and reject all remaining graphs.

Section 4.2 ignores the input to the agents and studies the computability of graph properties by the MPP model. Section 4.2.1 focuses on weakly connected interaction graphs. It is first proved that the class of computable graph properties is closed under complement, union, and intersection operations. Node and edge parity, bounded out-degree by a constant, existence of a node with more incoming than outgoing neighbors, and existence of some directed path of length at least $k = \mathcal{O}(1)$ are some examples of properties whose computability is proven. Moreover, the existence of symmetry in two specific interaction graphs is revealed and is exploited to prove that there exists no MPP, whose states eventually stabilize, to compute the graph language $2C$, consisting of all weakly connected interaction graphs that contain some 2-cycle. Finally, in Section 4.2.2, it is shown that no nontrivial graph property is computable in a graph universe that includes disconnected graphs.

4.1   SYMMETRIC NONDETERMINISTIC SPACE(n^2)

Definition 4.1 [CMS09c]   A *mediated population protocol* (MPP) is a 7-tuple $(X, Y, Q, S, I, O, \delta)$, where X, Y, Q, and S are all finite sets and

1. X is the *input alphabet*,

2. Y is the *output alphabet*,

3. Q is the set of *agent states*,

4. S is the set of *edge states*,

5. $I : X \to Q$ is the *input function*,

6. $O : Q \to Y$ is the *output function*,

7. $\delta : Q \times Q \times S \to Q \times Q \times S$ is the *transition function*.

If $\delta(a, b, c) = (a', b', c')$, we call $(a, b, c) \to (a', b', c')$ a *transition*, and we define $\delta_1(a, b, c) = a'$, $\delta_2(a, b, c) = b'$ and $\delta_3(a, b, c) = c'$.

The above definition does not include input for the edges. We assume that each edge is initially in one state from S as specified by some *edge initialization function* $\iota : E \to S$, which is not part of the protocol but generally models some preprocessing on the network that has taken place before the protocol's execution.

A *network configuration*, or simply a *configuration*, is a mapping $C : V \cup E \rightarrow Q \cup S$ specifying the state of each agent in the population and each edge in the set of permissible interactions. Let C and C' be configurations, and let u, υ be distinct agents. We say that C goes to C' via encounter $e = (u, \upsilon)$, denoted $C \overset{e}{\rightarrow} C'$, if

$$
\begin{aligned}
C'(u) &= \delta_1(C(u), C(\upsilon), C(e)) \\
C'(\upsilon) &= \delta_2(C(u), C(\upsilon), C(e)) \\
C'(e) &= \delta_3(C(u), C(\upsilon), C(e)) \\
C'(z) &= C(z), \ \text{for all } z \in (V - \{u, \upsilon\}) \cup (E - \{e\}),
\end{aligned}
$$

that is, C' is the result of the interaction of the pair (u, υ) under configuration C and is the same as C except for the fact that the states of u, υ, and (u, υ) have been updated according to δ_1, δ_2, and δ_3, respectively. We say that C can go to C' in one step, denoted $C \rightarrow C'$, if $C \overset{e}{\rightarrow} C'$ for some encounter $e \in E$. We write $C \overset{*}{\rightarrow} C'$ if there is a sequence of configurations $C = C_0, C_1, \ldots, C_t = C'$, such that $C_i \rightarrow C_{i+1}$ for all $i, 0 \leq i < t$, in which case, we say that C' is *reachable* from C.

An *execution* is a finite or infinite sequence of configurations $C_0, C_1, C_2, \ldots$, where C_0 is an initial configuration and $C_i \rightarrow C_{i+1}$, for all $i \geq 0$. We have both finite and infinite executions since the scheduler may stop in a finite number of steps or continue selecting pairs forever. Moreover, note that, according to the preceding definitions, the adversary scheduler may, for example, partition the agents into non-communicating clusters. If that's the case, then it is easy to see that no meaningful computation is possible. To avoid such unpleasant scenarios, a strong global *fairness condition* is imposed on the adversary to ensure the protocol makes progress. An infinite execution is *fair* if for every pair of configurations C and C' such that $C \rightarrow C'$, if C occurs infinitely often in the execution then so does C'. An adversary scheduler is fair if it always leads to fair executions. A *computation* is an infinite fair execution. An interaction between two agents is called *effective* if at least one of the initiator's, the responder's, and the edge's states is modified (that is, if C, C' are the configurations before and after the interaction, respectively, then $C' \neq C$). Similarly, a transition $(a, b, c) \rightarrow (a', b', c')$ is called effective if $a' \neq a$, or $b' \neq b$, or $c' \neq c$.

Note that the mediated population protocol model *preserves both uniformity and anonymity* properties. As a result, any MPP's *code* is of *constant size*, thus, can be stored in each agent (device) of the population and, additionally, there is not enough room in the states of the agents and the edges to store unique identifiers. Nevertheless, as we shall see, the MPP model can handle far more complicated computations than the population protocol model.

4.1.1   STABLE COMPUTATION

Mediated population protocols, like population protocols, do not halt. Instead, we require their output to stabilize. Stable computation is defined similarly as in the PP model.

Definition 4.2   A predicate p over $\mathcal{X}$ is said to be *stably computable* by the MPP model in a graph universe $\mathcal{U}$, if there exists a MPP $\mathcal{A}$ such that for any input assignment $x \in \mathcal{X}$ and any

$G = (V, E) \in \mathcal{U}$ s.t. $|V| = |x|$, any computation of $\mathcal{A}$ on G beginning from the initial configuration corresponding to x eventually reaches an output stable configuration in which all agents output $p(x)$.

Definition 4.3   A configuration C is called *state stable* if for every configuration C' s.t. $C \xrightarrow{*} C'$ it holds that $C' = C$.

   We say that a protocol $\mathcal{A}$ has *stabilizing states* if every computation of $\mathcal{A}$ eventually reaches a state stable configuration; that is, the states of all agents eventually stop changing. Note that any protocol that *state-stabilizes* also *output-stabilizes*, but the inverse is not generally true (stabilizing states is a stronger requirement).

   In some cases, a protocol, instead of stably computing a predicate p, may provide some different sort of guarantee. For example, whenever runs on some $x \in \mathcal{X}$ such that $p(x) = 1$, it may forever remain to configurations where at least one agent is in state a, and whenever $p(x) = 0$, it may forever remain to configurations where no agent is in state a. To formalize this:

Definition 4.4   [CMS09c, MCS10]   We say that a MPP $\mathcal{A}$ *guarantees* $t : \mathcal{C} \to \{0, 1\}$ *w.r.t.* $p : \mathcal{X} \to \{0, 1\}$ in a graph universe $\mathcal{U}$ if, for any input assignment $x \in \mathcal{X}$ and any $G = (V, E) \in \mathcal{U}$ s.t. $|V| = |x|$, any computation of $\mathcal{A}$ on G beginning from the initial configuration corresponding to x eventually reaches a configuration C, s.t. for all C', where $C \xrightarrow{*} C'$, it holds that $t(C') = t(C) = p(x)$.

4.1.2   PREDICATES ON INPUT ASSIGNMENTS

We assume here that the interaction graph is complete and that all edges are initially in a common state s_0, that is, the universe is $\{G \mid G \text{ is complete}\}$ and $\iota(e) = s_0$ for all $e \in E$. For simplicity, we make the convention that s_0 is the first state appearing in S (usually, it will be denoted by 0 or by s_0). Call this for sake of simplicity the SMPP model ('S' standing for "Symmetric"). We are interested in the computational power of the SMPP model. In particular, we provide an exact characterization of the predicates on input assignments that are stably computable.

Definition 4.5   [CMN$^+$10a]   Let **MPS** (standing for "Mediated Predicates in the fully Symmetric case") be the class of all stably computable predicates by the SMPP model.

Lemma 4.6   *All predicates in* **MPS** *are symmetric.*

Proof. Take any $p \in$ **MPS** and let $\mathcal{A}$ be the SMPP that stably computes it. Take also any input assignment $x = \sigma_1 \sigma_2 \ldots \sigma_n$ and let $\pi : V \to V$ be any permutation of $V = \{1, 2, \ldots, n\}$. Now consider the input assignment $x' = \sigma_{\pi(1)} \sigma_{\pi(2)} \ldots \sigma_{\pi(n)}$, which is a permutation of x. Take any fair, w.r.t. $\mathcal{A}$, infinite interaction sequence [1] $e_1, e_2, \ldots$, where $e_i \in E$, and replace each $e_i = (j, k)$ with $(\pi(j), \pi(k))$ to obtain a new infinite interaction sequence, which is well defined due to the fact that the interaction graph is complete. Now consider the two infinite executions of $\mathcal{A}$ that correspond to the two interaction sequences on inputs x and x', respectively. Obviously, $x'_w = x_{\pi(w)}$, so that for the initial configurations C'_0 and C_0, we have that $C'_0(w) = C_0(\pi(w))$ for all agents $w \in V$. Moreover, we have initially that $C'_0(j, k) = C_0(\pi(j), \pi(k))$ for all $(j, k) \in E$, which holds trivially since all edges are initially in s_0. Assume that the above holds for some interaction step i, that is, $C'_i(w) = C_i(\pi(w))$ for all $w \in V$ and $C'_i(j, k) = C_i(\pi(j), \pi(k))$ for all $(j, k) \in E$. It is not hard to see that the same must hold for step $i + 1$; consequently, both infinite executions pass in each step through the same multiset of states. This together with the fact that one execution is fair implies that the other must also be fair. So, we have obtained two computations of $\mathcal{A}$ on inputs x and x', respectively, that forever provide the same multisets of output symbols. Now, the fact that p is stably computable implies that $p(x) = p(x')$, which, in turn, implies that p has to be symmetric.   □

In the sequel, we build the machinery required to arrive at the exact characterization of **MPS** that is captured by Theorem 4.7.

Theorem 4.7   MPS = SNSPACE(n^2).

Proof. One direction follows from Theorem 4.22 and the inverse direction from Corollary 4.25.
□

We begin by providing an abstract proof idea of the above Theorem that briefly discusses most techniques that we develop in the sequel.

The "only if" part is easy. Any predicate in **MPS** is obviously symmetric, and additionally we can perform in $\mathcal{O}(n^2)$ space a nondeterministic search on the transition graph of the SMPP that stably computes the predicate.

The sufficiency of the conditions is somewhat more complicated. We have to show that for all symmetric languages $L \in$ **NSPACE(n^2)**, there exists a SMPP that stably computes p_L, defined as $p_L(x) = 1$ iff $x \in L$. The idea is to organize the agents into a spanning pseudo-path subgraph of the interaction graph (pseudo-path graphs are defined in the beginning of Section 4.1.2.2). To do that, the agents begin to form small pseudo-path graphs that in the sequel are merged together and are expanded to isolated nodes. When this process ends, the edges of the spanning pseudo-path graph will be active and all other $\mathcal{O}(n^2)$ edges will be inactive. Now the network can operate as a Turing machine of $\mathcal{O}(n^2)$ space by using the agents as the control units and the inactive edges as the cells. Whenever the inactive edges of some agent are exhausted, it passes control (via some active edge) to

---

[1] By a *fair interaction sequence*, we mean one that leads to a computation of $\mathcal{A}$.

its neighbor on the spanning pseudo-path graph. By also exploiting the nondeterminism inherent in the interaction pattern, the agents can simulate the nondeterministic TM that decides L. Note that, since the agents cannot detect termination of the spanning pseudo-path graph construction process, any time that the structure changes they reinitialize their computation in a systematic manner, so that reinitialized agents do not communicate with non-reinitialized ones, and by exploiting a backup of their input that is maintained throughout the computation. The final reinitialization happens when the spanning pseudo-path graph is formed an then the simulation is executed correctly.

4.1.2.1   MPS is a Proper Superset of SEM and a General Composition Theorem

We first show that **MPS** is a superset of **SEM** and then that the non-semilinear predicate ($N_c = N_a \cdot N_b$) belongs to **MPS**, where N_σ denotes the number of agents that initially obtain the input symbol σ. This (due to the fact that population protocols cannot handle multiplication of variables [AAE06]) establishes the following separation: **MPS** *is a proper superset of* **SEM**.

Lemma 4.8   [CMS09c]   SEM $\subseteq$ MPS.

Proof. Take any semilinear predicate p. Let $\mathcal{A}$ denote the population protocol that stably computes p. We construct a SMPP $\mathcal{B} = (X, Y, Q, S, I, O, \delta)$ that stably computes p. All components of $\mathcal{B}$ are equal to those of $\mathcal{A}$ except for S, which is not specified by $\mathcal{A}$, and δ, which has to be redefined. S is equal to $\{s_0\}$. Let δ' denote the transition function of $\mathcal{A}$. δ is defined as $\delta(a, b, s_0) = (\delta'_1(a, b), \delta'_2(a, b), s_0)$ for all $a, b \in Q$. Clearly, $\mathcal{B}$ ignores the edges and does the same as $\mathcal{A}$, thus, it stably computes p. Another, straightforward, way to see this is by noticing that the population protocol model is a special case of the mediated population protocol model. $\square$

Protocol 4 *VarProduct*

1: $X = \{a, b, c\}$
2: $Y = \{0, 1\}$
3: $Q = \{a, \dot{a}, b, c, \bar{c}\}$
4: $S = \{0, 1\}$
5: $I(\sigma) = \sigma$, for all $\sigma \in X$
6: $O(a) = O(b) = O(\bar{c}) = 1$ and $O(c) = O(\dot{a}) = 0$
7: $\delta: (a, b, 0) \rightarrow (\dot{a}, b, 1), (c, \dot{a}, 0) \rightarrow (\bar{c}, a, 0), (\dot{a}, c, 0) \rightarrow (a, \bar{c}, 0)$
8: // All transitions that do not appear have no effect, e.g., $\delta(a, b, 1) = (a, b, 1)$

Theorem 4.9   [CMS09c]   *Protocol* VarProduct *(see Protocol 4) provides w.r.t. predicate ($N_c = N_a \cdot N_b$) the following semilinear guarantee:*

- *If $N_c \neq N_a \cdot N_b$, then at least one agent remains in one of the states $\dot{a}$ and c.*

- *If $N_c = N_a \cdot N_b$, then no agent remains in these states.*

Proof. Notice that, due to the completeness of the interaction graph, the number of links leading from agents in state a to agents in state b equals $N_a \cdot N_b$. For each a, the protocol tries to erase b c's. Each a is able to remember the b's that has already counted (for every such b a c has been erased) by marking the corresponding links (note that this was clearly impossible in the population protocol model). If the c's were less than the product, then at least one $\dot{a}$ remains, and if the c's were more, at least one, c remains (in both cases, at least one agent that outputs 0 remains). If $N_c = N_a \cdot N_b$, then no agent remains in states $\dot{a}$ and c (every agent eventually outputs 1). $\qquad\square$

Remark 4.10 It is easy to see that Protocol *VarProduct* has stabilizing states.

Note that Theorem 4.9 alone does not complete the separation of **SEM** and **MPS**. The reason is that it does not show that the $SMPP$ model stably computes $(N_c = N_a \cdot N_b)$; what it truly shows is that whenever the predicate is true, a state stable configuration is reached for which another predicate t on configurations becomes true, and whenever it is false, a state stable configuration is reached for which t is also false. In fact, there is a way to exploit the guarantee and the stabilizing states in order to achieve the separation. This is captured by the following general composition theorem holding also for non-complete interaction graphs.

Theorem 4.11 [CMS09c] *Let $\mathcal{G}$ be some family of directed and connected interaction graphs. If there exists a MPP $\mathcal{A}$ with stabilizing states that, in $\mathcal{G}$, guarantees w.r.t. a predicate p a semilinear predicate t, then p is stably computable by the MPP model in $\mathcal{G}$.*

Proof. We show that $\mathcal{A}$ can be composed with a provably existing protocol $\mathcal{B}$ that stably computes t to give a new MPP $\mathcal{C}$ satisfying the following properties:

- $\mathcal{C}$ is formed by the composition of $\mathcal{A}$ and $\mathcal{B}$,

- its input is $\mathcal{A}$'s input,

- its output is $\mathcal{B}$'s output, and

- $\mathcal{C}$ stably computes p (i.e. all agents agree on the correct output) in $\mathcal{G}$.

Protocol $\mathcal{A}$ has stabilizing states and provides a guarantee t which is a semilinear predicate on $\mathcal{A}$'s configurations. Let $X_{\mathcal{A}} = X$ be the input alphabet of $\mathcal{A}$, $Q_{\mathcal{A}}$ the set of $\mathcal{A}$'s states, $\delta_{\mathcal{A}}$ the transition function of $\mathcal{A}$, and similarly for any other component of $\mathcal{A}$. We will use the indexes $\mathcal{B}$ and $\mathcal{C}$, for the corresponding components of the other two protocols.

Since predicate t is semilinear, according to a result in [AAC$^+$05], there is a population protocol $\mathcal{B}'$ that stably computes t with stabilizing inputs in $\mathcal{G}_{con}$. Note that $\mathcal{G} \subseteq \mathcal{G}_{con}$, so any predicate stably computable (both with or without stabilizing inputs) in $\mathcal{G}_{con}$ is also stably computable in $\mathcal{G}$. In fact, the same protocol $\mathcal{B}'$ stably computes t with stabilizing inputs in $\mathcal{G}$. Moreover, there also exists a mediated population protocol $\mathcal{B}$ (the one that is the same as $\mathcal{B}'$ but simply ignores the additional components of the new model) that stably computes t with stabilizing inputs in $\mathcal{G}$. Note that the input alphabet of $\mathcal{B}$ is $X_{\mathcal{B}} = Q_{\mathcal{A}}$, and its transition function is of the form $\delta_{\mathcal{B}} : (Q_{\mathcal{A}} \times Q_{\mathcal{B}}) \times (Q_{\mathcal{A}} \times Q_{\mathcal{B}}) \to Q_{\mathcal{B}} \times Q_{\mathcal{B}}$, since there is no need to specify edge states (formally, we should, but the protocol ignores them). In fact, $Q_{\mathcal{A}}$ also plays the role of $\mathcal{B}$'s inputs that eventually stabilize.

We define a mediated population protocol $\mathcal{C}$ as follows: $X_{\mathcal{C}} = X_{\mathcal{A}}$, $Y_{\mathcal{C}} = Y_{\mathcal{B}} = \{0, 1\}$, $Q_{\mathcal{C}} = Q_{\mathcal{A}} \times Q_{\mathcal{B}}$, $I_{\mathcal{C}} : X_{\mathcal{A}} \to Q_{\mathcal{C}}$ defined as $I_{\mathcal{C}}(x) = (I_{\mathcal{A}}(x), i_{\mathcal{B}})$ for all $x \in Q_{\mathcal{C}}$, where $i_{\mathcal{B}} \in Q_{\mathcal{B}}$ is the initial state of protocol $\mathcal{B}$, $S_{\mathcal{C}} = S_{\mathcal{A}}$, $O_{\mathcal{C}}(a, b) = O_{\mathcal{B}}(b)$, for all $q = (a, b) \in Q_{\mathcal{C}}$, and, finally, its transition function $\delta_{\mathcal{C}} : Q_{\mathcal{C}} \times Q_{\mathcal{C}} \times S_{\mathcal{C}} \to Q_{\mathcal{C}} \times Q_{\mathcal{C}} \times S_{\mathcal{C}}$ is defined as

$$\begin{aligned}
\delta_{\mathcal{C}}((a, b), (a', b'), s) = &((\delta_{\mathcal{A}_1}(a, a', s), \delta_{\mathcal{B}_1}((a, b), (a', b'))), \\
&(\delta_{\mathcal{A}_2}(a, a', s), \delta_{\mathcal{B}_2}((a, b), (a', b'))), \\
&\delta_{\mathcal{A}_3}(a, a', s)),
\end{aligned}$$

where for $\delta_{\mathcal{A}}(x, y, z) = (x', y', z')$ (in $\mathcal{A}$'s transition function), we have that $\delta_{\mathcal{A}_1}(x, y, z) = x'$, $\delta_{\mathcal{A}_2}(x, y, z) = y'$, $\delta_{\mathcal{A}_3}(x, y, z) = z'$, and similarly for $\delta_{\mathcal{B}}$.

Intuitively, $\mathcal{C}$ consists of $\mathcal{A}$ and $\mathcal{B}$ running in parallel. The state of each agent is a pair $c = (a, b)$, where $a \in Q_{\mathcal{A}}$, $b \in Q_{\mathcal{B}}$, and the state of each edge is a member of $S_{\mathcal{A}}$. Initially, each agent senses an input x from $X_{\mathcal{A}}$, and this is transformed according to $I_{\mathcal{C}}$ to such a pair, where $a = I_{\mathcal{A}}(x)$ and b is always a special $\mathcal{B}$'s initial state $i_{\mathcal{B}} \in Q_{\mathcal{B}}$. When two agents in states (a, b) and (a', b') interact through an edge in state s, then protocol $\mathcal{A}$ updates the first components of the agent states, i.e., a and a', and the edge state s, as if $\mathcal{B}$ didn't exist. On the other hand, protocol $\mathcal{B}$ updates the second components by taking into account the first components that represent its separate input ports at which the current input symbol of each agent is available at every interaction ($\mathcal{B}$ takes $\mathcal{A}$'s states for agent input symbols that may change arbitrarily between any two computation steps, but the truth is that they change due to $\mathcal{A}$'s computation). Since the first components of $\mathcal{C}$'s agent states eventually stabilize as a result of the fact that $\mathcal{A}$ has stabilizing states, protocol $\mathcal{B}$ will eventually obtain stabilizing inputs, consequently will operate correctly, and will stably compute t as if it had began computing on $\mathcal{A}$'s state stable configuration. But since t provides the correct answer for p if applied on $\mathcal{A}$'s state stable configuration, it is obvious that $\mathcal{C}$ must stably compute p in $\mathcal{G}$, and the theorem follows.   □

Corollary 4.12   [CMS09c]   *The non-semilinear predicate ($N_c = N_a \cdot N_b$) belongs to* **MPS***.*

Proof. Immediate from noticing that Theorem 4.9 and Remark 4.10 satisfy the requirements of Theorem 4.11.   □

Theorem 4.13   [CMS09c]   **SEM** *is a proper subset of* **MPS**.

Proof. By Lemma 4.8, **SEM** $\subseteq$ **MPS** and, by Corollary 4.12, together with the fact that ($N_c = N_a \cdot N_b$) is non-semilinear, ($N_c = N_a \cdot N_b$) $\in$ **MPS** − **SEM**.   □

4.1.2.2   Leader Nodes in Interaction Graphs

We are now going to establish a much better inclusion. In particular, we will show that any predicate in **SSPACE**(n) is also in **MPS**. In other words, the SMPP model is at least as strong as a linear space TM that computes symmetric predicates. We begin with some necessary definitions and a very basic notion of labels in interaction graphs.

Let $G = (V, E)$ be an interaction graph and let $d_G(u) \equiv |\{w \in V \mid (u, w) \in E \text{ or } (w, u) \in E\}|$ denote the degree of u w.r.t. G. A *pseudo-path graph* $L = (K, A)$ is a directed graph either satisfying $|K| = 1$ and $A = \emptyset$ or $|K| > 1$, $d_L(u) = d_L(v) = 1$ for some $u, v \in K$, and $d_L(w) = 2$ for all $w \in K - \{u, v\}$. In words, it is either an isolated node, which we call the *trivial* pseudo-path graph, or a directed graph that becomes a path graph when the directions of the links are ignored. A *pseudo-path subgraph* of G is a pseudo-path graph $L \subseteq G$ and is called *spanning* if $K = V$. Let $C_l(t)$ denote the *label component* of the state of $t \in V \cup E$ under configuration C.

We say that a pseudo-path subgraph of G is *correctly labeled* under configuration C, if it is trivial and its label is l with no active edges incident to it or if it is non-trivial and all the following conditions are satisfied:

1. Assume that $u, v \in K$ and $d_L(u) = d_L(v) = 1$. These are the only nodes in K with degree 1. Then one of u and v has label k_t (non-leader endpoint) and the other has either l_t or l_h (leader endpoint). The unique $e_u \in A$ incident to u, where u has w.l.o.g. label k_t, is an outgoing edge and the unique $e_v \in A$ incident to v is outgoing if $C_l(v) = l_t$ and incoming if $C_l(v) = l_h$.

2. For all $w \in K - \{u, v\}$ (internal nodes), it holds that $C_l(w) = k$.

3. For all $a \in A$, it holds that $C_l(a) \in \{p, i\}$ (active edges) and for all $e \in E - A$ such that e is incident to a node in K it holds that $C_l(e) = 0$ (inactive edges).

4. Let $v = u_1, u_2, \ldots, u_r = u$ be the path from the leader to the non-leader endpoint (resulting by ignoring the directions of the arcs in A). Let $P_L = \{(u_i, u_{i+1}) \mid 1 \le i < r\}$ be the corresponding directed path from v to u. Then for all $a \in A \cap P_L$, it holds that $C_l(a) = p$ (proper edges) and for all $a' \in A - P_L$ that $C_l(a') = i$ (inverse edges).

See Figure 4.2 for some examples of correctly labeled pseudo-path subgraphs. The meaning and service of each label will become clear in the following discussion.

We describe now a SMPP, called *Spanning Process*, that constructs a correctly labeled spanning pseudo-path subgraph of any complete interaction graph G. The correctness of the protocol is captured by Theorem 4.16. We provide a high level description of the protocol $\mathcal{A}$ in order to avoid its many low-level details. All agents are initially in state l, thought of as being *simple leaders*. All

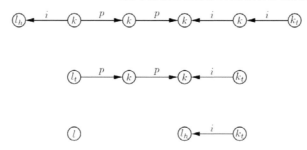

Figure 4.2: We assume that the above depicted graph, call it G, is complete. We have chosen not to draw the inactive edges for the sake of visibility. Therefore, all edges not appearing have label 0; that is, they are inactive. The top six nodes form a correctly labeled pseudo-path subgraph of G. The reason is that the left endpoint has label l_h; that is, it is a head leader; the right endpoint has label k_t; that is, it is a tail non-leader (condition 1 satisfied); all intermediate nodes are (simple) non-leaders (condition 2 satisfied); the edges that follow the direction from left to right have label p; that is, they are proper; those that follow the direction from right to left have label i; that is, they are inverse, and all other edges incident to these nodes (those that do not appear) are inactive (conditions 3 and 4 satisfied). Similarly, all other appearing graphs are pseudo-path subgraphs of the complete graph G. Note that the left node at the bottom that seems to be isolated is in fact a node of G whose incident edges are all inactive. Moreover, it has label l; consequently, it constitutes a trivial pseudo-path subgraph of G.

edges are in state 0, and we think of them as being *inactive*, that is, not part of the pseudo-path subgraph to be constructed. An edge in state p is interpreted as *proper* while an edge in state i is interpreted as *inverse*, and both are additionally interpreted as *active*, that is, part of the pseudo-path subgraph to be constructed. An agent in state k is a (*simple*) *non-leader*, an agent in state k_t is a non-leader that is additionally the *tail* of some pseudo-path subgraph (*tail non-leader*), an agent in state l_t is a leader and a tail of some pseudo-path subgraph (*tail leader*), and an agent in state l_h is a leader and a *head* of some pseudo-path subgraph (*head leader*). All these will be clarified in the sequel. A *leader* is a simple, tail, or head leader.

When two simple leaders interact through an inactive edge, the initiator becomes a tail non-leader, the responder becomes a head leader, and the edge becomes inverse. When a head leader interacts as the initiator with a simple leader via some inactive edge the initiator becomes a non-leader, the responder becomes a head leader, and the edge becomes inverse. When the simple leader is the initiator, the head leader is the responder, and the edge is again inactive, the initiator becomes a tail leader, the responder becomes a non-leader, and the edge becomes proper. When a tail leader interacts as the initiator with a simple leader via an inactive edge, the initiator becomes a non-leader, the responder becomes a head leader, and the edge becomes inverse. When the simple leader is the initiator, the tail leader is the responder, and the edge is again inactive, the initiator becomes a tail leader, the responder becomes a non-leader, and the edge becomes proper. These transitions can be formally summarized as follows:

$$(l, l, 0) \rightarrow (k_t, l_h, i),$$
$$(l_h, l, 0) \rightarrow (k, l_h, i),$$
$$(l, l_h, 0) \rightarrow (l_t, k, p),$$
$$(l_t, l, 0) \rightarrow (k, l_h, i), \text{ and}$$
$$(l, l_t, 0) \rightarrow (l_t, k, p).$$

In this manner, the agents become organized in correctly labeled pseudo-path subgraphs (see again their definition and Figure 4.2).

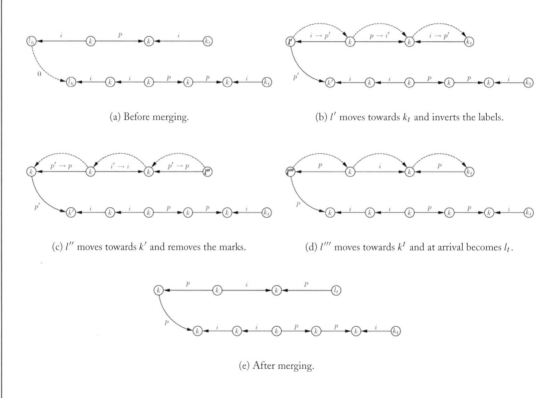

(a) Before merging.

(b) l' moves towards k_t and inverts the labels.

(c) l'' moves towards k' and removes the marks.

(d) l''' moves towards k^t and at arrival becomes l_t.

(e) After merging.

Figure 4.3: Two pseudo-path subgraphs are merged together.

We now describe how two such pseudo-path graphs, L_1 and L_2, are pieced together. Denote by $l(L) \in V$, and by $k_t(L) \in V$, the leader and tail non-leader endpoints of a correctly labeled pseudo-path graph L, respectively. When $l(L_1) = u$ interacts as the initiator with $l(L_2) = v$, through an inactive edge, v becomes a non-leader with a special mark, e.g., k' the edge becomes proper with a special mark, and u becomes a leader in a special state l', indicating that this state will travel towards $k_t(L_1)$ while making all proper edges that it meets inverse and all inverse edges proper. In order to know its direction, it marks each edge that it crosses. When it, finally, arrives at the endpoint, it goes to another special state and walks the same path in the inverse direction until it meets v again. This walk can be performed easily, without using the marks because now all edges have correct labels (states). To diverge from L_1's endpoint, it simply follows the proper links as the initiator (moving from their tail to their head), and the inverse links as the responder (moving from their head to their tail) while erasing all marks left from its previous walk. When it reaches v, it erases its mark, making its state k, and it goes to another special state, indicating that it again must walk towards $k_t(L_1)$ for the last time, performing no other operation this time. To do that, it follows the proper links as the responder (from their head to their tail) and the inverse links as the initiator (from their tail to their head). When it, finally, arrives at $k_t(L_1)$, it becomes a normal tail leader, and now it is easy to see that L_1 and L_2 have been correctly merged into a common correctly labeled pseudo-path graph. See Figure 4.3 for a graphical step by step example. The correctness of this process, called the *merging process*, is captured by Lemma 4.14.

Lemma 4.14 [CMN$^+$10a] *When the leader endpoints of two distinct correctly labeled pseudo-path subgraphs of G, $L_1 = (K_1, A_1)$ and $L_2 = (K_2, A_2)$ interact via $e \in E$, then, in a finite number of steps, L_1 and L_2 are merged into a new correctly labeled pseudo-path graph $L_3 = (K_1 \cup K_2, A_1 \cup A_2 \cup \{e\})$.*

Proof. We study all possible cases:

- L_1 and L_2 are both trivial (they are isolated simple leaders, where "isolated" means that all the edges incident to them are inactive): Then the initiator becomes a tail non-leader, the responder becomes a head leader, and the edge becomes inverse.

- L_1 is non-trivial and L_2 is trivial: First, assume that the leader of L_1 is a tail leader. If the tail leader is the initiator, then it becomes a non-leader, the responder becomes a head leader (the leader end-point of the new pseudo-path graph L_3), and the edge becomes inverse. Clearly, the added edge points towards the new leader of the path and is correctly inverse; all other edges correctly retain their direction labels, the old leader becomes internal, thus, correctly becomes a non-leader, and the other endpoint remains unaffected, thus, correctly remains a tail non-leader. The cases in which the leader of L_1 is a head leader and those where L_1's leader is the responder are handled similarly.

- L_2 is non-trivial and L_1 is trivial: This case is symmetric to the previous one.

- L_1 and L_2 are both non-trivial: Assume w.l.o.g. that L_1's leader is the initiator. Then L_2's leader will become a non-leader, which is correct since it will constitute an internal node of the new pseudo-path graph L_3, which will be the result of the merging process. But first, it becomes a marked non-leader in order to inform L_1's leader where to stop its movement. L_1's leader goes to a special state that only has effective interactions through active edges. This ensures that it only has effective interactions with its neighbors in the new pseudo-path graph

L_3. Additionally, the edge via which the pseudo-path graphs L_1 and L_2 were merged goes to a marked proper state. The goal of the merging process is to change all direction labels of L_1, that is, make the proper inverse and the inverse proper. The reason is that L_1's tail non-leader endpoint will now become L_3's leader endpoint, and if remain unchanged, L_1's direction labels will be totally wrong for the new pseudo-path graph. L_2's direction labels must remain unchanged since their new leader will be in the same side as before; thus, they will still be correct w.r.t., the direction of the path from L_3's new leader endpoint and its non-leader endpoint. When L_1's leader interacts via a non-marked edge, it knows that it interacts with a neighbor that it has not visited yet and which lies on the direction towards L_1's tail non-leader endpoint. Thus, it changes the edge's label; if it is proper it makes it inverse and contrariwise, marks it in order to know its direction towards that endpoint, and jumps to its neighboring node; that is, the neighbor becomes the special leader, and the node itself becomes a non-leader. In this manner, the leader keeps moving step by step towards L_1's non-leader endpoint while at the same time fixing the direction labels. Eventually, due to fairness, it will reach the endpoint. At this point, it goes to another special leader state whose purpose is to walk the same path in the inverse direction until it meets again the old leader of L_2, which is marked, and, thus, can be identified. It simply follows the marked links while erasing the marks of the links that it crosses. When it finally meets the unique marked agent of L_3, it unmarks it, thus, makes it a normal non-leader, unmarks the only edge that still remains marked, which is the edge that joined L_1 and L_2, and goes to another special leader state whose purpose is to walk again back to L_1's endpoint and then become a normal tail leader, that is, L_3's tail leader. This can be done easily because now all links have correct direction labels. In fact, it knows that if it interacts as the responder via a proper link or as the initiator via an inverse link, then it must cross that link because, in both cases, it will move on step closer to L_1's endpoint. All other interactions are ignored by this special leader. It is easy to see that due to fairness and due to the fact that it can only move towards L_1's endpoint, it will eventually reach it. When this happens, it becomes a normal tail leader. It must be clear that all internal nodes of L_3 are non-leaders, one endpoint has remained a tail non-leader while the other has become a tail leader; all direction labels are correct, and all other edges that are not part of L_3, but are incident to it, have remained inactive. Thus, L_3 is correctly labeled.

$\square$

Lemma 4.15 [CMN$^+$10a]   *Correctly labeled pseudo-path graphs never become smaller.*

Proof. Let r denote the number of nodes of a pseudo-path graph L_1. For $r = 1$, the trivial pseudo-path graph consists of an isolated simple leader. The only effective interaction is with another leader, which is either an isolated node or the leader of another pseudo-path graph L_2. In both cases, clearly, no pseudo-path graph becomes smaller because either L_1 obtains another node, or L_1 and L_2 get merged to form a new pseudo-path graph whose number of nodes is L_2's nodes plus one. For $r > 1$, L_1 is a normal pseudo-path graph with a leader, either a tail leader or a head leader. If L_1 is the result of some merging and is still running the merging process, then, according to Lemma 4.14, this process will eventually come to an end, and L_1 will then have a head or a tail leader. Then the only effective interaction is between L_1's leader and another leader, which either adds another node to L_1 or merges L_1 with another pseudo-path graph, and in both cases, no pseudo-path graph becomes smaller. □

Theorem 4.16 [CMN$^+$10a]   *There is a SMPP $\mathcal{A}$ that constructs a correctly labeled spanning pseudo-path subgraph of any complete interaction graph G.*

Proof.   By definition, we consider isolated simple leaders as trivial pseudo-path graphs. Thus, initially, G is partitioned into n correctly labeled trivial pseudo-path graphs. According to Lemma 4.15, correctly labeled pseudo-path graphs never become smaller, and according to Lemma 4.14, when their leaders interact, they are merged into a new pseudo-path graph containing all nodes of the interacting pseudo-path graphs plus an additional edge joining them. Moreover, given that there are two correctly labeled pseudo-path subgraphs in the current configuration, there is always the possibility (due to fairness) that these pseudo-path graphs may get merged because they are correctly labeled which implies that there are always inactive edges joining their leader endpoints, and there is no other possible effective interaction between two pseudo-path graphs. In simple words, two pseudo-path graphs can only get merged, and there is always the possibility that merging actually takes place. It is easy to see that this process has to end, due to fairness, in a finite number of steps, having constructed a correctly labeled spanning pseudo-path subgraph of G. □

4.1.2.3   Simulate A Linear Space Turing Machine
We now show that correctly labeled pseudo-path graphs allow for Mediated Protocols to simulate a linear space Turing Machine.

Theorem 4.17 [CMN$^+$10a]   *Assume that the interaction graph $G = (V, E)$ is a correctly labeled pseudo-path graph of n agents, where each agent takes its input symbol in a second state component [2]. Then there is a MPP $\mathcal{A}$ that when running on such a graph simulates a deterministic TM $\mathcal{M}$ of $\mathcal{O}(n)$ (linear) space that computes symmetric predicates.*

Proof. $\mathcal{A}$ exploits the fact that G is correctly labeled. It knows that there is a unique leader in one endpoint, called the *left endpoint*, which is either a head leader or a tail leader. Moreover, it knows that the other endpoint, the *right endpoint*, is a tail non-leader and that all other (internal) agents are simple non-leaders. All these are w.r.t. to $\mathcal{A}$'s label component. $\mathcal{A}$ also knows that the agents' second components contain, initially, their initial state, which is the same as their input symbol. It

---

[2]The first component is used for the labels of the spanning process and is called *label component*.

additionally knows that the edges have correct direction labels, which implies that those following the direction of the path from the leader endpoint to the non-leader endpoint are proper, while the remaining are inverse.

The leader starts simulating the TM. Since $\mathcal{M}$ computes symmetric predicates, it gives the same output for all permutations of any input vector's symbols. We already know from Exercise 1.5 that if all edges were proper, then there is a population protocol, and, thus, a MPP, that simulates $\mathcal{M}$. It remains to show that having inverse edges cannot not harm the simulation. The explanation is as follows. Assume that an agent u has $\mathcal{M}$'s head over the last symbol of its state component (each agent can use a constant number of such symbols due to uniformity property). Now, assume that $\mathcal{M}$ moves its head to the right. Then u must pass control to its right neighbor. To do so, it simply follows a proper edge as the initiator of an interaction or an inverse edge as the responder of an interaction. Similarly, when control must be passed to the left neighbor, the agent follows an inverse edge as the initiator of an interaction or a proper edge as the responder of an interaction. It is easy to check that in this manner, the correct directions can always be followed. Finally, $\mathcal{A}$ can detect the endpoints by their distinct labels. In fact, since the MPP model can also store states on the edges, it can use an additional edge component for the simulation in order to double the available space. □

It must be clear now, that if the agents could detect termination of the spanning process then they would be able to simulate a deterministic TM of $\mathcal{O}(n)$ (linear) space that computes symmetric predicates. But, unfortunately, they are unable to detect termination, because if they could, then termination could also be detected in any non-spanning pseudo-path subgraph constructed in some intermediate step (it can be proven by symmetry arguments together with the fact that the agents cannot count up to the population size). Fortunately, we can overcome the impossibility of detecting termination by applying a technique known as the *reinitialization technique*.

Let us first outline the approach that will be followed in Theorem 4.18. Whenever two correctly labeled pseudo-path subgraphs get merged, we know that a new correctly labeled pseudo-path graph will be constructed in a finite number of steps. Moreover, termination of the merging process can be detected (see the proof of Lemma 4.14). When the merging process comes to an end, the unique leader of the new pseudo-path graph does the following. It makes the assumption that the spanning process has come to an end (an assumption that is possibly wrong since the pseudo-path subgraph may not be spanning yet), restores its state component to its input symbol (thus, restarting the TM simulation), and informs its right neighbor to do the same. Restoring the input symbol can be trivially achieved because the agents can forever keep their input symbols in a read-only *input backup* component. The correctness of this idea is based on the fact that the reinitialization process also takes place when the last two pseudo-path subgraphs get merged into the final spanning pseudo-path subgraph. What happens then is that the TM simulation starts again from the beginning like it had never been executed during the spanning process, and Theorem 4.17 guarantees that the simulation will run correctly if not restarted in future steps. Clearly, it will never be restarted again because no other merging process will ever take place (a unique spanning pseudo-path subgraph is active and all other edges are inactive).

Theorem 4.18   [CMN+10a]   SSPACE(n) *is a subset of* **MPS**.

Proof. Take any $p \in$ **SSPACE**(n). By Theorem 4.17, we know that there is a MPP $\mathcal{A}$ that stably computes p on a pseudo-path graph of n nodes. We have to show that there exists a SMPP $\mathcal{B}$ that stably computes p. We construct $\mathcal{B}$ to be the composition of $\mathcal{A}$ and another protocol $\mathcal{I}$ that is responsible for executing the spanning and reinitialization processes.

Each agent's state consists of three components: a read-only *input backup*, one used by $\mathcal{I}$, and one used by $\mathcal{A}$. Thus, $\mathcal{A}$ and $\mathcal{I}$ are, in some sense, executed in parallel in different components.

Protocol $\mathcal{I}$ does the following. It always executes the spanning process, and when two pseudo-path graphs get merged and the merging process comes to an end, it executes the following reinitialization process. The new leader u that resulted from merging becomes marked, e.g., l_i^*. Recall that the new pseudo-path graph has also correct labels. When u meets its right neighbor, u sets its $\mathcal{A}$ component to its input symbol (by copying it from the input backup), becomes unmarked, and passes the mark to its right neighbor (correct edge labels guarantee that each agent distinguishes its right and left neighbors). When the marked agent interacts with its own right neighbor, it does the same, and so on, until the two rightmost agents interact; in which case, they are both reinitialized at the same time, and the special mark is lost. It is easy to see that this process guarantees that all agents in the pseudo-path graph become reinitialized, and before completion, non-reinitialized agents do not have effective interactions with reinitialized ones (the special marked agent acts always as the separator between reinitialized and non-reinitialized agents). Note that if other reinitialization processes are pending from previous reinitialization steps, then the new one erases them. This can be done easily because the new reinitialization signal will always be traveling from left to right, and all old signals will be found to its right; in this manner, we know which of them has to be erased. Another possible approach is to block the leader from participating in another merging process before completion of the current pending reinitialization process. This approach is also correct: fairness guarantees that the reinitialization process will terminate in a finite number of steps; thus, the merging process will not be blocked forever.

From Theorem 4.16, we know that the spanning process executed by $\mathcal{I}$ results in a correctly labeled spanning pseudo-path subgraph of G. The spanning process, as already mentioned, terminates when the merging of the last two pseudo-path subgraphs takes place and merging also correctly terminates in a finite number of steps (Lemma 4.14). Moreover, from the above discussion we know that when this happens, the reinitialization process will correctly reinitialize all agents of the spanning pseudo-path subgraph, thus, all agents in the population. But then, independently of its computation so far (in its own component), $\mathcal{A}$ will run from the beginning on a correctly labeled a pseudo-path graph of n nodes (this pseudo-path graph will not be modified again in the future); thus, it will stably compute p. Finally, if we assume that $\mathcal{B}$'s output is $\mathcal{A}$'s output, then we conclude that the SMPP $\mathcal{B}$ also stably computes p, thus, $p \in$ **MPS**. See Figure 4.4 for a graphical step by step example. $\qquad\square$

4.1.2.4 An Exact Characterization: MPS = SNSPACE(n^2)

We now extend the ideas used in the previous two sections in order to establish that **SSPACE**(n^2) is a subset of **MPS**, showing that **MPS** is a surprisingly wide class. Finally, we improve to **SNSPACE**(n^2) and show that the latter inclusion holds with equality, thus, arriving at the following exact characterization for **MPS**: *A predicate is in* **MPS** *iff it is symmetric and is in* **NSPACE**(n^2).

To simplify reading the proof, we first provide a proof idea:

The "only if" part is easy. Any predicate in **MPS** is obviously symmetric, and additionally, we can perform in $\mathcal{O}(n^2)$ space a nondeterministic search on the *transition graph* of the SMPP that stably computes the predicate.

The sufficiency of the conditions is somewhat more complicated. We have to show that for all symmetric languages $L \in$ **NSPACE**(n^2), there exists a SMPP that stably computes p_L, defined as $p_L(x) = 1$ iff $x \in L$. We have already shown in Lemma 1.4 that p_L is symmetric iff L is symmetric. The idea is to organize the agents into a spanning pseudo-path subgraph of the interaction graph. To do that, the agents begin to form small pseudo-path graphs that in the sequel are merged together and are expanded to isolated nodes. When this process ends, the edges of the spanning pseudo-path graph will be active, and all other $\mathcal{O}(n^2)$ edges will be inactive. Now the network can operate as a Turing machine of $\mathcal{O}(n^2)$ space by using the agents as the control units and the inactive edges as the cells. Whenever the inactive edges of some agent are exhausted, it passes control (via some active edge) to its neighbor on the spanning pseudo-path graph. By also exploiting the nondeterminism inherent in the interaction pattern, the agents can simulate the nondeterministic TM that decides L. Note that since the agents cannot detect termination of the spanning pseudo-path graph construction process any time that the structure changes, they reinitialize their computation in a systematic manner, so that reinitialized agents do not communicate with non-reinitialized ones and by exploiting a backup of their input that is maintained throughout the computation. The final reinitialization happens when the spanning pseudo-path graph is formed an then the simulation is executed correctly.

Theorem 4.19 [CMN$^+$10a] *Assume that the complete interaction graph $G = (V, E)$ contains a correctly labeled spanning pseudo-path subgraph, where each agent takes its input symbol in a second* state *component. Then there is a MPP $\mathcal{A}$ that when running on such a graph simulates a deterministic TM $\mathcal{M}$ of $\mathcal{O}(n^2)$ space that computes symmetric predicates.*

Proof. For simplicity and w.l.o.g., we assume that $\mathcal{A}$ begins its execution from the leader endpoint, and that initially, the simulation moves all n input symbols to the leftmost outgoing inactive edges ($n - 2$ leaving from the leader and two more leaving from the second agent of the pseudo-path graph). Consider w.l.o.g. that the left endpoint is a tail leader and the right one the tail non-leader. Each agent can distinguish its neighbors in the pseudo-path graph (in particular, it knows which

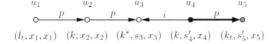

(a) Just after merging. The leader endpoint has the special star mark. The reinitialization process begins.

(b) u_1 becomes reinitialized and u_2 obtains the star mark. Note that u_1's first component obtains a bar mark to block u_1 from participating in another merging process.

(c) Nothing happens, since only u_1 has been reinitialized (u_2 still has the star mark).

(d) u_2 becomes reinitialized and passes the mark to u_3.

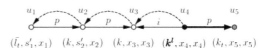

(e) Both u_4 and u_5 have not been reinitialized yet. A simulation step is executed but this is unimportant since both u_4 and u_5 will be reinitialized in future steps and cannot communicate with reinitialized agents (the star mark acts as a separator).

(f) u_3 becomes reinitialized and passes the mark to u_4.

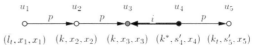

(g) A simulation step is executed normally because both have been reinitialized.

(h) Both become reinitialized and u_4 goes to k^l. The "left" mark will travel to u_1 to remove its mark and indicate the end of the reinitialization process.

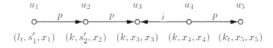

(i) After completion of the reinitialization process. The leader is again ready for merging.

Figure 4.4: Caption on the next page.

Figure 4.4: An example of the reinitialization process just after two pseudo-path graphs have been merged together. The agents are named $(u_1, u_2, \ldots, u_5)$. Each agent's state is a 3-vector (c_1, c_2, c_3) where component c_1 contains the label of the agent, c_2 the state of the TM simulation, and c_3 the input backup. The bold edge indicates the pair that has just interacted. The black agent is the initiator and the gray the responder. The states of the corresponding agents are updated in each figure according to their previous states and the state of the edge joining them.

is the left and which is the right one) from its remaining neighbors, since the latter are via inactive edges. Moreover, the endpoints of the pseudo-path graph can be identified because the pseudo-path graph is correctly labeled (one endpoint is a leader, the other is a tail non-leader, and all intermediate agents are non-leaders). Finally, we assume that the edge states consist now of two components, one used to identify them as active/inactive and the other used by the simulation.

In contrast to Theorem 4.17, the simulation also makes use of the inactive edges. The agent in control of the simulation is in a special state denoted with a star '$*$'. Since the simulation starts from the left endpoint (tail leader), its state will be l_t^*. When the star-marked leader interacts with its unique right neighbor on the pseudo-path graph, the neighbor's state is updated to a *r-marked* state (i.e. k^r). The k^r agent then interacts with its own right neighbor, which is unmarked and the neighbor updates its state to a special *dot* state (i.e. $\dot{k}$) whereas the other agent (in state k^r) is updated to k. Then the only effective interaction is between the star-marked leader (l_t^*) and the dot non-leader ($\dot{k}$), which can only happen via the inactive edge joining them. In this way, the inactive edge's state component used for the simulation becomes a part of the TM's tape. In fact, $\mathcal{M}$'s tape consists only of the inactive edges and is accessed in a systematic fashion, which is described below.

If the simulation has to continue to the right, the interaction $(l_t^*, \dot{k})$ sends the dot agent to state k^r. If it has to proceed left, the dot agent goes to state k^l. An agent in state k^r interacts with its *right* neighbor, sending it to dot state whereas a k^l agent does the same for its *left* neighbor. In this way, the dot mark is moving left and right between the agents by following the active edges in the appropriate interaction role (initiator or responder) as described in Theorem 4.16 for the special states traversing through the pseudo-path graph. The dot mark's (state's) position in the pseudo-path graph determines which outgoing inactive edge of l_t^* will be used. The sequence in which the dot mark is traversing the graph is the sequence in which l_t^* visits its outgoing inactive edges. Therefore, if it has to visit the next inactive edge, it moves the dot mark to the right (via a k^r state) or to the left (via a k^l state) if it has to visit the previous one. It should be noted that the dot marked agent plays the role of the TM's head since it points the edge (which would correspond to a tape's cell in $\mathcal{M}$) that is visited. As stated above only the inactive edges hold the contents of the TM's tape. The active ones are used for allowing the special states (symbols) traverse the pseudo-path graph.

Consider the case where the dot mark reaches the right non-leader endpoint ($\dot{k}_t$) and the simulation after the interaction $(l_t^*, \dot{k}_t)$ demands to proceed right. Since l_t^*'s outgoing edges have all been visited by the simulation, the execution must continue on the next agent (right neighbor of leader endpoint l_t) in the pseudo-path graph. This is achieved by having another special state traversing from right to left (since we are in the right non-leader endpoint) until it finds l_t^*. Then it removes its star mark (state) and assigns it to its right neighbor, which now takes control of the simulation visiting its own inactive edges. A similar process takes place when the simulation, controlled by any non-leader agent, reaches the left leader endpoint and needs to proceed to the left cell.

When the control of the simulation reaches a non-leader agent (e.g., from the left leader endpoint side) in order to visit its first edge, it places the dot mark to the left leader endpoint and then to the next (on the right) non-leader and so forth. If the dot mark reaches the star-marked agent (in the previous example from the left endpoint side), then it moves the dot to the closer (in the pseudo-path graph) agent that can "see" via an inactive edge towards the right non-leader endpoint. In this way, each agent visits its outgoing edges in a specific sequence (from leader to non-leader when the simulation moves right and the reverse when it moves left), providing the $\mathcal{O}(n^2)$ space needed for the simulation. See Figure 4.5 for a graphical example.

Note that the assumption that only inactive edges are used by the simulation to hold $\mathcal{M}$'s tape is not restrictive. The previously described mechanism can be extended (using a few more special states and little more complicated interaction sequences) to also use the active edges, as well as the agents, for the simulation. However, the inactive edges of each agent towards the rest of the population are asymptotically sufficient for the simulation discussed so far.   □

We present now an SMPP that simulates a deterministic TM by using asymptotically all its distributed memory as its tape cells. The correctness of the simulation is proved in Theorem 4.21, which concludes that **SSPACE**(n^2) $\subseteq$ **MPS**. The main idea is similar to that in the proof of Theorem 4.18 (based again on the reinitialization technique). We assume that the edge states now consist of two components, one used to identify them as active/inactive and the other used by the simulation (protocol $\mathcal{A}$ from Theorem 4.19).

This time, the reinitialization process attempts to reinitialize not only all agents of a pseudo-path graph but also all of their outgoing edges. We begin by describing the reinitialization process in detail. Whenever the merging process of two pseudo-path graphs comes to an end, resulting to a new pseudo-path graph L, the leader endpoint of L goes to a special *blocked* state, let it be l^b, blocking L from getting merged with another pseudo-path graph while the reinitialization process is being executed. Keep in mind that L will only get ready for merging just after completion of the reinitialization process. By interacting with its unique right neighbor in state k via an active edge, it propagates the blocked state towards that neighbor, updating its state to k^b and reinitializing the agent. The block state propagates in the same way towards the tail non-leader reinitializing and updating all intermediate non-leaders to k^b from left to right. Once it reaches this endpoint, a new special state k_0 is generated, which traverses L in the inverse direction. Once k_0 reaches the leader endpoint, it disappears, and the leader updates its state to l^*.

Now reinitialization of the inactive edges begins. When the leader in l^* interacts with its unique right neighbor (via the active edge joining them), it updates its neighbor's state to a special

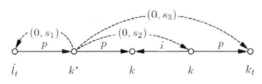

(a) The agent in k^* controls now the simulation.

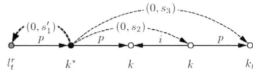

(b) A step of the simulation is executed on the inactive edge. The TM says "right" so k^* must next run the simulation on the first inactive edge to the right.

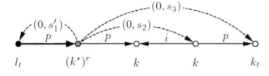

(c) Mark r travels to the right until it meets the first agent that has an incoming inactive edge from k^*.

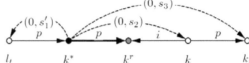

(d) The mark still travels.

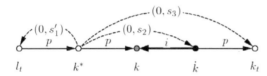

(e) The correct agent was found. The special dot mark will make the simulation run on the next inactive edge.

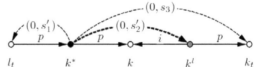

(f) A step of the simulation is executed. The TM says now "left" so the simulation must next use again the previous inactive edge.

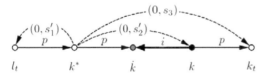

(g) The dot mark is placed on the wrong agent (because we only use for the simulation the inactive outgoing edges of k^*).

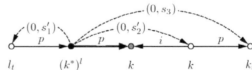

(h) The error is detected because the interaction happened through an active edge. The l mark continues its travel to the left.

Figure 4.5: Caption on the next page.

Figure 4.5: An example of simulating a $\mathcal{O}(n^2)$-space deterministic TM. The simulation is performed on the second (state) component of the inactive edges (those whose first component is 0). The bold edge indicates the pair that has just interacted. The black agent is the initiator and the gray the responder. The states of the corresponding agents are updated in each figure according to their previous states and the state of the edge joining them. We only present the effective interactions that take place; it is possible that between two subsequent figures a finite number of ineffective interactions have taken place. Fairness guarantees that an effective interaction that is always possible to occur will eventually occur (*Continues.*).

bar state (e.g., $\bar{k}$). When the agent with the bar state interacts with its own right neighbor, which is unmarked, the neighbor updates its state to a special *dot* state (e.g., $\dot{k}$). Now the bars cannot propagate, and the only effective interaction is between the star leader and the dot non-leader. This interaction reinitializes the state component of the edge used for the simulation and makes the responder non-leader a bar non-leader. Then the new bar non-leader turns its own right neighbor to a dot non-leader, the second outgoing edge of the leader is reinitialized in this manner, and so on, until the edge joining the star leader (left endpoint) with the dot tail non-leader (right endpoint) is reinitialized. What happens then is that the bars are erased one after the other from right to left (keep in mind that all outgoing edges of the leader have been reinitialized), and finally, the star moves one step to the right. So the first non-leader has now the star, and it reinitializes its own inactive outgoing edges from left to right in a similar manner. The process repeats the same steps over and over, until the right endpoint of L reinitializes all of its outgoing edges. When this happens, $\mathcal{A}$ will execute its simulation on the correct reinitialized states. Though it is clear that the above process is correctly executed when L is spanning because all outgoing edges have their heads on the pseudo-path graph, it is not so clear that it correctly terminates when L is not spanning. The reason is that in the latter case, there will always be inactive edges between agents of L and agents of some other pseudo-path subgraph L'. It is crucial to prove that no problem will occur because, otherwise, there is a clear risk that the reinitialization process on L will not terminate. This would render the spanning process incapable of merging L with some other pseudo-path graph, and a spanning pseudo-path graph would never get formed.

Lemma 4.20 [CMN$^+$10a] *Let L and L' be two distinct pseudo-path subgraphs of G, and assume that L runs a reinitialization process. The process always terminates in a finite number of steps.*

Proof. If L' is not running a reinitialization process then there can be no conflict between L and L'. The reason is that the reinitialization process has some effective interaction via an inactive edge only when the edge's tail is in a star state and its head is in a dot state. But these states can only appear in a pseudo-path graph while it is executing a reinitialization process. Thus, if this is the case, L's reinitialization process will get executed as if L' didn't exist.

If L' is also running its own reinitialization process, then there are two possible conflicts:

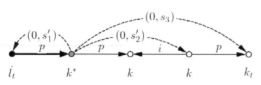

(i) The dot mark is placed at the leader endpoint.

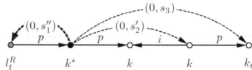

(j) A step of the simulation is executed. The TM says again "left" but it is already at the leftmost agent. A special R mark is created to change the agent that has control of the simulation.

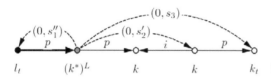

(k) The agent that has control was detected. The L mark will pass control to the left neighbor.

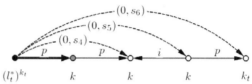

(l) The star mark was passed to the left. The left endpoint has now control of the simulation and will use its own inactive outgoing edges. The 'k_t' mark indicates that it must continue from its last outgoing edge (acts like an artificial dot mark over the non-leader endpoint.

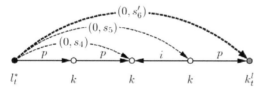

(m) A step of the simulation is executed. The TM says again "left".

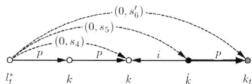

(n) The dot mark was passed to the left.

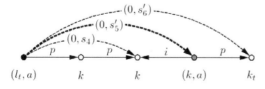

(o) A step of the simulation is executed. The TM accepts and an accepting component is created in both agents.

(p) The accepting component is in a finite number of steps (due to fairness) propagated to all agents and the population also accepts.

Figure 4.5: *Continued.* An example of simulating a $\mathcal{O}(n^2)$-space deterministic TM.

1. *A star agent of L interacts with a dot agent of L'*: In this case, the dot agent of L' simply becomes a bar non-leader, and the star agent of L maintains its state. Thus, L's reinitialization process is not affected.

2. *A star agent of L' interacts with a dot agent of L*: Now the opposite happens, and L's reinitialization process is clearly affected. But what really happens is that the dot agent of L becomes a bar non-leader via a wrong interaction. But this does not delay the progress of the reinitialization process; it only makes it take one step forward without reinitializing the correct edge.

In the first case, the process is not affected at all, and in the second, the process cannot be delayed (it simply takes some steps without reinitializing the corresponding edges); thus, it always terminates in a finite number of steps (due to fairness and by taking into account the discussion preceding this lemma), and L will be in finite time ready to participate in another merging process.   □

Theorem 4.21 [CMN$^+$10a]   **SSPACE**(n^2) *is a subset of* **MPS**.

Proof. Lemma 4.20 guarantees that the spanning process terminates with a spanning pseudo-path subgraph with active edges, while all remaining edges in G are inactive. In this case, since a unique pseudo-path subgraph exists (the spanning one), there can be no conflict, and it must be clear that all agents and all edges will get correctly reinitialized. When the last reinitialization process ends, protocol $\mathcal{A}$ starts its last execution, this time on the correct reinitialized system. We finally ensure that the simulation does not ever alter the agent labels used by the spanning and reinitialization processes. These labels are read-only from the viewpoint of $\mathcal{A}$. In the proof of Theorem 4.19, we made $\mathcal{A}$ put marks on the labels in order to execute correctly. Now we simply think of these marks as placed in a separate subcomponent of $\mathcal{A}$ that is ignored by the other processes. The theorem follows by taking into account Theorem 4.19 stating that this construction is all that $\mathcal{A}$ needs to get correctly executed.   □

We next show how one can add some nondeterminism to the above simulation and, as a consequence, further improve the inclusion of Theorem 4.21.

Theorem 4.22 [CMN$^+$10a]   **SNSPACE**(n^2) $\subseteq$ **MPS**.

Proof. In Theorems 4.19 and 4.21, it has been shown that the SMPP model can simulate a deterministic TM $\mathcal{M}$ of $\mathcal{O}(n^2)$ space. Some modifications are now presented that will allow the simulation of a nondeterministic TM $\mathcal{N}$ of the same memory size. $\mathcal{N}$ is similar to $\mathcal{M}$. Note that $\mathcal{N}$ is a decider for some predicate in **SNSPACE**(n^2); thus, it always halts. The modifications for $\mathcal{N}$ concern the agents states' components and the reinitialization process after each pseudo-path graph merging.

Each agent state $c \in Q$ has an additional (fourth) component c_4 (from now on, it will be referred as *choice component*), which is initialized to $t_{max} - 1$, where t_{max} is the greatest number of nondeterministic choices that $\mathcal{N}$ will ever face. It should be noted that any agent has to be able to store $\mathcal{N}$'s transition function (which includes the nondeterministic transitions) in order to perform a part of $\mathcal{N}$'s execution because that requires updating the corresponding components of its inactive outgoing edges ($\mathcal{N}$'s tape cells), according to this function. Also note that this assumption holds for the deterministic TM $\mathcal{M}$, and it is vital for both simulations. Obviously, there is a fixed upper bound on the number of nondeterministic choices (independent of the population size), and thus the agents can store them in their memories. In addition, t_{max} can be easily extracted from $\mathcal{N}$'s transition function stored in any agent.

As regards the reinitialization process, it changes as follows: Every time a leader is reinitialized, it sets its state's choice component to $t_{max} - 1$. Each time during the reinitialization that the star mark passes from an agent v to its right neighbor u (considering w.l.o.g. that reinitialization takes place from left to right), u sets its choice component to v's choice component -1. If the newly computed choice component is less than 0, then the corresponding agent sets this component to $t_{max} - 1$. This component's update is additional to the work each agent does during those interactions as described for the deterministic TM's simulation. From Theorem 4.21, we have that the reinitializations will eventually stop and that the final reinitialization takes place on a correctly labeled spanning pseudo-path subgraph of the interaction graph G. Since the reinitialization process is performed from the leader endpoint to the non-leader endpoint, the last reinitialization ends up with a pseudo-path graph where the choice components of the agents, starting from the leader, will be $t_{max} - 1, t_{max} - 2, \ldots, 1, 0, t_{max} - 1, \ldots$ and so forth. After that last reinitialization, the choice components will not change any further.

To view it more systematically, consider that each agent in the pseudo-path graph has a position according to its distance from the leader endpoint. Leader has the position 0, its neighbor has 1, the non-leader neighbor of leader's neighbor has 2, and so forth. Then the formula that determines the choice component's value for each agent is $(t_{max} - 1) - (position \mod t_{max})$. Note, however, that the agents do not know this formula nor their position and assign their choice components value during the reinitialization process as described in the previous paragraph. Position is dependent on the population size and therefore cannot be stored in a constant memory agent. The formula is given purely for clarifying the choice components' values after the termination of a reinitialization.

Whenever a nondeterministic choice has to be made between t candidates where $t \leq t_{max}$ by definition of t_{max}, the agent in control of $\mathcal{N}$'s simulation maps the numbers $0, 1, \ldots, t - 1$ to those candidates and waits for an arbitrary interaction. The choice component of the agent participating in the next interaction with the agent in control will provide the nondeterministic choice. This is achieved by having the agent in control of the simulation choose the candidate mapped to $v(c_4)$ mod t where v is the other participant of the interaction and $v(c_4)$ denotes the choice component of agent v. Note that since t_{max} is the greatest number of nondeterministic choices that can appear during $\mathcal{N}$'s execution, any time a nondeterministic choice has to be made, all possible choices will be available, provided that there are enough agents ($2t_{max} \leq n$ so that it is possible to see any choice number from $0, \ldots, t_{max} - 1$, no matter which agent has control of the simulation since an agent cannot interact with itself).

As in $\mathcal{M}$, any time the simulation reaches an accept state, all agents change their output to 1 and the simulation halts. Moreover, any time the simulation reaches a reject state, it is being reinitialized since the fact that a branch of the nondeterministic computation tree rejects does not mean that all branches reject. Fairness guarantees that, by making the nondeterministic choices in the previously described way, all possible paths in the tree representing $\mathcal{N}$'s nondeterministic computation will eventually be followed. Correctness lies in the following two cases:

1. *If $\mathcal{N}$ rejects then every agent's output stabilizes to* 0. Upon initialization, each agent's output is 0 since $\mathcal{N}$'s output function is the same as $\mathcal{M}$'s and can only change if $\mathcal{N}$ reaches an accept state. But all branches of $\mathcal{N}$'s computation reject, thus, no accept state is ever reached, and every agent's output forever remains to 0.

2. *If $\mathcal{N}$ accepts then every agent's output stabilizes to* 1. Since $\mathcal{N}$ accepts, there is a sequence of configurations S, starting from the initial configuration C that leads to a configuration C' in which each agent's output is set to 1 (by simulating directly the branch of $\mathcal{N}$ that accepts). Notice from $\mathcal{M}$'s description that when an agent reaches the q_{accept} state, it never alters its state again, and therefore its output remains on 1, so it suffices to show that the simulation will eventually reach C'. Assume on the contrary that it does not. Since $\mathcal{N}$ always halts, the simulation will be at the initial configuration C infinitely many times. Due to fairness, C' will also appear infinitely many times, which leads to a contradiction. Thus the simulation will eventually reach C', and the output will stabilize to 1.

$\square$

We now deal with the inverse direction of Theorem 4.7. That is, we are going to show that **MPS** $\subseteq$ **SNSPACE**(n^2). This, as alluded to in the proof idea of Theorem 4.7, is a not so difficult task. First recall that m denotes the number of edges of the interaction graph.

Definition 4.23   [CMS09c]   Let **DMP** (**UMP**) be the class of predicates stably computable by the MPP model in any family $\mathcal{G}$ of directed (undirected) and connected interaction graphs.

Theorem 4.24   [CMS09c]   *All predicates in **DMP** and **UMP** are also in the class **NSPACE**(m), where m denotes the number of edges of the interaction graph.*

It is not hard to prove the above theorem, and you are asked to do so in Exercise 4.5. Theorem 4.24 has the following immediate consequence.

Corollary 4.25   [CMS09c]   **MPS** *is a subset of* **SNSPACE**(n^2).

Proof. Any $p \in$ **MPS** is symmetric (see Lemma 4.6), and according to Theorem 4.24 belongs to **NSPACE**(m). Finally, notice that **MPS** deals with complete interaction graphs, in which $m = \mathcal{O}(n^2)$.   □

We have now arrived at the exact characterization of **MPS** stated in Theorem 4.7, that is, **MPS** = **SNSPACE**(n^2). One direction follows from Theorem 4.22, and the inverse direction from Corollary 4.25.

4.2   STABLY DECIDABLE NETWORK PROPERTIES

In this section, we deal with the self-awareness ability of the MPP model. In particular, as outlined in the beginning of the chapter, we want to study what a MPP is able to know about the underlying topology when this topology is not necessarily restricted to belong to some "easy" family of graphs. To turn this intuition into a formal model, we assume here that the output alphabet is by definition binary, that is, $Y = \{0, 1\}$, that $\iota(e) = s_0$ for all $e \in E$, and that $I(\sigma) = q_0$, for all $\sigma \in X$ (due to this, we do not specify some input alphabet nor an input function; rather we only assume that the initial configuration is always $C_0(u) = q_0$ for $u \in V$). For the sake of simplicity, we may also give to this special case its own name: call it *Graph Decision Mediated Population Protocol* (GDMPP) model. All the following definitions hold w.r.t. a fixed graph universe $\mathcal{U}$.

Definition 4.26   A *graph language* L is a subset of $\mathcal{U}$ containing interaction graphs that possibly share some common property.

Some examples of graph languages are the following:

- The graph language, consisting of all strongly connected members of $\mathcal{U}$.

- $L = \{G \in \mathcal{U} \mid G$ contains a directed hamiltonian path$\}$.

- $L = \{G \in \mathcal{U} \mid G$ has an even number of edges$\}$.

- $L = \{G \in \mathcal{U} \mid |V(G)| = |E(G)|\}$.

A graph language is said to be *trivial* if $L = \emptyset$ or $L = \mathcal{U}$.

Definition 4.27   [CMS10b]   Let L be a graph language consisting of all $G \in \mathcal{U}$, for which, in any computation of a GDMPP $\mathcal{A}$ on G, all agents eventually output 1. Then L is *the language stably recognized by* $\mathcal{A}$. A graph language is said to be *stably recognizable* by the GDMPP model (also called *GDMPP-recognizable*) if some GDMPP stably recognizes it.

Thus, any protocol *stably recognizes* the graph language, consisting of those graphs on which the protocol always answers "accept", i.e., eventually all agents output the value 1 (possibly the empty language).

Definition 4.28   [CMS10b]   We say that a GDMPP $\mathcal{A}$ *stably decides* a graph language $L \subseteq \mathcal{U}$ (or equivalently a predicate $p_L : \mathcal{U} \to \{0, 1\}$, defined as $p_L(G) = 1$ iff $G \in L$) if for any $G \in \mathcal{U}$ and any computation of $\mathcal{A}$ on G, all agents eventually output 1 if $G \in L$ and all agents eventually output 0 if $G \notin L$. A graph language is said to be *stably decidable* by the GDMPP model (also called *GDMPP-decidable*) if some GDMPP $\mathcal{A}$ stably decides it.

4.2.1   WEAKLY CONNECTED GRAPHS

In this section, we study the interesting case in which the graph universe is not allowed to contain disconnected graphs. Thus, here the graph universe is $\mathcal{G}_{con}$ (recall its definition from Section 1.2), and, thus, a graph language can only be a subset of $\mathcal{G}_{con}$. The main reason for selecting this specific universe for devising our protocols is that if we also allow disconnected graphs, then, as we shall see, it can be proven that no graph language is stably decidable. This is stated and proved in Section 4.2.2.

4.2.1.1   Stably Decidable Graph Languages
Our goal is to show the stable decidability of some interesting graph languages by providing protocols for them and proving their correctness. To begin, we prove some closure results to obtain a useful tool for our purpose.

Theorem 4.29   [CMS10b]   *The class of stably decidable graph languages is closed under complement, union, and intersection operations.*

The proof of this theorem is identical to the same result for classical population protocols.

Remark 4.30   In each application of the union and intersection operations, the size of the resulting protocol is equal to the product of the sizes of the composed protocols. As a result, closure w.r.t. to these operations can only hold for a constant number of subsequent applications.

In some cases, it is not easy to devise a protocol that respects the predicate output convention, that is, to ensure that all agents eventually agree on the correct output value. In such cases, we can use the following variation of Theorem 4.11 that facilitates the proof of existence of GDMPP protocols that stably decide a language.

Theorem 4.31   [CMS10b]   *If there exists a GDMPP $\mathcal{A}$ with stabilizing states that w.r.t. to a language L guarantees a semilinear predicate, then L is GDMPP-decidable.*

Proof. Immediate from the proof of Theorem 4.11. $\mathcal{A}$ can be composed with a provably existing GDMPP $\mathcal{B}$ whose stabilizing inputs are $\mathcal{A}$'s agent states to give a new GDMPP $\mathcal{C}$ that stably decides L w.r.t. the predicate output convention. Note that $\mathcal{B}$ is, in fact, a GDMPP, since its stabilizing inputs are not real inputs (GDMPPs do not have inputs). It simply updates its state components by taking also into account the eventually stabilizing state components of $\mathcal{A}$. Thus, their composition, $\mathcal{C}$, is also a GDMPP. □

Theorem 4.32   Node Parity [CMS10b]   *The graph languages $N_{even} = \{G \in \mathcal{G} \mid |V(G)| \text{ is even}\}$ and $N_{odd} = \overline{N}_{even}$ are stably decidable.*

Proof. Assume that the initial agent state is 1. Then there is a protocol that stably decides N_{even} in the case where G is complete. This is the parity protocol of Exercise 1.9 (do you see why?). But as you were asked to show in Exercise 3.2, there must exist another protocol that stably decides N_{even} in the general case, i.e., on any graph $G \in \mathcal{G}_{con}$, by simply swapping states to ensure that any two states eventually meet (the fairness assumption does not suffice when the interaction graph is not complete; rather the protocol itself must ensure that all states meet each other). Thus, L is stably decidable by the population protocol model that does not use inputs and whose output alphabet is $\{0, 1\}$, and since this model is a special case of the GDMPP model, N_{even} is stably decidable. Moreover, since the class of stably decidable graph languages is closed under complement (see Theorem 4.29), it follows that $N_{odd} = \overline{N}_{even}$ is also stably decidable. □

Theorem 4.33   Edge Parity [CMS10b]   *The graph languages $E_{even} = \{G \in \mathcal{G} \mid |E(G)| \text{ is even}\}$ and $E_{odd} = \overline{E}_{even}$ are stably decidable.*

Proof. By exploiting the closure under complement, it suffices to prove that E_{even} is stably decidable by presenting a GDMPP that stably decides it. The initial agent state is $(0, 0)$, consisting of two components where the first one is the *data bit* and the second the *live bit* similarly to the main idea of the majority protocol of Example 1.6. An agent with live bit 0 is said to be *asleep*, and an agent with live bit equal to 1 is said to be *awake*. The initial edge state is 1, which similarly means that all edges are initially awake. We divide the possible interactions in the following four groups (we also present their effect):

1. Both agents are asleep and the edge is awake:

   • The initiator wakes up, both agents update their data bit to 1, and the edge becomes asleep.

2. Both agents are asleep and the edge is asleep:

   • Nothing happens.

3. One agent is awake and the other is asleep:

   - The asleep agent becomes awake and the awake asleep. Both set their data bits to the modulo 2 sum of the data bit of the agent that was awake before the interaction and the edge's state, and if the edge was awake becomes asleep.

4. Both agents are awake:

   - The responder becomes asleep, they both set their data bits to the modulo 2 sum of their data bits and the edge's state, and if the edge was awake becomes asleep.

It is easy to see that the initial modulo 2 sum of the edge bits (initially, they are all equal to 1) is preserved and is always equal to the modulo 2 sum of the bits of the awake agents and the awake edges. The first interaction creates the first awake agent, and from that time, there is always at least one awake agent and eventually remains only one. Moreover, all edges eventually become asleep, which simply means that eventually, the one remaining awake agent contains the modulo 2 sum of the initial edge bits, which is 0 iff the number of edges is even. All the other agents are asleep, which means that they copy the data bit of the awake agent, thus eventually they all contain the correct data bit. The output map is defined as $O(0, \cdot) = 1$ (meaning even edge parity) and $O(1, \cdot) = 0$ (meaning odd edge parity). □

Theorem 4.34 Constant Neighbors - Some Node [CMS10b] *The graph language $N_k^{out} = \{G \in \mathcal{G} \mid G$ has some node with at least k outgoing neighbors$\}$ is stably decidable for any $k = \mathcal{O}(1)$ (the same holds for $\overline{N}_k^{out}$).*

Proof. Initially, all agents are in q_0 and all edges in 0. The set of agent states is $Q = \{q_0, \ldots, q_k\}$, the set of edge states is binary, and the output function is defined as $O(q_k) = 1$ and $O(q_i) = 0$ for all $i \in \{0, \ldots, k-1\}$. We now describe the transition function. In any interaction through an edge in state 0, the initiator visits an unvisited outgoing edge, so it marks it by updating the edge's state to 1 and increases its own state index by one, e.g., initially $(q_0, q_0, 0)$ yields $(q_1, q_0, 1)$, and, generally, $(q_i, q_j, 0) \rightarrow (q_{i+1}, q_j, 1)$, if $i + 1 < k$ and $j < k$, and $(q_i, q_j, 0) \rightarrow (q_k, q_k, 1)$, otherwise. Whenever two agents meet through a marked edge, they do nothing, except for the case where only one of them is in the special alert state q_k. If the latter holds, then both go to the alert state since in this case the protocol has located an agent with at least k outgoing neighbors. To conclude, all agents count their outgoing edges and initially output 0. Iff one of them marks its k-th outgoing edge, both end points of that edge go to an alert state q_k that propagates to the whole population and whose output is 1, indicating that G belongs to N_k^{out}. Obviously, the protocol that we have just described stably decides N_k^{out}, thus, both N_k^{out} and $\overline{N}_k^{out}$ are stably decidable. □

Note that $\overline{N}_k^{out}$ contains all graphs that have no node with at least $k = \mathcal{O}(1)$ outgoing neighbors, in other words, all nodes have fewer than k outgoing edges, which is simply the well-known bounded by k out-degree predicate.

Theorem 4.35   Constant Neighbors - All Nodes [CMS10b]   *The graph language $K_k^{out} = \{G \in \mathcal{G}$ | Any node in G has at least k outgoing neighbors\} is stably decidable for any $k = \mathcal{O}(1)$ (the same holds for $\overline{K}_k^{out}$).*

Proof. Note, first of all, that another way to think of K_k^{out} is $K_k^{out} = \{G \in \mathcal{G}_{con}$ |. No node in G has less than k outgoing neighbors\}, for some $k = \mathcal{O}(1)$. The protocol we describe is similar to the one described in the proof of Theorem 4.34. The only difference is that when an agent counts its k-th outgoing neighbor as the initiator of an interaction, it goes to the special alert state q_k, but the alert state is not propagated (e.g., the responder of this interaction keeps its state). It follows that, eventually, any node that has marked at least k outgoing edges will be in the alert state, while any other node that has less than k outgoing edges will be in some state q_i, where $i < k$. Clearly, the protocol has stabilizing states and provides the following semilinear guarantee:

- If $G \notin K_k^{out}$, then at least one agent remains in some state q_i, where $i < k$.

- If $G \in K_k^{out}$, no such state remains.

Thus, Theorem 4.31 applies, implying that there exists some GDMPP stably deciding K_k^{out} w.r.t. the predicate output convention. Thus, both K_k^{out} and $\overline{K}_k^{out}$ are stably decidable, and the proof is complete. □

Remark 4.36   [CMS10b]   By symmetry, the corresponding languages N_k^{in}, $\overline{N}_k^{in}$, K_k^{in}, and $\overline{K}_k^{in}$ concerning incoming neighbors are also GDMPP-decidable for all $k = \mathcal{O}(1)$.

Theorem 4.37   Compare Incoming and Outgoing Neighbors [CMS10b]   *The graph language $M_{out} = \{G \in \mathcal{G} \mid G$ has some node with more outgoing than incoming neighbors\} is stably decidable (the same holds for $\overline{M}_{out}$).*

Proof. Consider the following protocol: Initially, all agents are in state 0, which is the *equality* state. An agent can also be in state 1, which is the *more-outgoing* state. Initially, all edges are in state s_0, and S contains also o, i and b, where state o means that the edge has been used by the protocol only as outgoing so far; i means only as incoming, and b is for "both". Any agent always remembers if it has seen so far more outgoing edges or the same number of incoming and outgoing edges. So, if it is in equality state and is the initiator in an interaction where the edge has not been used at all (state s_0) or has been used only as an incoming edge (state i), which simply means that only the responder has counted it, then the agent goes to the more-outgoing state and updates the edge accordingly, to remember that it has counted it. Similarly, if an agent in the more-outgoing state is the responder of an interaction and the edge is in one of the states s_0 or o, then it goes to the equality state and updates the edge accordingly. If we view the interaction from the edge's perspective, then we distinguish the following cases:

1. The edge is in state s_0. Both the initiator and the responder can use it. If only the initiator uses it (both initiator and responder in equality state), then the edge goes to state o. If only the responder uses it (both in more-outgoing state), then the edge goes to state i. If both use it (initiator in equality and responder in more-outgoing), then it goes to state b. If no one uses it, it remains in s_0.

2. The edge is in state o. The initiator cannot use it since it has already counted it. If the responder is in more-outgoing state, then it counts it, thus the edge goes to state b. If, instead, it is in the equality state, the edge remains in state o.

3. The edge is in state i. The responder cannot use it. If the initiator is in equality state, then it counts it, thus the edge goes to state b. If, instead, it is in the more-outgoing state, the edge remains in state i.

4. The edge is in state b. Both the initiator and the responder have used it, thus nothing happens.

The equality state outputs 0 and the more-outgoing state outputs 1. If there exists a node with more outgoing edges, then it will eventually remain in the more-outgoing state giving 1 as output; otherwise, all nodes will eventually remain in equality state (although some of them may have more incoming edges), thus giving 0 as output. Computing that at least one more-outgoing state eventually remains is semilinear and the protocol, obviously, has stabilizing states, thus Theorem 4.31 applies, and we conclude that M_{out} is stably decidable. Closure under complement implies that $\overline{M}_{out}$ is also stably decidable. □

Remark 4.38 **[CMS10b]**   By symmetry, the corresponding languages $M_{in} = \{G \in \mathcal{G} \mid G$ has some node with more incoming than outgoing neighbors$\}$, and $\overline{M}_{in}$ are also stably decidable.

Theorem 4.39 **Directed Path of Constant Length [CMS10b]**   *The graph language* $P_k = \{G \in \mathcal{G} \mid G$ *has at least one directed path of at least k edges*$\}$ *is stably decidable for any* $k = \mathcal{O}(1)$ *(the same holds for* $\overline{P}_k$*).*

Proof. If $k = 1$, the protocol that stably decides P_1 is trivial, since it accepts iff at least one interaction happens (in fact, it can always accept since all graphs have at least two nodes and they are weakly connected, and thus $P_1 = \mathcal{G}_{con}$). We give a general protocol, $DirPath$ (Protocol 5), that stably decides P_k for any constant $k > 1$.

Protocol 5 *DirPath*

1: $Q = \{q_0, q_1, 1, \ldots, k\}, S = \{0, 1\},$
2: $O(k) = 1, O(q) = 0,$ for every $q \in Q - \{k\},$
3: δ:

$$(q_0, q_0, 0) \rightarrow (q_1, 1, 1)$$
$$(q_1, x, 1) \rightarrow (x - 1, q_0, 0), \text{ if } x \geq 2$$
$$\rightarrow (q_0, q_0, 0), \text{ if } x = 1$$
$$(x, q_0, 0) \rightarrow (q_1, x + 1, 1), \text{ if } x + 1 < k$$
$$\rightarrow (k, k, 0), \text{ if } x + 1 = k$$
$$(k, \cdot, \cdot) \rightarrow (k, k, \cdot)$$
$$(\cdot, k, \cdot) \rightarrow (k, k, \cdot)$$

Initially all nodes are in q_0 and all edges in 0. The protocol tries to expand disjoint paths. When rule $(q_0, q_0, 0) \rightarrow (q_1, 1, 1)$ applies, the initiator goes to q_1 indicating that it is a node of an active path, the responder goes to 1, indicating that it is the head of an active path of length 1 and the edge goes to 1, indicating that it is part of an active path. By inspecting the transition function, it is easy to see that the nodes of two disjoint active paths have no way of interacting with each other (in fact, the interactions happening between them leave their interacting components unaffected). This holds because all nodes in q_1 do nothing when communicating through an edge in state 0, and disjoint active paths can only communicate through edges in state 0. Moreover, the heads of the paths only expand by communicating with nodes in q_0, which, of course, cannot be nodes of active paths (all nodes of active paths are in q_1, except for the heads, which are in states from $\{1, \ldots, k - 1\}$). There are two main possibilities for an active path: either the protocol expands it, thus obtaining a node and an edge and increasing the head counter by one, or shrinks it, thus releasing a node and an edge and decreasing the head counter by one. Eventually, a path will either be totally released (all its nodes and edges will return to the initial states), or it will become of length k. In the first case, the protocol simply keeps working, but in the second, a path of length at least k was found and state k that outputs 1 is correctly propagated. The crucial point is that state k is the only state that outputs 1 and can only be reached and propagated by the agents iff there exists some path of length at least k. Moreover, if such a path exists, due to fairness assumption, the protocol will eventually manage to find it. $\qquad\square$

4.2.1.2 Non Stably Decidable Languages

Now we are about to prove that a specific graph language cannot be stably decided by GDMPPs with stabilizing states. First, we state and prove a useful lemma.

Lemma 4.40 **[CMS10b]** *For any GDMPP $\mathcal{A}$ and any computation (infinite fair execution) $C_0, C_1, C_2, \ldots$ of $\mathcal{A}$ on G (Figure 4.6(a)), there exists a computation $C'_0, C'_1, C'_2, \ldots, C'_i, \ldots$ of $\mathcal{A}$ on G' (Figure 4.6(b)) s.t.*

$$C_i(v_1) = C'_{2i}(u_1) = C'_{2i}(u_3)$$
$$C_i(v_2) = C'_{2i}(u_2) = C'_{2i}(u_4)$$
$$C_i(e_1) = C'_{2i}(t_1) = C'_{2i}(t_3)$$
$$C_i(e_2) = C'_{2i}(t_2) = C'_{2i}(t_4)$$

for any finite $i \geq 0$.

Proof. The proof is by induction on i. We assume that, initially, all nodes are in q_0 and all edges in s_0 (initial states). So the base case (for $i = 0$) holds trivially. Now, we make the following assumption: Whenever the scheduler of $\mathcal{A}$ on G (call it S_1) selects the edge e_1, we assume that the scheduler, S_2, of $\mathcal{A}$ on G' takes two steps; it first selects t_1 and then selects t_3. Whenever S_1 selects the edge e_2, S_2 first selects t_2 and then t_4. Formally, if $C_{i-1} \overset{e_1}{\to} C_i$, then $C'_{2(i-1)} \overset{t_1}{\to} C'_{2i-1} \overset{t_3}{\to} C'_{2i}$, and if $C_{i-1} \overset{e_2}{\to} C_i$, then $C'_{2(i-1)} \overset{t_2}{\to} C'_{2i-1} \overset{t_4}{\to} C'_{2i}$ for every finite $i \geq 1$. Obviously, S_2 is not a fair scheduler so to be able to talk about computation, we only require this predetermined behavior to be followed by S_2 for a finite number of steps. After this finite number of steps, S_2 goes on arbitrarily but in a fair manner.

Now assume that all conditions are satisfied for some finite step i (inductive hypothesis). We will prove that the same holds for step $i + 1$ to complete the proof (inductive step). There are two cases:

1. $C_i \overset{e_1}{\to} C_{i+1}$ (i.e., *in step $i + 1$ S_1 selects the edge e_1*): Then we know that S_2 first selects t_1 and then t_3 (in its corresponding steps $2i + 1$ and $2i + 2$). That is, its first transition is $C'_{2i} \overset{t_1}{\to} C'_{2i+1}$ and its second is $C'_{2i+1} \overset{t_3}{\to} C'_{2(i+1)}$. But from the inductive hypothesis, we know that $C'_{2i}(u_1) = C_i(v_1)$, $C'_{2i}(u_2) = C_i(v_2)$ and $C'_{2i}(t_1) = C_i(e_1)$, which simply means that interaction e_1 on G has the same effect as interaction t_1 on G' (u_1 has the same state as v_1, u_2 as v_2 and t_1 as e_1). Thus, $C'_{2i+1}(u_1) = C_{i+1}(v_1)$, $C'_{2i+1}(u_2) = C_{i+1}(v_2)$ and $C'_{2i+1}(t_1) = C_{i+1}(e_1)$. Moreover, in this step, t_3 and both its endpoints do not change state (since the interaction concerned t_1), thus $C'_{2i+1}(u_3) = C'_{2i}(u_3) = C_i(v_1)$ (the last equation comes from the inductive hypothesis), $C'_{2i+1}(u_4) = C'_{2i}(u_4) = C_i(v_2)$ and $C'_{2i+1}(t_3) = C'_{2i}(t_3) = C_i(e_1)$. When in the next step S_2 selects t_3, t_1 and both its endpoints do not change state, thus $C'_{2(i+1)}(u_1) = C'_{2i+1}(u_1) = C_{i+1}(v_1)$, $C'_{2(i+1)}(u_2) = C'_{2i+1}(u_2) = C_{i+1}(v_2)$ and $C'_{2(i+1)}(t_1) = C'_{2i+1}(t_1) = C_{i+1}(e_1)$. Now, let's see what happens to t_3 and its endpoints. Before the interaction, the state of u_3 is $C_i(v_1)$, the state of u_4 is $C_i(v_2)$ and the state of t_3 is $C_i(e_1)$,

which means that, in $C'_{2(i+1)}$, u_3 has gone to $C_{i+1}(v_1)$, u_4 to $C_{i+1}(v_2)$ and t_3 to $C_{i+1}(e_1)$. Finally, t_2 and t_4 have not participated in any of the two interactions of S_2, and thus they have maintained their states, that is $C'_{2(i+1)}(t_2) = C'_{2i}(t_2) = C_i(e_2) = C_{i+1}(e_2)$ (the last two equations follow from the inductive hypothesis, and the fact that, in step $i + 1$, S_1 selects e_1, which means that e_2 maintains its state, respectively), and, similarly, $C'_{2(i+1)}(t_4) = C_{i+1}(e_2)$.

2. $C_i \overset{e_2}{\to} C_{i+1}$ *(i.e. in step $i + 1$ S_1 selects the edge e_2):* This case is symmetric to the previous one.

□

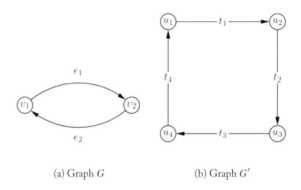

(a) Graph G (b) Graph G'

Figure 4.6: $G \in 2C$ and $G' \notin 2C$.

Let now $\mathcal{A}$ be a GDMPP that stably decides the graph language $2C = \{G \in \mathcal{G} \mid G$ has at least two nodes u, v s.t. both (u, v), $(v, u) \in E(G)\}$ (in other words, G has at least one 2-cycle)}. So for any computation of $\mathcal{A}$ on G, after finitely many steps, both v_1 and v_2 go to some state that outputs 1, since $G \in 2C$, and do not change their output value in any subsequent step (call the corresponding output stable configuration C_i, where i is finite). But according to Lemma 4.40, there exists a computation of $\mathcal{A}$ on G' that under configuration C'_{2i} has u_1, u_2, u_3 and u_4 giving output 1. We use this fact to prove the following impossibility result.

Theorem 4.41 [CMS10b] *There exists no GDMPP with stabilizing states to stably decide the graph language $2C = \{G \in \mathcal{G} \mid G$ has at least two nodes u, v s.t. both (u, v), $(v, u) \in E(G)\}$.*

Proof. Let $\mathcal{A}$ be a GDMPP with stabilizing states that stably decides $2C$. It follows that when $\mathcal{A}$ runs on G (Figure 4.6(a)) after a finite number of steps v_1 and v_2 obtain two states w.l.o.g. q_1 and q_2, respectively, that output 1 (since $\mathcal{A}$ stably decides $2C$) and do not change in any subsequent step (since $\mathcal{A}$ has stabilizing states). Assume that at that point e_1 is in s_1 and e_2 in s'_1. Assume also that there exists a subset $S_1 = \{s_1, s_2, \ldots, s_k\}$ of S, of edge states that can be reached by subsequent interactions of the pair (υ_1, υ_2) and a subset $S_2 = \{s'_1, s'_2, \ldots, s'_l\}$ of S, of edge states that can be reached by subsequent interactions of the pair (υ_2, υ_1), where k and l are both constants independent of n (note that S_1 and S_2 are not necessarily disjoint). It follows that for all $s_i \in S_1, (q_1, q_2, s_i) \to (q_1, q_2, s_j)$, where $s_j \in S_1$, and for all $s'_i \in S_2, (q_2, q_1, s'_i) \to (q_2, q_1, s'_j)$, where $s'_j \in S_2$. In words, none of these reachable edge states can be responsible for a change in some agent's state. According to Lemma 4.40, there exists a computation of $\mathcal{A}$ on G' (Figure 4.6(b)) such that after a finite number of steps u_1, u_3 are in q_1, u_2, u_4 are in q_2, t_1, t_3 are in s_1 and t_2, t_4 are in s'_1. Since $\mathcal{A}$ stably decides $2C$, at some subsequent finite step (after we let the protocol run in a fair manner in G'), some agent obtains a new state q_3, since if it didn't then, all agents would always remain to states q_1 and q_2 that output 1 (but in G', there is no 2-cycle and such a decision is wrong). This must happen through some interaction of the following two forms:

1. (q_1, q_2, s_i), where $s_i \in S_1$,

2. (q_2, q_1, s'_i), where $s'_i \in S_2$.

But this is a contradiction, since we showed earlier that no such interaction can modify the state of any of its end points. Intuitively, if there exists some way for $\mathcal{A}$ to modify one of q_1 and q_2 in G', then there would also exist some way for $\mathcal{A}$ to modify one of q_1 and q_2 in G after the system has obtained stabilizing states there, which is an obvious contradiction. □

As an immediate consequence (special case), we get the following corollary:

Corollary 4.42 [CMS10b] *There exists no GDMPP that in any computation on any $G \in 2C$ stabilizes to a single state, e.g., by propagating an alert state when it finds a 2-cycle, to stably decide the graph language $2C$.*

4.2.2 GRAPHS NOT EVEN WEAKLY CONNECTED

Here the graph universe is $\mathcal{G}_{all}$ (recall its definition from Section 1.2), and, thus, a graph language can only be a subset of $\mathcal{G}_{all}$. Any disconnected graph G in $\mathcal{G}_{all}$ consists of (weakly or strongly connected) components $G_1, G_2, \ldots, G_t$, where $t \geq 2$ (note also that any component must have at least two nodes, to allow computation).

Lemma 4.43 [CMS10b] *For any nontrivial graph language L, there exists some disconnected graph G in L where at least one component of G does not belong to L, or there exists some disconnected graph G' in $\overline{L}$ where at least one component of G' does not belong to $\overline{L}$ (or both).*

Proof. Let L be such a nontrivial graph language and assume that the statement does not hold. Then for any disconnected graph in L, all of its components also belong to L, and for any disconnected graph in $\overline{L}$, all of its components also belong to $\overline{L}$. There are two main cases:

1. L contains all connected graphs. But $\overline{L}$ is nontrivial, which means that it must contain at least one disconnected graph. We know that for any disconnected graph in $\overline{L}$, all of its connected components belong to $\overline{L}$, but this is a contradiction since all connected graphs belong to L.

2. L does not contain all connected graphs. There are now two possible subcases:

   (a) L contains at least one connected graph (but not all). This means that $\overline{L}$ contains also at least one connected graph. Let $G' = (V', E')$ be a connected graph from L and $G'' = (V'', E'')$ be a connected graph from $\overline{L}$. The disjoint union of G' and G'', $U = (V' \cup V'', E' \cup E'')$ is a disconnected graph consisting of two connected components, one belonging to L and one to $\overline{L}$. U itself must belong in one of L and $\overline{L}$ implying that all of its components must belong to L or all to $\overline{L}$, which is a contradiction.

   (b) L contains no connected graph. Thus, since L is nontrivial, it contains at least one disconnected graph whose connected components belong to L. But all connected graphs belong to $\overline{L}$, which is a contradiction.

$\square$

Theorem 4.44 **[CMS10b]** *Any nontrivial graph language $L \subset \mathcal{H}$ is not stably decidable by the GDMPP model.*

Proof. Let L be such a language and assume that there exists a GDMPP $\mathcal{A}_L$ that stably decides it. Thus, $\mathcal{A}_L$ has, eventually, all the agents of G giving output 1 if $G \in L$ and all giving output 0 if $G \notin L$. Moreover, the protocol $\mathcal{A}_{\overline{L}}$ that has the output map of $\mathcal{A}_L$ complemented stably decides $\overline{L}$. Those GDMPPs (and, in fact, any GDMPP) have no way to transmit data between agents of different components when run on disconnected graphs. In fact, it is trivial to see that, when run on disconnected graphs, those protocols essentially run individually on the different components of those graphs. This means that when, for example, $\mathcal{A}_L$ runs on a disconnected graph G, where G has at least two components $G_1, G_2, \ldots, G_t$, then $\mathcal{A}_L$ runs in t different copies, one for each component, and each such copy stably decides the membership of the corresponding component (on which it runs on) in L. The same holds for $\mathcal{A}_{\overline{L}}$. By Lemma 4.43, there exists at least one disconnected graph in L with at least one component in $\overline{L}$ or at least one disconnected graph in $\overline{L}$ with at least one component in L. If L contains such a disconnected graph then, obviously, $\mathcal{A}_L$ when run on this graph, call it G, has eventually all the nodes of the component(s) in $\overline{L}$ giving 0 as output. This is a contradiction because $G \in L$ and $\mathcal{A}_L$ stably decides L, which means that all agents should eventually output 1. If $\overline{L}$ contains such a disconnected graph, then the contradiction is symmetric. $\square$

As an immediate consequence of Theorem 4.44, we get the following corollary:

Corollary 4.45 **[CMS10b]**   *The graph language $C = \{G \in \mathcal{G}_{all} \mid G$ is (weakly) connected\} is not GDMPP-decidable.*

Proof. C is a nontrivial graph language and Theorem 4.44 applies.   □

Note that C is, in fact, the connectivity property, and it can have some meaning only if defined in $\mathcal{G}_{all}$. If it were stably decidable, we would be able to determine whether an interaction graph is connected or not, but according to the previous corollary, this is not the case in the GDMPP model.

4.3   EXERCISES

4.1.   (RQ) Is the predicate $(N_0 = N_1 \cdot N_2 \cdots N_k)$ stably computable by the MPP model for all $k = \mathcal{O}(1)$?

Hint: Try to generalize the idea of Protocol 4 (*VarProduct*).

4.2.   Mediated population protocols do not only stably compute predicates but can also stably solve some interesting graph construction problems. Consider the following problem:

Problem 4.46 Transitive Closure   Given a complete interaction graph $G = (V, E)$ and a precomputed subgraph $G' = (V', E')$ of G, find the transitive closure of G'; that is, find a new edge set E^* that will contain a directed edge (u, v) joining any nodes u, v, for which there is a non-null path from u to v in G' (note that always $E' \subseteq E^*$).

Here the edge initialization function $\iota : E \to \{0, 1\}$ specifies G' as the graph induced by $E' = \{e \in E \mid \iota(e) = 1\}$. Devise a MPP that with the help of a leader stably solves the above problem;

Hint: Here the edges' states must eventually stabilize and those that stabilize to the value 1 must correctly define the transitive closure of G'.

4.3.   One can extend the MPP model by assuming the existence of some cost function $c : E \to K$, where K is a finite subset of $\mathbb{Z}^+$ (nonnegative integers) whose cardinality is fixed and independent of n. Try now to solve the following problems:

Problem 4.47 Edges of Minimum Cost   Given an undirected connected interaction graph $G = (V, E)$ and a cost function $c : E \to K$ on the set of edges, design a protocol that finds the minimum cost edges of E.

Problem 4.48 Shortest Root-Leaf Path   Given that the interaction graph $G = (V, E)$ is a directed arborescence and a cost function $c : E \to K$ on the set of edges, design a protocol that finds the minimum cost path of the (nonempty) set $P = \{p \mid p$ is a path from the root to a leaf and $c(p) = \mathcal{O}(1)\}$, where $c(p) := \sum_{e \in p} c(e)$.

4.4. The proof of Theorem 4.22 as presented here is quite descriptive. Formalize it by presenting the whole transition function of the simulation.

4.5. Prove Theorem 4.24, that is, show that all predicates in **DMP** and **UMP** are also in the class **NSPACE**(m), where m denotes the number of edges of the interaction graph.

4.6. Define the stabilizing inputs variant of the MPP model. By exploiting the spanning line graph construction and the reinitialization technique, show that any MPP for fixed inputs can be adapted to work with stabilizing inputs. Note that this implies that MPPs can be composed "sequentially".

4.7. Prove that if the interaction graph has bounded degree by a constant then the Mediated Population Protocol model can simulate a distributed TM.

4.8. (RQ) Is the MPP model fault-tolerant? What preconditions are needed in order to achieve satisfactory fault-tolerance?

4.9. (RQ) The MPP model is of clear theoretical interest, but we do not yet know whether it is also of practical interest. Are there any realistic real-world scenarios for applying the MPP model? In what scenarios would a mediator be present, and how could one employ passive mobility in the presence of fixed communication links?

4.10. (RQ) It is clear that verifying Mediated Population Protocols is also hard (see Exercise 3.6). Prove the statement and propose methods for verifying MPPs.

4.11. Prove that, with the help of a leader, the graph language HAMILTONIAN PATH = $\{G \mid G$ contains some directed hamiltonian path$\}$ is GDMPP-recognizable.

Hint: The leader expands a directed path and checks in each step whether some node has not been reached yet.

4.12. Prove that, with the help of a leader, the graph languages $kC = \{G \mid G$ contains a directed cycle of length $k\}$, $k = \mathcal{O}(1)$, and TREE $= \{G \mid$ If we ignore the directions of the links, G is a spanning tree with no multiple edges$\}$ are GDMPP-decidable in $\mathcal{G}_{con}$.

4.13. Prove that connectivity cannot be stably decided by the GDMPP model even in the case where each connected component has a unique leader (unique for that component).

4.14. Consider the following variant of the GDMPP model. The interaction graph is always complete and an edge initialization function (that is, a preprocessing on the interaction graph) specifies the subgraph whose membership in a language has to be determined. Give a formal definition of this model and of stable decidability in this case, and devise a protocol to stably decide whether the specified subgraph is connected.

4.15. Prove that any graph language that is GDMPP-decidable is also stably decidable by the variant you defined in the previous exercise.

4.16. (RQ) Is the graph language $2C = \{G \in \mathcal{G} \mid G$ has at least two nodes u, υ s.t. both $(u, \upsilon), (\upsilon, u) \in E(G)$ stably decidable by the GDMPP model?

NOTES

The Mediated Population Protocol model was proposed by Chatzigiannakis, Michail, and Spirakis in 2009 [CMS09c]. Lemma 4.6 is similar to Corollary 3 of [AAD$^+$06]. The upper bound of Theorem 4.24 was proved in that work. The lower bound on **MPS**, of Theorem 4.22, appeared one year later and is due to Chatzigiannakis, Michail, Nikolaou, Pavlogiannis, and Spirakis [CMN$^+$10a]. To the best of our knowledge, the reinitialization technique was first used by Guerraoui and Ruppert in [GR09].

The GDMPP model was proposed by Chatzigiannakis, Michail, and Spirakis in 2009 [CMS09a]. That paper was a brief announcement and most of the results in the second part of this chapter appeared there as simple statements. One year later, the full paper appeared [CMS10b]. The bounded by k out-degree predicate was first proven to be stably decidable by the population protocol model. That result is due to Angluin, Aspnes, Chan, Fischer, Jiang, and Peralta [AAC$^+$05] (appears there as Lemma 3).

C H A P T E R   5

Passively Mobile Machines that Use Restricted Space

In this chapter, we assume that each agent is a TM. In particular, we discuss another theoretical model for passively mobile sensor networks, called the Passively mobile Machines (PM) model. To be more precise, it is a model of Passively mobile Machines (that we keep calling agents) with sensing capabilities, equipped with two-way communication. We mainly focus on PM protocols that use $\mathcal{O}(\log n)$ memory, which are known as PALOMA (PAssively mobile LOgarithmic space MAchines) protocols. The reason for studying such protocols is that having *logarithmic communicating machines* seems to be more realistic than communicating automata of constant memory. Moreover, *logarithmic* is, in fact, *extremely small*. Interestingly, as we shall see, it turns out that the agents of PALOMA protocols are able to organize themselves into a distributed nondeterministic TM of $\mathcal{O}(n \log n)$ space. The TM draws its nondeterminism by the nondeterminism inherent in the interaction pattern. The machine, similarly to that in Theorem 4.22, exploits the nondeterminism of the interaction pattern. Moreover, we will see that the space bound $\log n$ constitutes a special bound since it has some threshold behavior concerning the computational power of the PM model. This fact, together with the above discussion, renders the $\log n$ bound as the most appropriate for this kind of systems.

The chapter is organized in two parts. At the beginning of the first part, in Section 5.1, we provide a formal definition of the PM model. The section proceeds with a thorough description of the functionality of the systems under consideration and then provides definitions of configurations and fair executions. Moreover, stable computation by the PM model and the complexity class **PMSPACE**($f(n)$) (stably computable predicates by the PM model using $\mathcal{O}(f(n))$ space) are defined. In Subsection 5.1.1, two simple examples of PALOMA protocols are presented; since those compute non-semilinear predicates, it is established that PALOMA protocols are strictly stronger than population protocols. In Section 5.1.2, it is first proved that PM protocols can assume the existence of unique consecutive ids and knowledge of the population size at the space cost of $\mathcal{O}(\log n)$ (Theorem 5.14). By exploiting this knowledge and without increasing the order of required space, the PM model can simulate a TM of $\mathcal{O}(n \log n)$ space (Theorem 5.15), which establishes that **SSPACE**($n \log n$) is a subset of **PMSPACE**($\log n$). Section 5.1.3 goes one step further and shows that **SNSPACE**($n \log n$) $\subseteq$ **PMSPACE**($\log n$). In particular, it is proven that the PM model, using $\mathcal{O}(\log n)$ space, simulates the community protocol model (this inclusion is alternatively obtained by a direct simulation of a nondeterministic TM in Theorem 5.23). Finally, in Section 5.1.4, it is shown that **SNSPACE**($n \log n$) is an exact characterization for **PMSPACE**($\log n$), by proving that the corresponding language of any predicate in **PMSPACE**$(\log n)$, can be decided by a nondeterministic TM of $\mathcal{O}(n \log n)$ space.

The second part of the chapter focuses in the behavior of the PM model for different space bounds. Such a study is of particular interest since it is always important to know what computations is a model capable of dispatching according to the capabilities of the available hardware. For example, it is reasonable to ask whether more available memory to the agents would imply increased computational power. How are the computational capabilities affected under modifications of the available memory? Are there memory sizes possessing special properties making them outstanding and rendering them more appropriate than others?

It turns out that there are satisfying answers for most of these questions. In particular, we will see here:

- For $f(n) = \Omega(\log n)$, it holds that **PMSPACE**$(f(n)) =$ **SNSPACE**$(nf(n))$. Due to this, and by taking into account the symmetric space hierarchy theorem (Theorem 1.11), there is also a space hierarchy for the PM model. In simple words, for these space bounds, protocols with more memory available to them can compute more things.

- For $f(n) = o(\log n)$, it holds that **PMSPACE**$(f(n))$ is strictly smaller than **SNSPACE**$(nf(n))$, thus $\log n$ behaves as a computational threshold. This shows that the behavior of the model changes (is enhanced) at the space bound $\log n$. If we also take into account that memories of size $\log n$ are extremely small, then it seems that our selection to focus on this particular bound as the most realistic for this kind of systems is plausible.

- For $f(n) = o(\log \log n)$, it holds that **PMSPACE**$(f(n))$ is precisely the class of semilinear predicates! This naturally means that when the memories available to the protocols are strictly smaller than $\log \log n$ (asymptotically, of course) then these PM protocols are nothing more than population protocols, and although their memory is still dependent on the population size, they cannot exploit it as such; instead, they have to use it as a constant memory, much like population protocols do. This result also shows that for these small space bounds, there is no space hierarchy. Moreover, as we shall see, the first bound at which some space hierarchy of the PM model begins is $f(n) = \Omega(\log \log n)$. To establish this, we will have to devise such a protocol that computing the non-semilinear predicate $(\log N_a = c)$, where c is a constant. The gain is twofold: it also implies that **PMSPACE**$(f(n))$ is strictly wider than the class of semilinear predicates; thus, $\log \log n$ is another computational threshold.

An interesting problem that still remains open is what exactly happens between $\log \log n$ and $\log n$.

5.1   THE MODEL AND THE POWER OF LOG SPACE

In this section, we define formally the PM model and describe its functionality. We again provide definitions for general interaction graphs and unbounded memories, although we are interested in complete graphs and space-bounded by a logarithm of the population size.

Definition 5.1   [CMN$^+$10c]   A *Passively mobile Machines* (PM) protocol is a 6-tuple $(X, \Gamma, Q, \delta, \gamma, q_0)$ where X, Γ and Q are all finite sets and

1. X is the *input alphabet*, where $\sqcup \notin X$,

2. Γ is the *tape alphabet*, where $\sqcup \in \Gamma$ and $X \subset \Gamma$,

3. Q is the set of *states*,

4. $\delta : Q \times \Gamma^4 \to Q \times \Gamma^4 \times \{L, R\}^4 \times \{0, 1\}$ is the *internal transition function*,

5. $\gamma : Q \times Q \to Q \times Q$ is the *external transition function* (or *interaction transition function*), and

6. $q_0 \in Q$ is the *initial state*.

Each agent is equipped with the following:

- A *sensor* in order to sense its environment and receive a piece of the input.

- Four read/write *tapes*: the *working tape*, the *output tape*, the *incoming message tape*, and the *outgoing message tape*. We assume that all tapes are bounded to the left and unbounded to the right.

- A *control unit* that contains the state of the agent and applies the transition functions.

- Four *heads* (one for each tape) that read from and write to the cells of the corresponding tapes and can move one step at a time, either to the left or to the right.

- A binary *working flag* either set to 1 meaning that the agent is *working* internally or to 0 meaning that the agent is *ready* for interaction.

Initially, all agents are in state q_0, their working flag is set to 1, and all their cells contain the *blank symbol* $\sqcup$. We assume that all agents concurrently receive their sensed input (different agents may sense different data) as a response to a global start signal. The input to each agent is a symbol from X and is written on the leftmost cell of its working tape.

When its working flag is set to 1, we can think of an agent working as a usual multitape Turing Machine (but it additionally writes the working flag). In particular, while the working flag is set to 1, the internal transition function δ is applied, the control unit reads the symbols under the heads and its own state, updates all of them, moves each head one step to the left or to the right, and sets the working flag to 0 or 1, according to δ.

Again here, a fair adversary specifies the order according to which interactions take place. Assume now that two agents u and v are about to interact with u being the initiator of the interaction and v being the *responder*. Let $f : V \to \{0, 1\}$ be a function returning the current value of each agent's working flag. If at least one of $f(u)$ and $f(v)$ is equal to 1, then nothing happens because at least one agent is still working internally. Otherwise ($f(u) = f(v) = 0$), both agents are ready and an interaction is established. In the latter case, the external transition function γ is applied, the states of the agents are updated accordingly, the outgoing message of the initiator is copied to the leftmost cells of the incoming message tape of the responder (replacing its contents and writing $\sqcup$ to all other previously non-blank cells) and vice versa (we call this the *message swap*), and finally the working flags of both agents are again set to 1. These operations could be handled by the protocols themselves, but then protocol descriptions would become awkward. So, we simply think of them as automatic operations performed by the hardware. These operations are also considered as atomic, that is, the interacting agents cannot take part in another interaction before the completion of these operations and, moreover, either all operations totally succeed or are all totally aborted (in which case, the states of the interacting agents are restored).

Note that the assumption that the internal transition function δ is only applied when the working flag is set to 1 is weak. In fact, an equivalent way to model this is to assume that δ is of the form $\delta : Q \times \Gamma^4 \times \{0, 1\} \to Q \times \Gamma^4 \times \{L, R, S\}^4 \times \{0, 1\}$, that it is always applied, and that for all $q \in Q$ and $a \in \Gamma^4$, $\delta(q, a, 0) = (q, a, S^4, 0)$ is satisfied, where S means that the corresponding head "stays put". The same holds for the assumptions that γ is not applied if at least one of the interacting agents is working internally and that the working flags are set to 1 when some established interaction comes to an end; it is equivalent to an extended γ of the form $\gamma : Q^2 \times \{0, 1\}^2 \to Q^2 \times \{0, 1\}^2$, that is applied in every interaction, and for which $\gamma(q_1, q_2, f_1, f_2) = (q_1, q_2, f_1, f_2)$ if $f_1 = 1$ or $f_2 = 1$, and $\gamma(q_1, q_2, f_1, f_2) = (\gamma_1(q_1, q_2), \gamma_2(q_1, q_2), 1, 1)$ if $f_1 = f_2 = 0$, hold for all $q_1, q_2 \in Q$, and we could also further extend δ and γ to handle the exchange of messages, but for sake of simplicity, we have decided to leave such details out of the model.

Since each agent is a TM, we use the notion of a configuration to capture its "state". An *agent configuration* is a tuple $(q, l_w, r_w, l_o, r_o, l_{im}, r_{im}, l_{om}, r_{om}, f)$, where $q \in Q$, $l_i, r_i \in \Gamma^*$, and $f \in \{0, 1\}$. q is the state of the control unit, l_w (l_o, l_{im}, l_{om}) is the string of the working (output, incoming message, outgoing message) tape to the left of the head (including the symbol scanned), r_w (r_o, r_{im}, r_{om}) is the string of the working (output, incoming message, outgoing message) tape to the right of the head (excluding infinite sequences of blank cells), and f is the working flag indicating whether the agent is ready to interact ($f = 0$) or carrying out some internal computation ($f = 1$). Let $\mathcal{B}$ be the set of all agent configurations. Given two agent configurations $A, A' \in \mathcal{B}$, we say that A *yields* A' if A' follows A by a single application of δ.

Similarly to the PP and MPP models, a *population configuration* is a mapping $C : V \to \mathcal{B}$, specifying the agent configuration of each agent in the population. Let C, C' be population configurations and let $u \in V$. We say that C *yields* C' via *agent transition u*, denoted $C \overset{u}{\to} C'$, if $C(u)$ yields $C'(u)$ and $C'(w) = C(w), \forall w \in V - \{u\}$.

Denote by $q(A)$ the state component of an agent configuration A and similarly for the other components (e.g., $l_w(A), r_{im}(A), f(A)$, and so on). Let $s_{tp}(A) = l_{tp}(A)r_{tp}(A)$; that is, we obtain by concatenation the whole contents of tape $tp \in \{w, o, im, om\}$. Given a string s and $1 \le i, j \le |s|$ denote by $s[\ldots i]$ its prefix $s_1 s_2 \cdots s_i$ and by $s[j \ldots]$ its suffix $s_j s_{j+1} \cdots s_{|s|}$. If $i, j > |s|$ then $s[\ldots i] = s \sqcup^{i-|s|}$ (i.e. $i - |s|$ blank symbols appended to s) and $s[j \ldots] = \varepsilon$. For any external transition $\gamma(q_1, q_2) = (q_1', q_2')$, define $\gamma_1(q_1, q_2) = q_1'$ and $\gamma_2(q_1, q_2) = q_2'$. Given two population configurations C and C', we say that C *yields* C' via encounter $e = (u, v) \in E$, denoted $C \overset{e}{\to} C'$, if one of the following two cases holds:

Case 1 (only for this case, we define $C^u \equiv C(u)$ to avoid excessive number of parentheses):

- $f(C(u)) = f(C(v)) = 0$, which guarantees that both agents u and v are ready for interaction under the population configuration C.

- $C'(u) = (\gamma_1(q(C^u), q(C^v)), l_w(C^u), r_w(C^u), l_o(C^u), r_o(C^u), s_{om}(C^v)[\ldots |l_{im}(C^u)|],$
  $s_{om}(C^v)[|l_{im}(C^u)| + 1 \ldots], l_{om}(C^u), r_{om}(C^u), 1),$

- $C'(v) = (\gamma_2(q(C^u), q(C^v)), l_w(C^v), r_w(C^v), l_o(C^v), r_o(C^v), s_{om}(C^u)[\ldots |l_{im}(C^v)|],$
  $s_{om}(C^u)[|l_{im}(C^v)| + 1 \ldots], l_{om}(C^v), r_{om}(C^v), 1),$ and

- $C'(w) = C(w), \forall w \in V - \{u, v\}$.

Case 2:

- $f(C(u)) = 1$ or $f(C(v)) = 1$, which means that at least one agent between u and v is working internally under the population configuration C, and

- $C'(w) = C(w), \forall w \in V$. In this case, no effective interaction takes place; thus, the population configuration remains the same.

Generally, we say that C *yields* (or *can go in one step to*) C', and write $C \to C'$, if $C \overset{e}{\to} C'$ for some $e \in E$ (via encounter) or $C \overset{u}{\to} C'$ for some $u \in V$ (via agent transition), or both. The definitions of reachability, execution, fairness, and computation remain the same as before.

We assume that the input alphabet X, the tape alphabet Γ, and the set of states Q are all sets whose cardinality is fixed and independent of the population size (i.e., all of them are of cardinality $\mathcal{O}(1)$). Thus, protocol descriptions have also no dependence on the population size and the PM model *preserves uniformity*. Moreover, PM protocols are *anonymous* (though here there is plenty of room on the tapes to create there unique ids).

The definitions concerning input assignments [1] and stable computation remain the same as in the previous models. In what follows, we assume that the interaction graph is complete.

Definition 5.2   [CMN$^+$10c]   Let **PMSPACE**$(f(n))$ be the class of all predicates that are stably computable by some PM protocol that uses $\mathcal{O}(f(n))$ space in every agent (and in all of its tapes).

Remark 5.3   All agents are identical and do not initially have unique ids, thus, stably computable predicates by the PM model on complete interaction graphs have to be symmetric.

In fact, although we provide general definitions, we are mainly interested in the class **PMSPACE**$(\log n) :=$ **PMSPACE**$(\log n)$, and we call a PM protocol a *PALOMA* protocol (standing for PAssively mobile LOgarithmic space MAchines) if it always uses $\mathcal{O}(\log n)$ space. The main result proved in this section is the following exact characterization for **PMSPACE**$(\log n)$: it is equal to **SNSPACE**$(n \log n)$. In fact, the proof that we give easily generalizes and also provides an exact characterization for **PMSPACE**$(f(n))$, when $f(n) = \Omega(\log n)$: **PMSPACE**$(f(n))$ is equal to **SNSPACE**$(nf(n))$ (the latter characterization is presented in the sequel).

5.1.1   A FIRST INCLUSION FOR PMSPACE$(\log n)$

Example 5.4   Multiplication of Variables [CMN$^+$10c]   We present now a PM protocol that stably computes the predicate $(N_c = N_a \cdot N_b)$ using $\mathcal{O}(\log n)$ space (on the complete interaction graph of n nodes); that is, all agents eventually decide whether the number of cs in the input assignment is the product of the number of as and the number of bs. We give a high-level description of the protocol.

Initially, all agents have one of a, b, and c written on the first cell of their working memory (according to their sensed value). That is, the set of input symbols is $X = \Sigma = \{a, b, c\}$. Each agent that receives input a goes to state a and becomes ready for interaction (sets its working flag to 0). Agents in state a and b both do nothing when interacting with agents in state a and agents in state b. An agent in c initially creates in its working memory three binary counters, the a-counter that counts the number of as, the b-counter, and the c-counter, initializes the a and b counters to 0, the c-counter to 1, and becomes ready. When an agent in state a interacts with an agent in state c, a becomes $\bar{a}$ to indicate that the agent is now sleeping, and c does the following (in fact, we assume that c goes to a special state c_a in which it knows that it has seen an a, and that all the following are done internally, after the interaction; finally the agent restores its state to c and becomes again ready for interaction): it increases its a-counter by one (in binary), multiplies its a and b counters, which can be done in binary in logarithmic space (binary multiplication is in $LOGSPACE$), compares the result with the c-counter, copies the result of the comparison to its output tape, that is, 1 if they

---

[1]The assumption that also here the input to each agent is a single symbol has been made for the sake of simplicity and is w.l.o.g. However, the definitions here can be easily modified to allow the agents to take whole strings as input.

are equal and 0, otherwise, and finally, it copies the comparison result and its three counters to the outgoing message tape, and becomes ready for interaction. Similar things happen when a b meets a c (interchange the roles of a and b in the above discussion). When a c meets a c, the responder becomes $\bar{c}$ and copies to its output tape the output bit contained in the initiator's message. The initiator remains to c, adds the a-counter contained in the responder's message to its a-counter, the b and c counters of the message to its b and c counters, respectively, multiplies again the updated a and b counters, compares the result to its updated c counter, stores the comparison result to its output and outgoing message tapes, copies its counters to its outgoing message tape, and becomes ready again. When a $\bar{a}, \bar{b}$ or $\bar{c}$ meets a c they only copy to their output tape the output bit contained in c's message and become ready again (eg $\bar{a}$ remains $\bar{a}$), while c does nothing.

Note that the number of cs is at most n which means that the c-counter will become at most $\lceil \log n \rceil$ bits long, and the same holds for the a and b counters, so $\mathcal{O}(\log n)$ memory is required in each tape.

Theorem 5.5 **[CMN$^+$10c]** *The above PM protocol stably computes the predicate $(N_c = N_a \cdot N_b)$ using $\mathcal{O}(\log n)$ space.*

Proof. Given a fair execution, eventually only one agent in state c will remain, its a-counter will contain the total number of as, its b-counter the total number of bs, and its c-counter, the total number of cs. By executing the multiplication of the a and b counters and comparing the result to its c-counter, it will correctly determine whether $(N_c = N_a \cdot N_b)$ holds, and it will store the correct result (0 or 1) to its output and outgoing message tapes. At that point, all other agents will be in one of the states $\bar{a}, \bar{b}$, and $\bar{c}$. All these, again due to fairness, will eventually meet the unique agent in state c and copy its correct output bit (which they will find in the message they get from c) to their output tapes. Thus, eventually all agents will output the correct value of the predicate, having used $\mathcal{O}(\log n)$ memory. □

Corollary 5.6 **[CMN$^+$10c]** **SEM** *is a proper subset of* **PMSPACE**$(\log n)$.

Proof. PALOMA   protocols   simulate   population   protocols   and $(N_c = N_a \cdot N_b) \in$ **PMSPACE**$(\log n)$, which is non-semilinear. □

5.1.2   ASSIGNING UNIQUE IDS BY REINITIATING COMPUTATION

In this section, we first prove that PM protocols can assume the existence of unique consecutive ids and knowledge of the population size at the space cost of $\mathcal{O}(\log n)$ (Theorem 5.14). In particular, we present a PM protocol that correctly assigns unique consecutive ids to the agents and informs them of the correct population size using only $\mathcal{O}(\log n)$ memory, without assuming any initial knowledge of none of them. We show that this protocol can simulate any PM protocol that assumes the existence of these ids and knows the population size. At the end of the section, we exploit this result to prove that **SSPACE**$(n \log n) \subseteq$ **PMSPACE**$(\log n)$.

Definition 5.7 [CMN$^+$10c]   Let *IPM* ('I' standing for "Ids") be the extension of the PM model in which the agents have additionally the unique ids $\{0, 1, \ldots, n - 1\}$ and in which each agent knows the population size (these are read-only information stored in a separate read-only tape).

Definition 5.8 [CMN$^+$10c]   Let **IPMSPACE**$(f(n))$ be the class of all predicates that are stably computable by some IPM protocol that uses $\mathcal{O}(f(n))$ space in every agent (and in all of its tapes, excluding the space used for the read-only tape) and denote by **SIPMSPACE**$(f(n))$ its symmetric subclass.

Pick any $p \in$ **SIPMSPACE**$(\log n)$. Let $\mathcal{A}$ be the IPM protocol that stably computes it in $\mathcal{O}(\log n)$ space. We now present a PM protocol $\mathcal{I}$ (see Protocol 6), containing protocol $\mathcal{A}$ as a subroutine, that stably computes p, by also using $\mathcal{O}(\log n)$ space. $\mathcal{I}$ is always executed and its job is to assign unique ids to the agents, to inform them of the correct population size and to control $\mathcal{A}$'s execution (e.g. restarts its execution if needed). $\mathcal{A}$, when $\mathcal{I}$ allows its execution, simply reads the unique ids and the population size provided by $\mathcal{I}$ and executes itself normally. We first present $\mathcal{I}$ and then prove that it eventually correctly assigns unique ids and correctly informs the agents of the population size, and that when this process comes to a successful end, it restarts $\mathcal{A}$'s execution in all agents without allowing non-reinitialized agents to communicate with the reinitialized ones. Thus, at some point, $\mathcal{A}$ will begin its execution reading the correct unique ids and the correct population size (provided by $\mathcal{I}$), thus, it will get correctly executed and will stably compute p.

We begin by describing $\mathcal{I}$'s variables. id is the variable storing the id of the agent (from which $\mathcal{A}$ reads the agents' ids), sid the variable storing the id that an agent writes in its outgoing message tape in order to send it, and rid the variable storing the id that an agent receives via interaction. Recall the model's convention that all variables used for sending information, like sid, preserve their value in future interactions unless altered by the agent. Initially, $id = sid = 0$ for all agents. All agents have an input backup variable $binput$ which they initially set to their input symbol and make it read-only. Thus, each agent has always available its input via $binput$ even if the computation has proceeded. $working$ represents the block of the working tape that $\mathcal{A}$ uses for its computation and $output$ represents the contents of the output tape. $initiator$ is a binary flag that after every interaction becomes true if the agent was the initiator of the interaction and false otherwise (this is easily implemented by exploiting the external transition function). ps is the variable storing the population size, sps the one used to put it in a outgoing message, and rps the received one. Initially, $ps = sps = 0$.

Protocol 6 $\mathcal{I}$

1: **if** $rid = id$ **then** // two agents with the same ids interact
2:     **if** $initiator = 1$ **then** // the initiator
3:         $id \leftarrow id + 1, sid \leftarrow id$ // increases its id by one and writes it in the outgoing message tape
4:         $ps \leftarrow id + 1, sps \leftarrow ps$ // sets the population size equal to its updated id plus 1
5:     **else** // the responder
6:         $ps \leftarrow id + 2, sps \leftarrow ps.$
7:     **end if**
8:     // both clear their working block and copy their input symbol into it
9:     // they also clear their output tape
10:     $working \leftarrow binput, output \leftarrow \emptyset$
11: **else** // two agents whose ids differ interact
12:     **if** $rps > ps$ **then** // the one who knows an outdated population size
13:         $working \leftarrow binput, output \leftarrow \emptyset$ // is reinitialized
14:         $ps \leftarrow rps, sps \leftarrow ps$ // and updates its population size to the greater value
15:     **else if** $rps = ps$ **then** // they know the same population size
16:         // so they are both reinitialized and can proceed executing $\mathcal{A}$
17:         **print** $\mathcal{A}$ for 1 step
18:     **end if**
19: **end if**

We now describe $\mathcal{I}$'s functionality. Whenever a pair of agents with the same id interact, the initiator increases its id by one and both update their population size value to the greater id plus one. Whenever two agents with different ids and population size values interact, they update their population size variables to the greater size. Thus the correct size (greatest id plus one) is propagated to all agents. Both interactions described above reinitialize the participating agents (restore their input and erase all data produced by the subroutine $\mathcal{A}$, without altering their ids and population sizes). Subroutine $\mathcal{A}$ runs whenever two agents of different ids and same population sizes interact, using those data provided by $\mathcal{I}$.

Lemma 5.9 [CMN$^+$10c] *(i) $\mathcal{I}$ assigns the ids $\{0, 1, \ldots, n-1\}$ in a finite number of steps. (ii) The id-assignment process ends with an interaction (u, v) of two agents u and v that both have the id $n-2$. (iii) This is the last interaction that modifies some agent's id. (iv) When this interaction happens, u and v know n and all other agents know a population size that is strictly smaller than n.*

Proof. (i) Initially, all agents have the id 0. Each agent's id can only be incremented. Moreover, an id that has appeared in the population can never be completely eliminated (it is only incremented when sure that it also exists in another agent). As long as id $n-1$ has not appeared, by the pigeonhole principle, there will be at least two agents with the same id. Thus, eventually (in a finite number of steps), due to fairness, two such agents will interact and one of them will increase its id by one. Clearly, the above process must end in a finite number of steps with an agent having id $n - 1$. When this happens, the agents are assigned the unique ids $\{0, 1, \ldots, n - 1\}$. If not, then at least one id $i < n - 1$ is missing from the population. But i should have appeared because then $n - 1$ could not have been reached. But this is a contradiction because once an id appears, then it can never be completely eliminated.

(ii) Assume not. Then it must end by some interaction between two agents u and υ that both have the same id $i < n - 2$. After the interaction, u has the id $i + 1$, υ the id i, and the agents in general have the uids $\{0, 1, \ldots, n - 1\}$. This implies that id $i + 1$ did not exist in the population just before this interaction. But for $n - 1$ to exist, it must be the case that $i + 1 < n - 1$ had appeared at some point. But then, it could have never been completely eliminated, which is a contradiction.

(iii) Just after the unique consecutive ids $\{0, 1, \ldots, n - 1\}$ have been assigned, no agents have the same id. Ids are only modified when two agents with the same id interact. Thus, no agent will again change its id in all subsequent steps.

(iv) u and υ obviously know n after their interaction (that terminates the id-assignment process), because u, that sets $id = n - 1$, sets ps equal to $id + 1$, and υ that keeps its id (that is, it still has $id = n - 2$), sets $ps = id + 2$. At the same time, for all other agents $w \in V - \{u, \upsilon\}$, it holds that their ps variables contain a value less than n, because, if not, then there should be an agent other than u with id $n - 1$, which is impossible (due to the correctness of the id-assignment process). □

Lemma 5.10 **[CMN$^+$10c]** *After the last id-modification has taken place (via interaction (u, υ)) all agents eventually get informed of the correct population size, and whenever some agent i, who knows the correct population size, propagates the population size to agent j, j becomes reinitialized and cannot become reinitialized again in the future.*

Proof. Protocol 6 states that after the last id-modification has taken place, whenever an agent j interacts with another agent k that knows a larger population size, j updates its population size to the corresponding value of k and gets reinitialized, that is, restores $\mathcal{A}$'s working blocks to the respective input symbols (by executing $working \leftarrow binput$), and clears its output tapes (denoted by $output \leftarrow \emptyset$ in the code). This interaction pattern propagates the largest population size value to all agents. Since ids cannot change any more, the largest population size known by agents u and υ cannot change either because the population size increases as the number of different ids increases. Consequently, an agent that knows the correct population size cannot be reinitialized any more. Hence, once any agent j that does not know the correct population size (thus by Lemma 5.9, it knows a strictly smaller value) interacts with an agent i who knows the correct value (initially u and υ), j learns the correct population size and gets reinitialized for the last time. □

In the following Lemma, we call an interaction *effective* if protocol $\mathcal{A}$ is executed in at least one of the participating agents. Moreover, we call an agent *finally reinitialized* if it has been reinitialized for the last time.

Lemma 5.11 [CMN$^+$10c]   *After the unique consecutive ids $\{0, 1, \ldots, n-1\}$ have been assigned, finally reinitialized agents, have* effective *interactions with each other, while, on the other hand, their interactions with non finally reinitialized agents have no effect w.r.t. to $\mathcal{A}$'s execution.*

Proof. After the unique ids have been successfully assigned, it is like the population is partitioned in two classes, the class FR of finally reinitialized agents, which know the correct population size and NFR of the non finally reinitialized ones (which do not know the correct population size). Initially (just after the unique ids have been successfully assigned), $FR = \{n-2, n-1\}$ and $NFR = \{0, 1, \ldots, n-3\}$; that is, all agents except $n-1$ and $n-2$, who know the correct population size n, are considered as non finally reinitialized. An agent $i \in NFR$ moves to FR iff it interacts with an agent in FR. This interaction reinitializes i for the last time, as shown in Lemma 5.10, and updates it with the correct population size. Therefore, no interaction between agents in different classes can be effective. Similarly, by inspecting Protocol 6, it is easy to see that agents in FR have effective interactions with each other.   □

It is easy to see that $\mathcal{I}$, except for calling $\mathcal{A}$, only performs some variable assignments, which cannot lead into an infinite loop. But while the correct ids have not yet been assigned to the agents, some interacting agents may contain inconsistent data, which could make subroutine $\mathcal{A}$ fall into an infinite loop. This would disable $\mathcal{I}$'s capability to reinitialize it, if needed.

Lemma 5.12 [CMN$^+$10c]   *No agent ever falls into some infinite loop.*

Proof. $\mathcal{A}$ is always executed for one step only.   □

Lemma 5.13 [CMN$^+$10c]   *Given that $\mathcal{I}$'s execution is fair, $\mathcal{A}$'s execution is fair as well.*

The proof of Lemma 5.13 is left as Exercise 5.2. Now, by combining the above lemmata, we can prove the following:

Theorem 5.14 [CMN$^+$10c]   **PMSPACE**$(\log n) = $ **SIPMSPACE**$(\log n)$.

Proof. **PMSPACE**$(\log n) \subseteq$ **SIPMSPACE**$(\log n)$ holds trivially, so it suffices to show that **SIPMSPACE**$(\log n) \subseteq$ **PMSPACE**$(\log n)$. For any $p \in$ **SIPMSPACE**$(\log n)$ let $\mathcal{A}$ be the IPM protocol that stably computes it in $\mathcal{O}(\log n)$ space. We previously showed that there is a PM protocol $\mathcal{I}$, containing protocol $\mathcal{A}$ as a subroutine (see Protocol 6), so that: $\mathcal{I}$ correctly assigns the unique consecutive ids $\{0, 1, \ldots, n-1\}$ to the agents (Lemma 5.9) and informs them of the correct population size (Lemma 5.10). Then each agent that learns the correct population size by interacting with an agent that already knows it becomes finally reinitialized, in the sense that it starts executing $\mathcal{A}$ from the beginning and cannot get reinitialized again in future steps (Lemma 5.10). During this propagation process, $\mathcal{I}$ does not allow non finally reinitialized agents, that possibly contain outdated information, to have some effective interaction with finally reinitialized agents (Lemma 5.11). Moreover, due to the intermittent execution of $\mathcal{A}$, no agent could have ever become busy for an infinite number of steps, thus, it is guaranteed that the reinitializations can always be applied (Lemma 5.12). Finally, provided that $\mathcal{I}$'s execution is fair, so is $\mathcal{A}$'s execution, which is simulated by $\mathcal{I}$ (Lemma 5.13). $\mathcal{I}$ uses $\mathcal{O}(\log n)$ memory for $\mathcal{A}$'s execution and $\mathcal{O}(\log n)$ memory for storing the unique ids and the population size, thus $\mathcal{O}(\log n)$ in total. Since $\mathcal{A}$ stably computes p, the same holds for $\mathcal{I}$, that correctly simulates $\mathcal{A}$, and the theorem follows. □

We now show that any symmetric predicate in $SPACE(n \log n)$ also belongs to **SIPMSPACE**$(\log n)$. The idea is this: The IPM model needs $\mathcal{O}(\log n)$ space to simulate a deterministic TM $\mathcal{M}$ of $\mathcal{O}(n \log n)$ space. Intuitively, the agents are lined up so that any two consecutive agents have consecutive ids, and a simulation token specifies the agent that is responsible for the simulation. While agent u carries out the simulation, any motion of the tape head of $\mathcal{M}$ corresponds to passing the simulation token to one of its neighbouring agents. That way, the tape head of $\mathcal{M}$ alters the tapes of the agents in a modular way. We proceed with the formal proof.

Theorem 5.15 [CMN$^+$10c]   SSPACE$(n \log n)$ *is a subset of* **SIPMSPACE**$(\log n)$.

Proof. Let $p : X^* \to \{0, 1\}$ be any predicate in **SSPACE**$(n \log n)$ and $\mathcal{M}$ be the deterministic TM that decides p by using $\mathcal{O}(n \log n)$ space. We construct an IPM protocol $\mathcal{A}$ that stably computes p. Let x be any input assignment in X^*. Each agent receives its input symbol according to x (e.g., u receives the symbol $x(u)$). The agents have the unique ids $\{0, 1, \ldots, n-1\}$ and know the population size n. Moreover, we assume for the sake of simplicity that the agents are equipped with an extra tape, the *simulation tape* that is used during the simulation. The agent that has the unique id 0 starts simulating $\mathcal{M}$.

In the general case, assume that currently the simulation is carried out by an agent u having the id i_u. Agent u uses its simulation tape to write symbols according to the transition function of $\mathcal{M}$. Any time the head of $\mathcal{M}$ moves to the right, u moves the head of the simulation tape to the right, pauses the simulation, writes the current state of $\mathcal{M}$ to its outgoing message tape, and passes the simulation to the agent v having id $i_v = (i_u + 1) \mod n$. Any time the head of $\mathcal{M}$ moves to the left, u pauses the simulation, writes the current state of $\mathcal{M}$ to its outgoing message tape, and passes the simulation to the agent v having id $i_v = (i_u - 1) \mod n$. From agent v's perspective, in the first case, it just receives the state of $\mathcal{M}$, copies it to its working tape and starts the simulation, while in the second case, it additionally moves the head of the simulation tape one cell to the left before it starts the simulation.

It remains to cover the boundary case in which the head of the simulation tape is over the special symbol that indicates the beginning of the tape. In that case, the agent moves the head to the right and continues the simulation himself (notice that this can only happen to the agent that begins the simulation, that is, the one having the id 0).

Whenever, during the simulation, $\mathcal{M}$ accepts, then $\mathcal{A}$ also accepts; that is, the agent that detects $\mathcal{M}$'s acceptance, writes 1 to its output tape and informs all agents to accept. If $\mathcal{M}$ rejects, it also rejects. Finally, note that $\mathcal{A}$ simulates $\mathcal{M}$ not necessarily on input $x = \sigma_0 \sigma_1 \ldots \sigma_{n-1}$ but on some x', which is a permutation of x. The reason is that agent with id i does not necessarily obtain σ_i as its input. The crucial remark that completes the proof is that $\mathcal{M}$ accepts x if and only if it accepts x', because p is symmetric.

Because of the above process, it is easy to verify that the kth cell of the simulation tape of any agent u having the id i_u corresponds to the $[n(k-1) + i_u + 1]$th cell of $\mathcal{M}$. Thus, it is immediate that whenever $\mathcal{M}$ alters $\mathcal{O}(n \log n)$ tape cells, any agent u will alter $\mathcal{O}(\log n)$ cells of its simulation tape. □

Theorem 5.16   [CMN$^+$10c]   **SSPACE**$(n \log n)$ *is a subset of* **PMSPACE**$(\log n)$.

Proof. Follows from **SSPACE**$(n \log n) \subseteq$ **SIPMSPACE**$(\log n) =$ **PMSPACE**$(\log n)$. □

Corollary 5.17   [CMN$^+$10c]   **SNSPACE**$(\sqrt{n \log n})$ *is a subset of* **PMSPACE**$(\log n)$.

Proof. Follows from Theorem 5.16 and Savitch's theorem (Theorem 1.8). □

5.1.3   A BETTER INCLUSION FOR PMSPACE$(\log n)$

Here, we show with two different approaches that **SNSPACE**$(n \log n)$ is a subset of **PMSPACE**$(\log n)$, thus, improving the inclusion of Theorem 5.16.

5.1.3.1   PALOMA Protocols Simulate Community Protocols

We begin by showing that the PM model simulates the Community Protocol model by using $\mathcal{O}(\log n)$ memory in each agent. This is the first approach of establishing that **SNSPACE**$(n \log n) \subseteq$ **PMSPACE**$(\log n)$. Recall that by **CP**, we denote the class of predicates that are stably computable by the Community Protocol model and that we have already established in Theorem 3.15 that **CP** is equal to **SNSPACE**($n \log n$).

Definition 5.18 [CMN⁺10c]   Let **RCP** denote the class of all symmetric predicates that are stably computable by a restricted version of the community protocol model in which the agents can only have the unique ids $\{0, 1, \ldots, n - 1\}$.

We first show that the community protocol model that is restricted in the above fashion is equivalent to the community protocol model.

Lemma 5.19 [CMN⁺10c]   **RCP** = **CP**.

Proof. **RCP** $\subseteq$ **CP** holds trivially. It remains to show that **CP** $\subseteq$ **RCP**. Since the community protocol model can only perform comparisons on ids, it follows that if we replace any vector of unique ids $(id_0, id_1, \ldots, id_{n-1})$ indexed by agents, where $id_0 < id_1 < \ldots < id_{n-1}$, by the unique ids $(0, 1, \ldots, n - 1)$ (thus preserving the ordering of the agents w.r.t. their ids), then the resulting computations in both cases must be identical.   □

Lemma 5.20 [CMN⁺10c]   **RCP** *is a subset of* **SIPMSPACE**($\log n$).

Proof. PALOMA protocols that already have the unique ids $\{0, 1, \ldots, n - 1\}$ and know the population size can do whatever community protocols that have the same unique ids can, and additionally can perform operations on ids (they can store them in the agents' memories and perform some internal computation on them).   □

Since, according to Theorem 5.14, **SIPMSPACE**($\log n$) is equal to **PMSPACE**($\log n$), we have arrived at the following result.

Theorem 5.21 [CMN⁺10c]   **CP** *is a subset of* **PMSPACE**($\log n$).

Proof. Follows from **CP** = **RCP** $\subseteq$ **SIPMSPACE**($\log n$) = **PMSPACE**($\log n$).   □

Theorem 5.22 [CMN⁺10c]   **SNSPACE**($n \log n$) *is a subset of* **PMSPACE**($\log n$).

Proof. By Theorem 3.15, **SNSPACE**($n \log n$) is equal to **CP**. Then we simply take into account Theorem 5.21.   □

5.1.3.2   A Direct Approach

Note that the proof of Theorem 5.22 depends on the following result: A Storage Modification Machine can simulate a Turing Machine. The reason is that the omitted proof of Theorem 3.15 constitutes an indirect proof of the fact that **SNSPACE**$(n \log n)$ is a subset of **CP**. In particular, the theorem follows by showing that community protocols can simulate a Storage Modification Machine, and then the above result concerning storage modification machines is used to establish that community protocols can simulate a nondeterministic TM. Here, and in order to avoid this dependence, we generalize the ideas used in the proof of Theorem 5.14 and provide a direct simulation of a nondeterministic TM of $\mathcal{O}(n \log n)$ space by the PM model where agents use $\mathcal{O}(\log n)$ space.

Theorem 5.23 [CMN$^+$10c]   SNSPACE$(n \log n)$ *is a subset of* **PMSPACE**$(\log n)$.

Proof. By considering Theorem 5.14, it suffices to show that **SNSPACE**$(n \log n)$ is a subset of **SIPMSPACE**$(\log n)$. We have already shown that the IPM model can simulate a deterministic TM $\mathcal{M}$ of $\mathcal{O}(n \log n)$ space by using $\mathcal{O}(\log n)$ space (Theorem 5.15). We now present some modifications that will allow us to simulate a nondeterministic TM $\mathcal{N}$ of the same memory size. Keep in mind that $\mathcal{N}$ is a decider for some predicate in **SNSPACE**$(n \log n)$; thus, it always halts. Upon initialization, each agent enters a reject state (writes 0 to its output tape), and the simulation is carried out as in the case of $\mathcal{M}$.

Whenever a nondeterministic choice has to be made, the corresponding agent gets ready and waits for participating in an interaction. The id of the other participant will provide the nondeterministic choice to be made. One possible implementation of this idea is the following. Since there is a fixed upper bound on the number of nondeterministic choices (independent of the population size), the agents can store them in their memories. Any time a nondeterministic choice has to be made between k candidates the agent assigns the numbers $0, 1, \ldots, k - 1$ to those candidates and becomes ready for interaction. Assume that the next interaction is with an agent whose id is i. Then the nondeterministic choice selected by the agent is the one that has assigned the number $i \mod k$. Fairness guarantees that, in this manner, all possible paths in the tree representing $\mathcal{N}$'s nondeterministic computation will eventually be followed.

Any time the simulation reaches an accept state, all agents change their output to 1 and the simulation halts. Moreover, any time the simulation reaches a reject state, it is being reinitiated. The correctness of the above procedure is captured by the following two cases.

1. *If $\mathcal{N}$ rejects then every agent's output stabilizes to* 0. Upon initialization, each agent's output is 0 and can only change if $\mathcal{N}$ reaches an accept state. But all branches of $\mathcal{N}$'s computation reject; thus, no accept state is ever reached, and every agent's output forever remains to 0.

2. *If $\mathcal{N}$ accepts then every agent's output stabilizes to* 1. Since $\mathcal{N}$ accepts, there is a sequence of configurations S, starting from the initial configuration C that leads to a configuration C' in which each agent's output is set to 1 (by simulating directly the branch of $\mathcal{N}$ that accepts).

Notice that when an agent sets its output to 1, it never alters its output tape again, so it suffices to show that the simulation will eventually reach C'. Assume on the contrary that it does not. Since $\mathcal{N}$ always halts the simulation will be at the initial configuration C infinitely many times. Due to fairness, by an easy induction on the configurations of S, C' will also appear infinitely many times, which leads to a contradiction. Thus the simulation will eventually reach C' and the output will stabilize to 1.

$\square$

5.1.4 AN EXACT CHARACTERIZATION FOR PMSPACE$(\log n)$

We first notice that **PMSPACE**$(\log n) \subseteq$ **NSPACE**$(n \log n)$.

Theorem 5.24 [CMN$^+$10c] *All predicates in* **PMSPACE**$(\log n)$ *are in the class* **NSPACE**$(n \log n)$.

The proof is similar to those that achieve the corresponding inclusions for the MPP model (Theorem 4.24) and the community protocol model (Theorem 3.13), so we only present the core idea. It suffices to show that the language corresponding to any predicate in **PMSPACE**$(\log n)$ can be decided by a nondeterministic TM of $\mathcal{O}(n \log n)$ space. The TM guesses the next configuration and checks whether it has reached one that is output stable. Note that $\mathcal{O}(n \log n)$ space suffices, because a population configuration consists of n agent configurations each of size $\mathcal{O}(\log n)$.

Theorem 5.25 [CMN$^+$10c] **PMSPACE**$(\log n) =$ **SNSPACE**$(n \log n)$.

Proof. Follows from Theorems 5.22 (or, equivalently, Theorem 5.23), which establishes that **SNSPACE**$(n \log n) \subseteq$ **PMSPACE**$(\log n)$, and 5.24, which establishes that **PMSPACE**$(\log n) \subseteq$ **NSPACE**$(n \log n)$, but for all $p \in$ **PMSPACE**$(\log n)$, p is symmetric (similarly to Lemma 4.6), thus, **PMSPACE**$(\log n) \subseteq$ **SNSPACE**$(n \log n)$. $\square$

5.2 BELOW LOG SPACE, ABOVE LOG SPACE AND A SPACE HIERARCHY

Theorem 5.26 [CMN$^+$10c] *For any space function $f : \mathbb{N} \to \mathbb{N}$, any predicate in* **PMSPACE**$(f(n))$ *is also in* **SNSPACE**$(2^{f(n)}(f(n) + \log n))$.

Proof. Take any $p \in \textbf{PMSPACE}(f(n))$. Let $\mathcal{A}$ be the PM protocol that stably computes predicate p in space $\mathcal{O}(f(n))$. As usual, $L_p = \{(s_1, s_2, \ldots, s_n) \mid s_i \in X \text{ for all } i \in \{1, \ldots, n\} \text{ and } p(s_1, s_2, \ldots, s_n) = 1\}$ is the language corresponding to p. We describe a nondeterministic TM $\mathcal{N}$ that decides L_p in $g(n) = \mathcal{O}(2^{f(n)}(f(n) + \log n))$ space.

Note that each agent has a memory of size $\mathcal{O}(f(n))$. So, by assuming a binary tape alphabet $\Gamma = \{0, 1\}$, an assumption which is w.l.o.g., there are $2^{\mathcal{O}(f(n))}$ different agent configurations each of size $\mathcal{O}(f(n))$. $\mathcal{N}$ stores a population configuration by storing all these agent configurations, consuming for this purpose $\mathcal{O}(f(n)2^{f(n)})$ space, together with a number per agent configuration representing the number of agents in that agent configuration under the current population configuration. These numbers sum up to n and each one of them requires $\mathcal{O}(\log n)$ bits, thus, $\mathcal{O}(2^{f(n)} \log n)$ extra space is needed, giving a total of $\mathcal{O}(2^{f(n)}(f(n) + \log n))$ space needed to store a population configuration. The reason that such a representation of population configurations suffices is that when k agents are in the same internal configuration there is no reason to store it k times. The completeness of the interaction graph allows us to store it once and simply indicate the number of agents that are in this common internal configuration, that is, k.

Now $\mathcal{N}$ simply does the same as the nondeterministic TMs of Theorems 4.24 and 5.24 with the only difference being that it stores configurations according to the new encoding that we have just defined. □

Corollary 5.27 [CMN$^+$10c]   *For any function $f(n) = o(\log n)$, it holds that* $\textbf{PMSPACE}(f(n)) \subsetneq$ $\textbf{SNSPACE}(nf(n))$.

Proof. By considering Theorem 5.26 and the symmetric space hierarchy theorem (Theorem 1.11), it suffices to show that $2^{f(n)}(f(n) + \log n) = o(nf(n))$ for $f(n) = o(\log n)$. We have that

$$2^{f(n)}(f(n) + \log n) = 2^{o(\log n)}\mathcal{O}(\log n) = o(n)\mathcal{O}(\log n),$$

which obviously grows slower than $nf(n) = n \cdot o(\log n)$. □

So, for example, if $f(n) = \log \log n$, then $\textbf{PMSPACE}(\log \log n) \subseteq \textbf{SNSPACE}(\log^2 n)$, which is strictly smaller than $\textbf{SNSPACE}(nf(n)) = \textbf{SNSPACE}(n \log \log n)$ by the symmetric space hierarchy theorem. Another interesting example is obtained by setting $f(n) = c$. In this case, we obtain the $\textbf{SNSPACE}(\log n) = \textbf{SNL}$ upper bound for population protocols of Exercise 1.3.

Although the above upper bounds are relatively tight for $f(n) \leq \log n$ space functions, the bounds for $f(n) > \log n$ have worse behavior in relation to the $nf(n)$ taken for space function $\log n$. In the theorem below, tighter upper bounds are shown for $f(n) = \Omega(\log n)$ by using the better encoding of population configurations provided by Theorem 5.26.

Theorem 5.28 [CMN$^+$10c]   *For any space function $f(n)$, it holds that* $\textbf{PMSPACE}(f(n))$ *is a subset of* $\textbf{SNSPACE}(nf(n))$.

Proof. This proof is similar to the proof of Theorem 5.24, establishing that **PMSPACE**$(\log n)$ is a subset of **SNSPACE**$(n \log n)$. Using similar arguments, it can be easily shown that all predicates in **PMSPACE**$(f(n))$ are in **SNSPACE**$(nf(n))$. In particular, there is a nondeterministic TM $\mathcal{N}'$ of space $\mathcal{O}(nf(n))$ that can decide the language L_p corresponding to any predicate $p \in$ **PMSPACE**$(f(n))$. $\mathcal{N}'$ holds the internal configurations of the n agents each of which needs $\mathcal{O}(f(n))$ space, and therefore each population configuration fits in $\mathcal{O}(nf(n))$ cells of $\mathcal{N}'$'s tape. $\mathcal{N}'$ starts with the initial configuration C, guesses the next C' and checks whether it has reached a configuration in which all agents give the correct output for p. When $\mathcal{N}'$ reaches such a configuration C, it computes the complement of a similar reachability problem: it verifies that there exists no configuration reachable from C in which p is violated. This condition can also be verified in $\mathcal{O}(nf(n))$ space since **NSPACE** is closed under complement for all space functions $g(n) = \Omega(\log n)$ (see the Immerman-Szelepcsényi theorem - Theorem 1.9). Note that for any reasonable function $f(n)$, $g(n) = nf(n) \geq \log n$, as required by the Immerman-Szelepcsényi theorem. $\square$

The upper bounds shown above are obviously better for space functions $f(n) = \Omega(\log n)$ than those presented by Theorem 5.26. Note however, that Theorem 5.28 also holds for $f(n) = o(\log n)$ and for those space functions the upper bounds are worse than those of Theorem 5.26. In order to realize this, consider the function $f(n) = c$ (the memory of each agent is independent of the population size, thus this is equivalent to the PP model). According to Theorem 5.28, the upper bound is the trivial **SNSPACE**(n), whereas the Theorem 5.26 decreases the upper bound to **SNSPACE**$(\log n)$. This behavior is expected due to the configuration representation of the population used by those theorems. When the configuration is stored as n-vector where each element of the vector holds the internal configuration of an agent (representation used in Theorem 5.28), then as the memory size grows the additional space needed is a factor n of that growth. On the other hand, when a configuration is represented as a vector of size equal to the number of all possible internal configurations where each element is the number of agents that are in the corresponding internal configuration (as in Theorem 5.26), then the size of the vector grows exponentially to the memory growth. Therefore, tighter upper bounds are obtained by Theorem 5.28 for space constructible functions $f(n) = \Omega(\log n)$ and by Theorem 5.26 for $f(n) = o(\log n)$. Note that for $f(n) = \log n$, the bounds by both theorems are the same.

The next theorem shows that for space functions $f(n) = \Omega(\log n)$ the PM model can simulate a nondeterministic TM of space $\mathcal{O}(nf(n))$ by using $\mathcal{O}(f(n))$ space. The theorem is not so hard to prove if one uses the arguments used in the proof of Theorem 5.14. Intuitively, with memory at least $\log n$ in each agent, we can always assign unique ids and propagate the population size; thus, we will always be able to organize the population into a distributed nondeterministic TM, where each one of the n agents offers $\mathcal{O}(f(n))$ to the simulation.

Theorem 5.29 [CMN⁺10c]   *For all $f(n) = \Omega(\log n)$, it holds that* **SNSPACE**$(nf(n))$ *is a subset of* **PMSPACE**$(f(n))$.

Proof. In Theorem 5.23, a nondeterministic TM of $\mathcal{O}(n \log n)$ space is simulated by the PALOMA model, given that all agents know the population size and have unique ids. Moreover, in Theorem 5.14, a construction has been presented that allows the PALOMA protocols to assume the existence of unique ids and knowledge of the population size. The same construction can be also applied to those protocols that use $\mathcal{O}(f(n))$ space, for $f(n) = \Omega(\log n)$. The reason is that in this space the agents can store again both unique ids and the population size. Thus, again here the same protocol $\mathcal{I}$ of Theorem 5.14 can be used. □

By combining the previous two theorems, we have that:

Theorem 5.30 **[CMN⁺10c]** *For all* $f(n) = \Omega(\log n)$, *it holds that* **PMSPACE**$(f(n)) =$ **SNSPACE**$(nf(n))$.

Proof. Follows from Theorems 5.28 and 5.29. □

Thus, by combining now Corollary 5.27 and Theorem 5.30, we arrive at the following corollary.

Corollary 5.31 *The space bound $f(n) = \Theta(\log n)$ acts as a threshold of the computational power of the PM model.*

Considering the above analysis and Corollary 5.31, it is worth noting that PALOMA protocols, seem to belong to a golden section between realistic requirements, w.r.t. implementation, and computational power offered.

Theorem 5.32 **Space Hierarchy Theorem of the PM model [CMN⁺10c]** *For any two functions $f, g : \mathbb{N} \rightarrow \mathbb{N}$, where $f(n) = \Omega(\log n)$ and $g(n) = o(f(n))$, there is a predicate p in* **PMSPACE**$(f(n))$ *but not in* **PMSPACE**$(g(n))$.

Proof. From Theorem 1.11, we have that for any such functions f, g, there is a language $L \in$ **SNSPACE**$(nf(n))$ so that $L \notin$ **SNSPACE**$(ng(n))$. From Theorem 5.30, we have that **SNSPACE**$(nf(n)) =$ **PMSPACE**$(f(n))$; therefore, $p_L \in$ **PMSPACE**$(f(n))$ (where p_L is the symmetric predicate that corresponds to the symmetric language L). We distinguish two cases. If $g(n) = \Omega(\log n)$, then from Theorem 5.30, we have that **SNSPACE**$(ng(n)) =$ **PMSPACE**$(g(n))$ and so $L \notin$ **PMSPACE**$(g(n))$ or equivalently $p_L \notin$ **PMSPACE**$(g(n))$. If $g(n) = o(\log n)$, then from Corollary 5.27, we have that **PMSPACE**$(g(n)) \subsetneq$ **SNSPACE**$(ng(n)) \subsetneq$ **SNSPACE**$(nf(n)) =$ **PMSPACE**$(f(n))$. □

5.2.1   BEHAVIOR OF THE PM MODEL FOR SPACE $o(\log \log n)$

Now we are ready to prove that $\mathbf{SEM} = \mathbf{PMSPACE}(f(n))$, when $f(n) = o(\log \log n)$. Since $\mathbf{SEM} \subseteq \mathbf{PMSPACE}(f(n))$ holds trivially, we will only deal with the $\mathbf{PMSPACE}(f(n)) \subseteq \mathbf{SEM}$ direction.

Theorem 5.33   *Any PM protocol $\mathcal{A}$ that uses $f(n) = o(\log \log n)$ space can only compute semilinear predicates.*

The formal proof is quite involved, so we begin by discussing an intuitive proof idea.

Proof Idea. For each execution and each agent configuration C_u of an agent u in that execution, we define a binary tree of "ancestor agent configurations," which has C_u as its root and each node is either a leaf, corresponding to an initial agent configuration, or a parent node C_v, which has as children, the agent configurations whose interaction produced C_v.

Define the *depth $d(C)$* of an agent configuration C as the height of the shortest tree with C at its root.

If we only consider trees that have *minimum size* (w.r.t. the number of nodes) among all trees of the same depth, then no agent configuration appears twice on the same path, because else we could replace the subtree rooted at the later occurrence with the smaller subtree rooted at the earlier one. But then any such tree yields an execution that has the following property: *(Property P)* "It has at least $d(C)$ distinct agent configurations and must have started from a population of at most $2^{(d(C)-1)}$ initial agents."

Now consider the complementary cases:

(a) For any C, the depth $d(C)$ (of *distinct* configurations) is bounded by a constant. But there is only a constant number of binary trees of a depth bounded by a constant. So the protocol has only finitely reachable agent configurations. Then this passively mobile protocol can be converted to a *finite-states* protocol (i.e., a standard population protocol).

(b) $d(C)$ grows with the population size, n, in some executions. The longest path in the tree of C may (in an execution) have all nodes representing (agent) configurations of the same agent, u. This means that some other agents produced agent configurations that caused the existence of the $d(C)$ *distinct* configurations of this agent u. At the worst, in some execution, all n agents may have been involved in the tree of C, i.e., the tree has n nodes (by fairness, all agents will meet with u). But then u has to have local memory enough to keep *at least* $\log n$ *distinct configurations* by Property P, i.e., $\Omega(\log \log n)$ local memory (in any reasonable, at least binary, tape alphabet).

We will prove Theorem 5.33 rigorously, but first, and in order to further simplify the reading of the proof, we present a summary of it.

Initially, we define an agent configuration graph, whose nodes are the internal configurations of the agents. This graph depends on the protocol $\mathcal{A}$ (that uses $o(\log \log n)$ memory) and the population size n and contains all reachable agent configurations under which the working flag is 0. Two such configurations are joined by an edge (u, v) if there exists some configuration if there exists some interaction with some other configuration w after which u will become v (after executing its internal computation). Moreover, w constitutes the label of the corresponding edge.

The proof proceeds by showing that as n grows, the agent configuration graph is modified in the following systematic fashion: only new nodes and edges are added; thus, it continues to have a common subgraph with smaller ns. This is rational since if at the new population size n we ignore some nodes, then the remaining nodes will behave in precisely the same manner as they did for smaller ns (that is, they will have precisely the same reachability properties).

Then each node a of the agent configuration graph is associated to a value $r(a)$, which is defined as the minimum sum of node and label value that gives a. That is, for all u and v such that there exists the edge (u, a) and its label is v, it holds that $r(a) = \min(r(u) + r(v))$. All initial configurations take value 1; intuitively, nodes that are reachable by an interaction of initial configurations take value 2, those that are reachable by an initial and one that is reachable in one step take value 3, and so on; thus these values express reachability distance.

The next step is to prove that all nodes are assigned a value by the above rule (it holds since they are all reachable) and that (the most important) for any protocol $\mathcal{A}$ that uses $o(\log \log n)$ memory, there exists a n_0 such that for all $n > n_0$, the maximum value that appears in the agent configuration graph is less than $n/2$.

Then it is proved that any configuration a in an agent configuration graph for population n that is reachable in $r(a) - 1$ steps is also reachable in some population of size $r(a)$. Inductively, this also seems rational: all initial configurations are reachable in 0 steps, so they can also appear in a population of size 1 (the unique agent simply has to take the required input), those that are reachable by the interaction of to initial ones (so, in one step) may also appear in a population of size 2, provided that the two agents get the right inputs, and so on.

The next step is the heart of the proof: It is proven that, for any protocol $\mathcal{A}$ that uses $o(\log \log n)$ space, there exists a n_0 s.t., for all $n > n_0$, the corresponding agent configuration graph is in some sense complete; that is, for any two reachable agent configurations, those configurations can appear in the same population configuration and thus they may interact. The idea is this: Consider any two such reachable agent configurations for population n. As already mentioned, both must have some values $< n/2$. This means that (due to the previous result), both are reachable in some population of size less than $n/2$. Thus, if we consider population n as two separate populations each of size $n/2$ (we break n in two halves), which are not allowed communication for a finite number of steps, then it is possible that one agent configuration appears in one population and the other agent configuration appears in the other, and so it is possible that there is eventually an interaction between them. Note that this does not hold for memories that are at least $\log \log n$ because there the above $n/2$ bound does not hold.

Now the proof is almost complete. The final step is to show that, due to the above discussion, there exists some n_0 s.t., for all $n > n0$; the number of different agent configurations ceases to grow (then obviously that n_0 may be considered as a constant and $\mathcal{A}$ can be simulated by a protocol of constant memory, thus, anything computed by it must be semilinear). Assume that the number of different configurations could grow for $n' > n$, and let k be a new configuration for n' (which didn't exist for n) and which first appears via an interaction of agent configurations that also existed for n (obviously, a new configuration must appear by already existing ones because the new agent configuration graph only adds new nodes and edges). By the previous result, these two configurations could also have appeared and interacted in population n, which implies that k should also belong to the agent configuration graph of population n. Thus, there is no new configuration, such a configuration cannot exist, and the proof is complete.

It is now time to present a rigorous proof of Theorem 5.33.

Definition 5.34   Let $\mathcal{A}$ be a PM protocol executed in a population V of size n. Define *agent configuration graph*, $R_{\mathcal{A},V} = \{U, W, F\}$, a graph such that:

- U is the set of the agent configurations that can occur in any execution of $\mathcal{A}$ such that the working flag is set to 0.

- W is the set of edges (u, v), $u, v \in U$ so that there exists an edge (u, v) when there exists an agent configuration w, so that an interaction between two agents with configurations u, w will lead the first one to configuration v.

- $F : W \rightarrow \{u_1, u2, \ldots\}, u_i \in U \times \{i, r\}$ is an edge labeling function so that when an agent k being in configuration u enters configuration v via a single interaction with an agent being in configuration w, and k acts as $x \in \{i, r\}$ (initiator-responder) in the interaction, then $\{w, x\} \in F((u, v))$, while $F((u, v)) = \emptyset$ in any other case. Notice that F is a function since we only deal with deterministic protocols.

In other words, U contains the configurations that an agent may enter in any possible execution when we do not take into consideration the ones that correspond to internal computation, while W defines the transitions between those configuration through interactions defined by F. Note that the model's description excludes infinite sequences of blank cells from the agent configurations. Also, notice that, in general, $R_{\mathcal{A},V}$ depends not only on the protocol $\mathcal{A}$, but also on the population V. We call a $u \in U$ *initial node* iff it corresponds to an initial agent configuration.

Definition 5.35   Two agent configuration graphs $R_{\mathcal{A},V} = \{U, W, F\}$ and $R_{\mathcal{A}',V'} = \{U', W', F'\}$ are called *equal*, denoted by $R_{\mathcal{A},V} = R_{\mathcal{A}',V'}$, iff $U = U'$, $W = W'$ and $F(e) = F'(e), \forall e \in W$.

Because of the uniformity property, we can deduce the following theorem:

Theorem 5.36   *Let $R_{\mathcal{A},V}, R_{\mathcal{A},V'}$ be two agent configuration graphs corresponding to a protocol $\mathcal{A}$ for any two different populations V, V' of size n and n', respectively, where $n < n'$. Then, there exists a subgraph R^* of $R_{\mathcal{A},V'}$ such that $R^* = R_{\mathcal{A},V}$, and whose initial nodes contains all the initial nodes of $R_{\mathcal{A},V'}$.*

Proof. Indeed, let V_1', V_2' be a partitioning of V' such that $V_1' = V$, and observe the agent configuration graph that is yielded by the execution of $\mathcal{A}$ in V_1'. Since both populations execute the same protocol $\mathcal{A}$, the transitions are the same, thus all edges in $R_{\mathcal{A},V}$ will be present in $R_{\mathcal{A},V_1'}$ between the common pairs of nodes, and their F labels will be equal as well since $V_1' = V$. Therefore, $R_{\mathcal{A},V} = R_{\mathcal{A},V_1'}$. Moreover, since the initial nodes are the same for both populations, they must be in $R_{\mathcal{A},V_1'}$. Finally, $R_{\mathcal{A},V_1'}$ is a subgraph of $R_{\mathcal{A},V'}$, as $V_1' \subset V'$, and the proof is complete.   □

The above theorem states that while we explore populations of greater size, the corresponding agent configuration graphs are only enhnanced with new nodes and edges, while the old ones are preserved.

Given an agent configuration graph, we associate each node a with a value $r(a)$ inductively, as follows:

Base Case For any initial node a, $r(a) = r_{init} = 1$.

Inductive Step For any other node a, $r(a) = min(r(b) + r(c))$ such that a is reachable from b through an edge that contains c in its label, and b, c have already been assigned an r value.

Lemma 5.37   *Let $R_{\mathcal{A},V} = \{U, W, F\}$ be an agent configuration graph. Every node in $R_{\mathcal{A},V}$ get associated with an r value.*

Proof. Assume for the sake of the contradiction that there is a maximum, non empty set of nodes $U' \subset U$ such that $\forall v \in U'$, v does not get associated with an r value. Then $B = U - U'$, and $C = (B, U')$ defines a cut, with all the initial nodes being in B. We examine any edge (u, v) with label L that crosses the cut, having an arbitrary $(w, x) \in L$. Obviously, $u \in B$ and $v \in U'$, and u is associated with a value $r(u)$. Since v is not associated with any r value, the same must hold for node w (otherwise, $r(v) = r(u) + r(w)$). We now examine the first agent c that enters a configuration corresponding to some $v \in U'$. Because of the above observation, this could only happen through an interaction with an agent being in a configuration that is also in U', which creates the contradiction.   □

Note that for any given protocol and population size, the r values are *unique* since the agent configuration graph is unique. The following lemma captures a bound in the r values when the corresponding protocol uses $f(n) = o(\log \log n)$ space.

Lemma 5.38   *Let r_{max-i} be the i-th greatest r value associated with any node in an agent configuration graph. For any protocol $\mathcal{A}$ that uses $f(n) = o(\log \log n)$, there exists a n_0 such that for any population of size $n > n_0$, $r_{max} < \frac{n}{2}$.*

Proof. Since $f(n) = o(\log \log n)$, $\lim_{n \to \infty} \frac{f(n)}{\log \log n} = 0$, so $\lim_{n \to \infty} \frac{\log \log n}{f(n)} = \infty$ and $\lim_{n \to \infty} \frac{\log n}{2^{f(n)}} = \infty$. It follows from the last equation that for any positive integer M, there exists a fixed n_0 such that $\frac{\log n}{2^{f(n)}} > M$ for any $n > n_0$.

Fix any such n and let $k = |U| \leq 2^{f(n)}$ in the corresponding agent configuration graph. Since any node is associated with an r value, there can be at most k different such values. Now observe that $r_{max} \leq 2 \cdot r_{max-1} \leq \cdots \leq 2^k \cdot r_{init} \leq 2^{2^{f(n)}} < 2^{\frac{\log n}{M}} \leq \sqrt[M]{n} \leq \frac{n}{2}$ for $n > max(n_0, 2)$ and $M \geq 2$.

□

Note that these r-values are a part of our theoretical analysis and are not stored on the population (there is not enough space on the agents to store them). In the following analysis, we consider for any practical purposes that $M = 2$.

Given a protocol $\mathcal{A}$ and a population V, we define the following property:

Definition 5.39 *Property $Q(a)$:* Given a node a in the agent configuration graph $R_{\mathcal{A},V}$, there exists a subpopulation of V of size $r(a)$ and a fair execution of the corresponding protocol $\mathcal{A}$ that will lead an agent to the configuration a.

The following lemma proves that the r values correspond to the above reachability property.

Lemma 5.40 *$Q(a)$ holds for any node of $R_{\mathcal{A},V}$.*

Proof. We prove the above lemma by generalized induction in the r values.

Base Case $Q(a)$ obviously holds for any initial node u, since $r_{init} = 1$.

Inductive Step We examine any non initial node u that has been associated with a value $r(u) = r(a) + r(b)$, for some a, b. The inductive hypothesis guarantees that $Q(a)$ and $Q(b)$ hold. Then, a population of size $r(a) + r(b)$ can lead two agents to configurations a and b, independently. Then an interaction between those agents will take one of them to configuration u, so $Q(u)$ holds too.

□

Lemmata 5.38 and 5.40 lead to the following:

Lemma 5.41 *For any protocol $\mathcal{A}$ that uses $f(n) = o(\log \log n)$, there exists a fixed n_0 such that for any population of size $n > n_0$, and any pair of agent configurations u, v, the interaction (u, v) can occur.*

Proof. Indeed, because of the Lemma 5.38, there exists a n_0 such that for any $n > n_0$, $r(a) < \frac{n}{2}$ for any a. With that in mind, Lemma 5.40 guarantees that in any such population, any interaction (u, v) can occur since any of the agent configurations u, v can occur independently, by partitioning the population in two subpopulations of size $\frac{n}{2}$ each.   □

We can now complete our proof of Theorem 5.33:

Proof. Because of the uniformity constraint, $\mathcal{A}$ can be executed in any population of arbitrary size. We choose a fixed n_0 as defined in Lemma 5.38 and examine the population L of size $n = n_0$. Let $R_{\mathcal{A},L}$ be the corresponding agent configuration graph. Let L' be any population of size $n' > n$ and $R_{\mathcal{A},L'}$ the corresponding agent configuration graph. Because of the theorem 5.36, $R_{\mathcal{A},L'}$ contains a subgraph K, such that $K = R_{\mathcal{A},L}$, and the initial nodes of $R_{\mathcal{A},L'}$ are in K. Let $U^* = U' - U$, and k the first agent configuration that appears in L' such that $k \in U^*$ through an interaction (u, v) (k can't be an initial configuration, thus it occurs through some interaction). Then $u, v \in U$, and the interaction (u, v) can occur in the population L too (Lemma 5.41), so that $k \in U$, which refutes our choice of k creating a contradiction. So, $U^* = \emptyset$, and the set of agent configurations does not change as we examine populations of greater size. Since the set of agent configurations remains described by the *fixed* $R_{\mathcal{A},L}$, the corresponding predicate can be computed by the Population Protocol model; thus, it is semilinear.   □

Theorem 5.33 guarantees that for any protocol that uses only $f(n) = o(\log \log n)$ space in each agent, there exists a population of size n_0 in which it stops using extra space. Since n_0 is fixed, we can construct a protocol based on the agent configuration graph which uses constant space[2], and thus can be executed in the Population Protocol Model.

So far, we have established that **PMSPACE**$(f(n)) \subseteq$ **SEM** when $f(n) = o(\log \log n)$. Since the inverse direction holds trivially, we can conclude that **PMSPACE**$(f(n)) = $ **SEM**.

Theorem 5.33 practically states that when the memories available to the protocols are strictly smaller than $\log \log n$ (asymptotically) then these PM protocols are nothing more than population protocols, and although their memory is still dependent on the population size, they cannot exploit it as such; instead, they have to use it as a constant memory much like population protocols do.

5.2.2   THE LOGARITHMIC PREDICATE

In this section, we shall present the non-semilinear logarithmic predicate, and will show how it can be computed by a PM protocol that uses $\mathcal{O}(\log \log n)$ space in each agent. Note that by combining this result with the one presented in the previous section, we establish that $\log \log n$ is a strict bound on the semilinear behavior of the model.

We define the logarithmic predicate as follows: During the initialization, each agent receives an input symbol from $X = \{a, 0\}$, and let N_a denote the number of agents that have received the symbol a. We want to compute whether $\log N_a = t$ for some arbitrary t. We give a high level protocol that computes this predicate, and prove that it can be correctly executed using $\mathcal{O}(\log \log n)$ space.

[2]Notice that this fixed agent configuration graph can be viewed as a deterministic finite automaton.

Each agent u maintains a variable x_u, and let out_u be the variable that uses to write its output. Initially, any agent u that receives a as his input symbol sets $x_u = 1$ and $out_u = 1$, while any other agent v sets $x_v = 0$ and $out_v = 1$.

The main protocol consists of two subprotocols, $\mathcal{A}$ and $\mathcal{B}$, that are executed concurrently. Protocol $\mathcal{A}$ does the following: whenever an interaction occurs between two agents, u, v, with u being the initiator, if $x_u = x_v > 0$, then $x_u = x_u + 1$ and $x_v = 0$. Otherwise, nothing happens. Protocol $\mathcal{B}$ runs in parallel, and computes the semilinear predicate of determining whether there exist two or more agents having $x > 0$. If so, it outputs 0; otherwise it outputs 1. Observe that $\mathcal{B}$ is executed on stabilizing inputs, as the $x-$variables fluctuate before they stabilize to their final value. However, we have already shown in Section 3.2 that the semilinear predicates are also computable under this constraint (see also Protocol 4 of Section 4.1.2.1).

Lemma 5.42   Space Complexity [CMN⁺10c]   *The main protocol uses $\mathcal{O}(\log \log n)$ space.*

Proof. As protocol $\mathcal{B}$ computes a semilinear predicate, it only uses $\mathcal{O}(c)$ space, with c being a constant. To examine the space bounds of $\mathcal{A}$, pick any agent u. We examine the greatest value that can be assigned to the variable x_u. Observe that in order for x_u to reach value k, there have to be at least 2 preexisting $x-$ variables with values $k - 1$. Through an easy induction, it follows that there have to be at least 2^k preexisting variables with the value 1. Since $2^k \leq N_a$, $k \leq \log N_a \leq \log n$, so x_u is upper bounded by $\log n$, thus consuming $\mathcal{O}(\log \log n)$ space.   □

Lemma 5.43   Correctness [CMN⁺10c]   *The output of the above protocol stabilizes to 1 if $\log N_a = t$ for some t, otherwise stabilizes to 0.*

Proof. If the output of the protocol is 1, then there exists exactly one agent with nonzero value k and, due to the above analysis, upon initiation of the computation there will be 2^{k-1} with value 1, and since only the corresponding agents will have received the symbol a as input, it will hold that $N_a = 2^{k-1} \Rightarrow \log N_a = k - 1$. On the other hand, if the output of the protocol is 0, then there will be $l \geq 2$ with nonzero variables $x_1 \neq x_2 \neq \ldots \neq x_l$, thus, due to them, initially there should have been $2^{x_1-1} + 2^{x_2-1} + \ldots + 2^{x_l-1}$ with input a, which implies that $N_a \neq 2^k$ for all k, because any number can be written uniquely as a sum of different powers of 2.   □

Thus, we have presented a non-semilinear predicate that can be computed by a PM protocol using $\mathcal{O}(\log \log n)$ space. Combining the results in this subsection with those one presented in the previous one, we obtain the following theorem:

Theorem 5.44   [CMN⁺10c]   **SEM = PMSPACE**$(f(n))$ *when* $f(n) = o(\log \log n)$. *Moreover,* **SEM $\subsetneq$ PMSPACE**$(f(n))$ *when* $f(n) = \mathcal{O}(\log \log n)$.

Theorem 5.44 exactly reflects the situation for the class of all regular languages **REG**, where **REG** = **SPACE**($o(\log\log n)$) $\subsetneq$ **SPACE**($\mathcal{O}(\log\log n)$) [SHL65, Alb85] and [Sze94] (Theorem 5.1.3, pages 29-30). The proof presented here, however, is quite different.

Figure 5.1 provides an overview of the classes that have been discussed throughout the text.

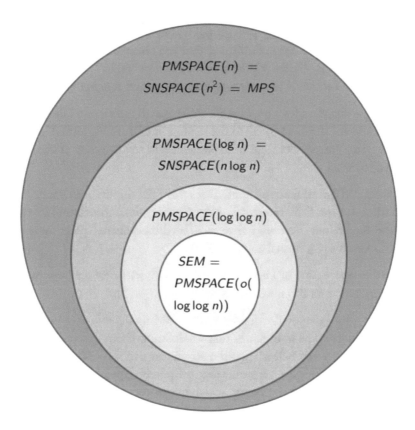

$PMSPACE(n) =$
$SNSPACE(n^2) = MPS$

$PMSPACE(\log n) =$
$SNSPACE(n\log n)$

$PMSPACE(\log\log n)$

$SEM =$
$PMSPACE(o($
$\log\log n))$

Figure 5.1: An overview of the classes.

5.3   EXERCISES

5.1.   Devise a PM protocol to stably compute the predicate ($N_1 = 2^t$), where $t \in \mathbb{Z}_{\geq 0}$, on the complete interaction graph of n nodes using $\mathcal{O}(\log n)$ space. That is, all agents must eventually decide whether the number of 1s in the input assignment is a power of 2.

5.2.   Prove Lemma 5.13.

5.3.   Redefine the PM model to work with whole strings as inputs.

5.4. (RQ) Define the transition graph for PM protocols (don't forget to take also into account the internal steps of the machines) and consider the following relativistic time notion: Define the *time performance* of a protocol $\mathcal{A}$ as the maximum number of distinct configurations (where a configuration is possibly distinct up to the cardinalities of agent configurations appearing in the population) appearing before the first output-stable configuration in any computation of $\mathcal{A}$ on n agents (so time is measured as a function of the population size, and we are interested in its behavior as n grows). What is the time performance of the protocol presented in Example 5.4 and of the one that you constucted in Exercise 5.1? Define and study time complexity classes of predicates much as we did for space (one option is to forget about space and another is to study time complexity as a function of the available space).

5.5. (RQ) Assume that the adversary scheduler selects each interaction independently (and possibly each internal step) according to the random uniform distribution. Study the expected time complexity (number of steps to convergence) of some natural predicates (like the ones presented so far).

5.6. (RQ) Is the PM model fault-tolerant? Does this hold for all space bounds? The necessary precondition for the fault-tolerance of the Community Protocol model was that the ids cannot be altered, but this does not seem to be the case here (the ids here are created and thus part of each agent's usual computation).

5.7. Improve the upper bound of Theorem 5.26, by noticing that the analysis we have performed, although sufficient for our purposes, is not optimal.

5.8. (RQ) What is the computational power of the PM model for space bounds $f(n)$ between $\log \log n$ and $\log n$? The only things that we do know about this particular space bound is that above $\log \log n$ and below $\log n$ the semilinear and the $nf(n)$ behaviors, respectively, of the model cease. However, it seems that the power depends on the number of different ids that can be assigned to the agents, which in turn, of course, depends on the actual space bound.

5.9. (RQ) Can PM protocols be generally composed? Is this true for all space bounds? One will probably have to define, first, a stabilizing inputs variant of the PM model.

NOTES

All results in this chapter are due to Chatzigiannakis, Michail, Nikolaou, Pavlogiannis, and Spirakis [CMN+10b, CMN+10c].

CHAPTER 6

Conclusions and Open Research Directions

6.1 CONCLUSIONS

In this monograph, we have presented some models for passively mobile sensor networks. We began with the Population Protocol model and provided an exact characterization of its computational power. We then presented some first variants, namely the stabilizing inputs version of population protocols that allows the composition of protocols and the Community Protocol model that enhances the computational power by allowing the existence of uids. The rest of the monograph was devoted to two new models, namely the Mediated Population Protocol model and the Passively mobile Machines model. Both are extensions of the population protocol model characterized by realistic and implementable additional components. In the former, the additional component is the existence of a mediator that stores information of the edges of the interaction graph, and in the latter, it is the assumption that the agents are no longer finite-state agents but multitape Turing machines whose storage capacity is specified according to the computational demands.

In what concerns the MPP model, we initially focused on complete interaction graphs and studied on them the computational power of the model. We concluded that the MPP model can simulate a nondeterministic Turing machine of $\mathcal{O}(n^2)$ space that decides symmetric languages. This entailed to show, first, that all agents can be organized into a straight line of active links. Then the agents simply reinitialize the simulation; they all play the role of head of the simulated machine and use the remaining $\mathcal{O}(n^2)$ links as read/write cells. The nondeterminism needed for the simulation stems from the inherent nondeterminism of the mobility pattern. But since the agents cannot split the computation into multiple copies, as nondeterminism demands, what they really do is to perform repeatedly nondeterministic searches on the TM's computational tree. Their output is initially "reject" and they turn it to "accept" as long as they encounter an accepting branch. Then their output is no longer modified. By proving that the inverse simulation is also possible (where the machine simulates the protocol), we concluded that the class **MPS** of stably computable predicates is precisely the class of symmetric predicates in **NSPACE**(n^2). Consequently, the MPP model constitutes a particularly powerful model. Moreover, we studied the stable decidability of graph properties by this model. We saw that in the universe containing also disconnected graphs no graph property is computable. Due to this fact, we focused on weakly connected graphs where we established the decidability of many interesting graph languages.

In what concerns the PM model, we focused again on complete interaction graphs trying again to assess its computational power. It seemed initially that the computational power depends on the memory available to the protocols. From the very beginning, we were particularly interested in the case where the memory used does not exceed a logarithm of the population size. The reasons for that preference were that this is precisely the memory needed by the agents in order to be able of storing unique ids and that the logarithm ensures realistic memory sizes (sufficiently small w.r.t. what contemporary technology can provide). We managed to arrive at an exact characterization of the class **PMSPACE**$(\log n)$, of all stably computable predicates in this case: The class **PMSPACE**$(\log n)$ is precisely the class of all symmetric predicates in **NSPACE**$(n \log n)$. By this, we established that the MPP and the PM model are in some sense equally strong as they both exploit their whole available distributed memory for the simulation of a nondeterministic TM. The simulation works by having the agents assign unique ids to themselves via the reinitialization technique. At the end they also know the size of the population. These are all that they need in order to get organized into a Turing machine.

Then, we went one step further trying to find out what happens as we change the memory that is available to PM protocols. The results presented here are very important because one of the most crucial questions in any distributed system is how much space is needed in order to solve any given problem (or how much time, but the notion of time is out of the scope of this monograph). In particular, we saw initially that if the available memory is at most $f(n)$, where $f(n)$ is at least $\log n$, then the corresponding class is equal to the class of symmetric predicates in **NSPACE**$(nf(n))$. Since there is space hierarchy in the symmetric subclass of **NSPACE**$(nf(n))$, we concluded that there is also a space hierarchy for the PM model. This practically means that, for those $f(n)$, as $f(n)$ grows the computational capabilities of the model increase. By observing that when $f(n)$ is strictly smaller that $\log n$ the agents cannot store unique ids, we suspected that the above behavior of increasing computational power does not hold for these space bounds. Indeed, by using an alternative encoding of configurations (one in which ordering has no meaning), we were able to establish better inclusions for these $f(n)$, concluding that the classes here are strictly smaller than **NSPACE**$(nf(n))$, and thus $\log n$ behaves as a threshold on computational power. Now the $\log n$ bound begins to stand out, constituting a space limit after which the computational capabilities strictly increase. Finally, we saw that for $f(n)$ strictly smaller than $\log \log n$, all computable predicates are semilinear, which makes the PM model for these bounds equivalent to the population protocol model, and that for $f(n)$ at least, $\log \log n$ the PM model computes a non-semilinear predicate, thus $\log \log n$ behaves as a threshold too.

6.2 OPEN RESEARCH DIRECTIONS

Many interesting problems remain open in the rapidly developing field of population protocols. Are the MPP and PM models fault-tolerant? What preconditions are needed in order to achieve satisfactory fault-tolerance? Are these preconditions realistic? Are there exact characterizations of the classes of graph languages that are stably decidable by these models? What is the class of stably decidable graph languages by the variant of the GDMPP model in which the interaction graph is always complete and the edge initialization function specifies the subgraph whose membership in the language has to be determined (the function marks only the links that constitute the subgraph)? What can be computed by the PM model in the stabilizing inputs case? Are there appropriate real-world scenarios for applying the MPP model, or it is just a model of pure theoretical interest? What is the computational power of the PM model for space bounds $f(n)$ between $\log \log n$ and $\log n$? As alluded to above, the only things that we do know about this particular space bound is that above $\log \log n$ and below $\log n$ the semilinear and the $nf(n)$ behaviors, respectively, of the model cease. [CDF$^+$09] revealed the need for the protocols to *adapt* when natural modifications in the mobility pattern occur, in order for the protocols to keep working correctly and/or fast. However, we do not yet know how to define nor how to achieve adaptivity. Moreover, the time complexity of protocols based on some random scheduling assumption has not been yet studied for any of the models presented in this monograph, except for the population protocol model. In the case of the population protocol model, there exist some interesting results [AAD$^+$04, AAD$^+$06, AAE08a, AAE08b] and some of the techniques already developed may be applicable to the other models, but there is still much work to be done towards this direction. Are there more efficient, possibly based on logic, verification methods for population protocols than those presented in [CMS10a] (those are based on searching of the transition graph)? We do not yet know of any verification method for MPPs, CPs, and PM protocols. However, some of the ideas presented in [CMS10a] may also be applicable to these models (possibly also the hardness results). Finally, one can study a variant of the classical model in which the agents interact in groups of $k > 2$ agents and not in pairs (like a broadcast medium). Of course, assuming a constant state space, the computational power of the model is semilinear (see, e.g., Theorem 9, [AAER07]). However, the time efficiency of this variant is open.

Bibliography

[AAC⁺05] D. Angluin, J. Aspnes, M. Chan, M. J. Fischer, H. Jiang, and R. Peralta. Stably computable properties of network graphs. In V. K. Prasanna, S. Iyengar, P. Spirakis, and M. Welsh, editors, *Distributed Computing in Sensor Systems: First IEEE International Conference, DCOSS 2005, Marina del Rey, CA, USA, June/July, 2005, Proceedings*, volume 3560 of *Lecture Notes in Computer Science*, pages 63–74. Springer-Verlag, June 2005. 17, 38, 54, 62, 95

[AAD⁺03] D. Angluin, J. Aspnes, Z. Diamadi, M. J. Fischer, and R. Peralta. Urn automata. Technical Report YALEU/DCS/TR-1280, Yale University Department of Computer Science, Nov. 2003.

[AAD⁺04] D. Angluin, J. Aspnes, Z. Diamadi, M. J. Fischer, and R. Peralta. Computation in networks of passively mobile finite-state sensors. In *23rd annual ACM Symposium on Principles of Distributed Computing (PODC)*, pages 290–299, New York, NY, USA, 2004. ACM. DOI: 10.1145/1011767.1011810 xiv, xv, 2, 6, 8, 16, 17, 54, 127

[AAD⁺06] D. Angluin, J. Aspnes, Z. Diamadi, M. J. Fischer, and R. Peralta. Computation in networks of passively mobile finite-state sensors. In *Distributed Computing*, pages 235–253. DOI: 10.1007/s00446-005-0138-3 2, 3, 16, 21, 25, 26, 27, 28, 29, 35, 54, 95, 127

[AAE06] D. Angluin, J. Aspnes, and D. Eisenstat. Stably computable predicates are semilinear. In *25th annual ACM Symposium on Principles of Distributed Computing (PODC)*, pages 292–299, New York, NY, USA, 2006. ACM Press. DOI: 10.1145/1146381.1146425 21, 23, 30, 31, 32, 33, 34, 35, 61

[AAE08a] D. Angluin, J. Aspnes, and D. Eisenstat. Fast computation by population protocols with a leader. *Distributed Computing*, 21[3]:183–199, September 2008. DOI: 10.1007/s00446-008-0067-z 42, 43, 46, 54, 127

[AAE08b] D. Angluin, J. Aspnes, and D. Eisenstat. A simple population protocol for fast robust approximate majority. *Distributed Computing*, 21[2]:87–102, July 2008. DOI: 10.1007/s00446-008-0059-z 17, 44, 45, 46, 127

[AAER07] D. Angluin, J. Aspnes, D. Eisenstat, and E. Ruppert. The computational power of population protocols. *Distributed Computing*, 20[4]:279–304, November 2007. DOI: 10.1007/s00446-007-0040-2 127

[AAFJ08] D. Angluin, J. Aspnes, M. J. Fischer, and H. Jiang. Self-stabilizing population protocols. *ACM Trans. Auton. Adapt. Syst.*, 3[4]:1–28, 2008.
DOI: 10.1145/1452001.1452003 17

[AB09] S. Arora and B. Barak. *Computational Complexity: A Modern Approach.* Cambridge
University Press; 1st edition, 2009.

[ACD+11] C. Àlvarez, I. Chatzigiannakis, A. Duch, J. Gabarró, O. Michail, S. Maria, and P. G.
Spirakis. Computational models for networks of tiny artifacts: A survey. *Computer
Science Review*, 5[1], January 2011. DOI: 10.1016/j.cosrev.2010.09.001

[ADGS09] C. Àlvarez, A. Duch, J. Gabarro, and M. Serna. Sensor field: A computational model. In *5th Intl Workshop on Algorithmic Aspects of Wireless Sensor Networks (ALGOSENSORS)*, pages 3–14, Berlin, Heidelberg, 2009. Springer-Verlag.
DOI: 10.1007/978-3-642-05434-1_3 17

[Alb85] M. Alberts. Space complexity of alternating turing machines. In L. Budach, editor,
Fundamentals of Computation Theory, volume 199 of *Lecture Notes in Computer Science*,
pages 1–7. Springer Berlin / Heidelberg, 1985. DOI: 10.1007/BFb0028785 123

[AR07] J. Aspnes and E. Ruppert. An introduction to population protocols. *Bulletin of
the European Association for Theoretical Computer Science*, 93:98–117, October 2007.
DOI: 10.1007/978-3-540-89707-1_5 5, 16, 17

[ASS10] C. Àlvarez, M. Serna, and P. G. Spirakis. On the computational power of constant
memory sensor fields. Technical Report FRONTS-TR-2010-10, 2010. 18

[ASSC02] I. F. Akyildiz, W. Su, Y. Sankarasubramaniam, and E. Cayirci. Wireless sensor
networks: a survey. *Computer Networks*, 38:393–422, 2002.
DOI: 10.1016/S1389-1286(01)00302-4

[BBK09] M. Bertier, Y. Busnel, and A.-M. Kermarrec. On gossip and populations. In S. Kutten
and J. Zerovnik, editors, *16th International Colloquium on Structural Information and
Communication Complexity (SIROCCO)*, volume 5869 of *Lecture Notes in Computer
Science*, pages 72–86. Springer-Verlag, 2009. DOI: 10.1007/978-3-642-11476-2_7

[BBCK10] J. Beauquier, J. Burman, J. Clement, and S. Kutten. On utilizing speed in networks
of mobile agents. In *29th annual ACM SIGACT-SIGOPS Symposium on Principles of
Distributed Computing (PODC)*, pages 305–314, New York, NY, USA, 2010. ACM.
DOI: 10.1145/1835698.1835775

[BCC+09] O. Bournez, P. Chassaing, J. Cohen, L. Gerin, and X. Koegler. On the convergence
of population protocols when population goes to infinity. *Applied Mathematics and
Computation*, 2009. DOI: 10.1016/j.amc.2009.04.056

[BCCK09a] O. Bournez, J. Chalopin, J. Cohen, and X. Koegler. Playing With Population Protocols. In *CSP*, pages 3–15, 2008. DOI: 10.4204/EPTCS.1.1

[BCCK09b] O. Bournez, J. Chalopin, J. Cohen, and X. Koegler. Population protocols that correspond to symmetric games. *CoRR*, abs/0907.3126, 2009.

[BCM⁺07] J. Beauquier, J. Clement, S. Messika, L. Rosaz, and B. Rozoy. Self-stabilizing counting in mobile sensor networks. In *26th annual ACM Symposium on Principles of Distributed Computing (PODC)*, pages 396–397, New York, NY, USA, 2007. ACM. DOI: 10.1145/1281100.1281191

[Bol98] B. Bollobás. *Modern Graph Theory*. Springer, corrected edition, July 1998.

[BZ83] D. Brand and P. Zafiropulo. On communicating finite-state machines. *J. ACM*, 30[2]:323–342, 1983. DOI: 10.1145/322374.322380

[CDF⁺09] I. Chatzigiannakis, S. Dolev, S. P. Fekete, O. Michail, and P. G. Spirakis. Not all fair probabilistic schedulers are equivalent. In *13th International Conference on Principles of Distributed Systems (OPODIS)*, volume 5923 of *Lecture Notes in Computer Science*, pages 33–47, Berlin, Heidelberg, 2009. Springer-Verlag. DOI: 10.1007/978-3-642-10877-8_5

[CLRS01] T. H. Cormen, C. E. Leiserson, R. L. Rivest, and C. Stein. *Introduction to Algorithms, Second Edition*. The MIT Press and McGraw-Hill Book Company, 2001.

[CMN⁺10a] I. Chatzigiannakis, O. Michail, S. Nikolaou, A. Pavlogiannis, and P. G. Spirakis. All symmetric predicates in $NSPACE(n^2)$ are stably computable by the mediated population protocol model. In *35th International Symposium on Mathematical Foundations of Computer Science (MFCS)*, volume 6281 of *Lecture Notes in Computer Science*, pages 270–281. Springer-Verlag, August 23–27 2010. DOI: 10.1007/978-3-642-15155-2_25

[CMN⁺10b] I. Chatzigiannakis, O. Michail, S. Nikolaou, A. Pavlogiannis, and P. G. Spirakis. Passively mobile communicating logarithmic space machines. Technical Report FRONTS-TR-2010-16, RACTI, Patras, Greece, 2010. http://fronts.cti.gr/aigaion/?TR=154, arXiv/1004.3395v1.

[CMN⁺10c] I. Chatzigiannakis, O. Michail, S. Nikolaou, A. Pavlogiannis, and P. G. Spirakis. Passively mobile communicating machines that use restricted space. Technical report, RACTI, Patras, Greece, 2010. http://arxiv.org/abs/1012.2440v1.

[CMS09a] I. Chatzigiannakis, O. Michail, and P. G. Spirakis. Brief announcement: Decidable graph languages by mediated population protocols. In I. Keidar, editor, *23rd*

International Symposium on Distributed Computing (DISC), volume 5805 of *Lecture Notes in Computer Science*, pages 239–240. Springer-Verlag, September 2009. DOI: 10.1007/978-3-642-04355-0_24

[CMS09b] I. Chatzigiannakis, O. Michail, and P. G. Spirakis. Exploring the computational limits of adaptive networked populations of tiny artefacts. In *Future and Emerging Technologies (FET)*, April 2009.

[CMS09c] I. Chatzigiannakis, O. Michail, and P. G. Spirakis. Mediated population protocols. In *36th International Colloquium on Automata, Languages and Programming (ICALP)*, volume 5556 of *Lecture Notes in Computer Science*, pages 363–374. Springer-Verlag, July 2009. DOI: 10.1007/978-3-642-02930-1_30

[CMS09d] I. Chatzigiannakis, O. Michail, and P. G. Spirakis. Recent advances in population protocols. In *34th International Symposium on Mathematical Foundations of Computer Science (MFCS)*, volume 5734 of *Lecture Notes in Computer Science*, pages 56–76, Berlin, Heidelberg, 2009. Springer-Verlag. DOI: 10.1007/978-3-642-03816-7_6

[CMS10a] I. Chatzigiannakis, O. Michail, and P. G. Spirakis. Algorithmic verification of population protocols. In *12th International Symposium on Stabilization, Safety, and Security of Distributed Systems (SSS)*, volume 6366 of *Lecture Notes in Computer Science*, pages 221–235. Springer-Verlag, September 2010. DOI: 10.1007/978-3-642-16023-3_19

[CMS10b] I. Chatzigiannakis, O. Michail, and P. G. Spirakis. Stably decidable graph languages by mediated population protocols. In *12th International Symposium on Stabilization, Safety, and Security of Distributed Systems (SSS)*, volume 6366 of *Lecture Notes in Computer Science*, pages 252–266. Springer-Verlag, September 2010. DOI: 10.1007/978-3-642-16023-3_21

[CS08] I. Chatzigiannakis and P. G. Spirakis. The dynamics of probabilistic population protocols. In *22nd international symposium on Distributed Computing (DISC)*, volume 5218 of *Lecture Notes in Computer Science*, pages 498–499, Berlin, Heidelberg, 2008. Springer-Verlag. DOI: 10.1007/978-3-540-87779-0_35

[DF01] Z. Diamadi and M. J. Fischer. A simple game for the study of trust in distributed systems. *Wuhan University Journal of Natural Sciences*, 6[1–2]:72–82, 2001. Also appears as Yale Technical Report TR-1207. DOI: 10.1007/BF03160228

[DGFGR06] C. Delporte-Gallet, H. Fauconnier, R. Guerraoui, and E. Ruppert. When birds die: Making population protocols fault-tolerant. In *IEEE 2nd Intl Conference on Distributed Computing in Sensor Systems (DCOSS)*, volume 4026 of *Lecture Notes in Computer Science*, pages 51–66. Springer-Verlag, June 2006. DOI: 10.1007/11776178_4

[Dol00] S. Dolev. *Self-stabilization*. MIT Press, Cambridge, MA, USA, 2000.

[EN94] J. Esparza and M. Nielsen. Decidability issues for petri nets - a survey. *Bulletin of the European Association for Theoretical Computer Science*, 52:244–262, 1994.

[FLP85] M. J. Fischer, N. A. Lynch, and M. S. Paterson. Impossibility of distributed consensus with one faulty process. *J. ACM*, 32[2]:374–382, 1985. DOI: 10.1145/3149.214121

[FNP+10] A. Filippas, S. Nikolaou, A. Pavlogiannis, O. Michail, I. Chatzigiannakis, and P. G. Spirakis. Computational models for wireless sensor networks: A survey. In *1st International Conference for Undergraduate and Postgraduate Students in Computer Engineering, Informatics, related Technologies and Applications (EUREKA!)*, 2010. Also FRONTS Technical Report, FRONTS-TR-2010-18, http://fronts.cti.gr/aigaion/? TR=156.

[FR74] M. Fischer and M. Rabin. Super-exponential complexity of presburger arithmetic. In *Symposium on Applied Mathematics*, volume VII of *SIAM-AMS Proceedings*, pages 27–41, 1974.

[Gef03] V. Geffert. Space hierarchy theorem revised. *Theor. Comput. Sci.*, 295:171–187, 2003. DOI: 10.1016/S0304-3975(02)00402-4

[GR09] R. Guerraoui and E. Ruppert. Names trump malice: Tiny mobile agents can tolerate byzantine failures. In *36th International Colloquium on Automata, Languages and Programming (ICALP)*, volume 5556 of *Lecture Notes in Computer Science*, pages 484–495. Springer-Verlag, July 2009. DOI: 10.1007/978-3-642-02930-1_40

[GS66] S. Ginsburg and E. H. Spanier. Semigroups, presburger formulas, and languages. *Pacific Journal of Mathematics*, 16:285–296, 1966.

[Hig52] G. Higman. Ordering by divisibility in abstract algebras. *Proccedings of the London Mathematical Society*, 3[2]:326–336, 1952. DOI: 10.1112/plms/s3-2.1.326

[HP79] J. E. Hopcroft and J.-J. Pansiot. On the reachability problem for 5-dimensional vector addition systems. *Theor. Comput. Sci.*, 8:135–159, 1979. DOI: 10.1016/0304-3975(79)90041-0

[IDE04] O. H. Ibarra, Z. Dang, and O. Egecioglu. Catalytic p systems, semilinear sets, and vector addition systems. *Theor. Comput. Sci.*, 312[2-3]:379–399, 2004. DOI: 10.1016/j.tcs.2003.10.028

[Imm88] N. Immerman. Nondeterministic space is closed under complementation. *SIAM J. Comput.*, 17[5]:935–938, 1988. DOI: 10.1137/0217058

[KMSP95] A. Kamath, R. Motwani, P. Spirakis, and K. Palem. Tail bounds for occupancy and the satisfiability threshold conjecture. *Random Struct. Algorithms*, 7:59–80, August 1995. DOI: 10.1002/rsa.3240070105

[Knu76] D. E. Knuth. Big omicron and big omega and big theta. *SIGACT News*, 8[2]:18–24, 1976. DOI: 10.1145/1008328.1008329

[Kra03] M. Kracht. *The Mathematics of Language*, volume 63 of *Studies in Generative Grammar*. de Gruyter Mouton, 2003.

[Kur81] T. Kurtz. *Approximation of Population Processes*. Society for Industrial and Applied Mathematics, Philadelphia, number 36 in cbms-nsf regional conference series in applied mathematics edition, 1981.

[KW07] H. Karl and A. Willig. *Protocols and Architectures for Wireless Sensor Networks*. Wiley-Interscience, 2007.

[Lam78] L. Lamport. Time, clocks, and the ordering of events in a distributed system. *Commun. ACM*, 21[7]:558–565, 1978. DOI: 10.1145/359545.359563

[Lan02] S. Lang. *Algebra (Revised Third Edition)*. Springer-Verlang, 2002.

[Liu85] C. L. Liu. *Elements of Discrete Mathematics*. McGraw-Hill Inc.,US; 2nd edition, 1985.

[Lyn96] N. A. Lynch. *Distributed Algorithms*. Morgan Kaufmann; 1st edition, 1996.

[MCS10] O. Michail, I. Chatzigiannakis, and P. G. Spirakis. Mediated population protocols. *Theor. Comput. Sci.*, 2010. To appear. DOI: 10.1016/j.tcs.2011.02.003

[Mic10] O. Michail. *New Models for Population Protocols*. Computer Engineering & Informatics Department (CEID), Computer Science & Technology Graduate Programme, University of Patras, 2010. PhD Thesis (in Greek).

[Min67] M. L. Minsky. *Computation: Finite and Infinite Machines*. Prentice-Hall, Inc., Upper Saddle River, NJ, USA, 1967.

[Pap94] C. H. Papadimitriou. *Computational Complexity*. Addison-Wesley, 1994.

[Par66] R. J. Parikh. On context-free languages. *J. ACM*, 13[4]:570–581, 1966. DOI: 10.1145/321356.321364

[Pre29] M. Presburger. Über die Vollständigkeit eines gewissen Systems der Arithmetik ganzer Zahlen, in welchem die Addition als einzige Operation hervortritt. In *Comptes-Rendus du I Congrès de Mathématiciens des Pays Slaves*, pages 92–101, 1929.

[QS82] J. P. Queille and J. Sifakis. A temporal logic to deal with fairness in transition systems. In *23rd Annual Symposium on Foundations of Computer Science (FOCS)*, pages 217–225. IEEE Computer Society, IEEE, November 1982. DOI: 10.1109/SFCS.1982.57

[QS83] J. P. Queille and J. Sifakis. Fairness and related properties in transition systems - A temporal logic to deal with fairness. *Acta Inf.*, 19:195–220, 1983. DOI: 10.1007/BF00265555

[Sav70] W. J. Savitch. Relationships between nondeterministic and deterministic tape complexities. *J. Comput. Syst. Sci.*, 4[2]:177–192, 1970. DOI: 10.1016/S0022-0000(70)80006-X

[Sch70] A. Schönhage. Universelle turing speicherung. In J. Dorr and G. Hotz, editors, *Automatentheorie und Formale Sprachen*, pages 369–383, 1970.

[Sch80] A. Schönhage. Storage modification machines. *SIAM J. Comput.*, 9[3]:490–508, 1980. DOI: 10.1137/0209036

[SHL65] R. E. Stearns, J. Hartmanis, and P. M. Lewis. Hierarchies of memory limited computations. In *Proceedings of the 6th Annual Symposium on Switching Circuit Theory and Logical Design (SWCT 1965)*, FOCS '65, pages 179–190, Washington, DC, USA, 1965. IEEE Computer Society. DOI: 10.1109/FOCS.1965.11

[Sip06] M. Sipser. *Introduction to the Theory of Computation, Second Edition, International Edition*. Thomson Course Technology, 2006.

[SL05] M. J. Sailor and J. R. Link. "Smart dust": nanostructured devices in a grain of sand. *Chem. Commun.*, pages 1375–1383, 2005. DOI: 10.1039/b417554a

[Spi10] P. G. Spirakis. *Theoretical Aspects of Distributed Computing in Sensor Networks*, chapter Population Protocols and Related Models. Springer-Verlag, 2010.

[Sze87] R. Szelepcsényi. The method of forcing for nondeterministic automata. *Bulletin of the European Association for Theoretical Computer Science*, 33:96–99, 1987.

[Sze94] A. Szepietowski. *Turing Machines with Sublogarithmic Space*. Springer-Verlag New York, Inc., 1994.

[Tar72] R. Tarjan. Depth-first search and linear graph algorithms. *SIAM J. Comput.*, 1[2]:146–160, 1972. DOI: 10.1137/0201010

[Vaz01] V. V. Vazirani. *Approximation Algorithms*. Springer, 1st ed., corr. 2nd printing edition, 2001.

[vEB89] P. van Emde Boas. Space measures for storage modification machines. *Inf. Process. Lett.*, 30[2]:103–110, 1989. DOI: 10.1016/0020-0190(89)90117-8

[vN49] J. von Neumann. Theory and organization of complicated automata. In A. Burks, editor, *Theory of Self-Reproducing Automata [by] John von Neumann*, pages 29–87 (Part One). University of Illinois Press, Urbana (1949), 1949. Based on transcripts of lectures delivered at the University of Illinois, in December 1949. Edited for publication by A.W. Burks.

[WLLP01] B. Warneke, M. Last, B. Liebowitz, and K. S. J. Pister. Smart dust: Communicating with a cubic-millimeter computer. *Computer*, 34[1]:44–51, 2001. DOI: 10.1109/2.895117

Acronyms

a.k.a.   also known as. 3

GDMPP   Graph Decision Mediated Population Protocol. 82

ids   identifiers. 12
iff   if and only if. 3
IPM   Passively mobile Machines with unique Ids. 104

MPP   Mediated Population Protocol. 12

NSMM   Nondeterministic Storage Modification Machine. 47

PALOMA   PAssively mobile LOgarithmic space MAchines. 97
PM   Passively mobile Machines. 12
PP   Population Protocol. 1

RQ   Research Question. 53

s.t.   such that. 3
SMM   Storage Modification Machine. 50
SMPP   Symmetric Mediated Population Protocol. 59

TM   Turing Machine. 1

uids   unique identifiers. 12

w.l.o.g.   without loss of generality. 4
w.r.t.   with respect to. 16

WSN   Wireless Sensor Network. 1

Authors' Biographies

OTHON MICHAIL

Othon Michail, born in 1984, obtained his Diploma and his MSc in Computer Science & Technology from the Department of Computer Engineering & Informatics of the University of Patras in 2007 and 2009, respectively. He recently (September 2010) obtained his Ph.D. from the same department under the supervision of Prof. Dr. Paul Spirakis. The title of his thesis is "New Models for Population Protocols". He is currently a member of the Research Unit 1 of the RACTI (since April 2009). His research interests include Theory of Computation in new models of computation (like wireless sensor networks and, in particular, population protocols), Computational Complexity, and Algorithms.

IOANNIS CHATZIGIANNAKIS

Ioannis Chatzigiannakis obtained his Ph.D. from the Department of Computer Engineering & Informatics of the University of Patras in 2003. He is currently Adjunct Faculty at the Computer Engineering & Informatics Department of the University of Patras (since October 2005). He is the Director of the Research Unit 1 of RACTI (since July 2007). He has coauthored over 70 scientific publications. His main research interests include distributed and mobile computing, wireless sensor networks, algorithm engineering and software systems. He has served as a consultant to major Greek computing industries. He is the Secretary of the European Association for Theoretical Computer Science since July 2008.

PAUL SPIRAKIS

Paul Spirakis, born in 1955, obtained his Ph.D. from Harvard University, in 1982. He is currently the Director of the RACTI and a Full Professor in the Patras University, Greece. He was acknowledged between the top 50 scientists worldwide in Computer Science with respect to "The best Nurturers in Computer Science Research", published by B. Kumar and Y.N. Srikant, ACM Data Mining, 2005. His research interests are Algorithms and Complexity and interaction of Complexity and Game Theory. Paul Spirakis has extensively published in most of the important Computer Science journals and most of the significant refereed conferences contributing to over 300 scientific publications. He was elected unanimously as one of the two Vice Presidents of the Council of the EATCS. He is a member of the ACM Europe Council and also a member of Academia Europaea.